ANGLISTIK UND ENGLISCHUNTERRICHT

Herausgegeben von
Gabriele Linke
Nicole Maruo-Schröder
Merle Tönnies

Band 95

MARIE HOLOGA
SOPHIA LANGE (Eds.)

Romantic Ethics and the 'Woke' Romantics

Universitätsverlag
WINTER
Heidelberg

Bibliografische Information der Deutschen Nationalbibliothek

Die Deutsche Nationalbibliothek verzeichnet diese Publikation
in der Deutschen Nationalbibliografie;
detaillierte bibliografische Daten sind im Internet
über *http://dnb.d-nb.de* abrufbar.

Herausgeber:
Prof. Dr. Gabriele Linke
Prof. Dr. Nicole Maruo-Schröder
Prof. Dr. Merle Tönnies

ISBN 978-3-8253-4970-7
ISSN 0344-8266

Dieses Werk einschließlich aller seiner Teile ist urheberrechtlich geschützt. Jede
Verwertung außerhalb der engen Grenzen des Urheberrechtsgesetzes ist ohne
Zustimmung des Verlages unzulässig und strafbar. Das gilt insbesondere für
Vervielfältigungen, Übersetzungen, Mikroverfilmungen und die Einspeicherung
und Verarbeitung in elektronischen Systemen.

© 2023 Universitätsverlag Winter GmbH Heidelberg
Imprimé en Allemagne · Printed in Germany
Druck: Memminger MedienCentrum, 87700 Memmingen

Gedruckt auf umweltfreundlichem, chlorfrei gebleichtem
und alterungsbeständigem Papier

Den Verlag erreichen Sie im Internet unter:
www.winter-verlag.de

In academic publishing as much as in academic life, change is, on the one hand, immanent and permanent while, on the other hand, continuity is indispensable. The job of series editors entails efforts in both directions: They are always on the watch for new topics and ideas and need to find volume editors for emergent fields and innovative approaches, and on top of that, the publication has to be adapted to the changing conditions of production, distribution and reception. But while responding to a- changing times, they also need, through their day-to-day work, to secure quality and continuity of form and content. The series *anglistik & englischunterricht* is no exception to these challenges of academic publishing, among which changes in the group of editors also occasion- ally feature.

Holger Rossow has been a member of the group of series editors since 2005, when the 'founding fathers' of the series, Gerd Stratmann and Erwin Otto, passed the torch to the next generation. Ever since, he has enriched our editorial work not only with perspectives from his own background in history, political science and cultural studies, but also by feeding his own expert knowledge on the complex and controversial history of globalisation into a volume on this issue. Furthermore, he provided substantial feedback as a reader and critic of numerous manuscripts on a wide range of topics, paying meticulous attention to details of content and language as well as form. Almost always he would spot some little problems everybody else had overlooked and pursue them unwaveringly until they were eliminated.

As co-editors, we have particularly appreciated the way Holger Rossow repeatedly smoothed out editing processes by speedily and competently answering mails from editors who were despairing at some persistent formatting problem. He had an eye for lay-outing and helped editors perfect the form of the printable manuscripts. His reliability and his quiet, matter-of-factual way of working have endeared him not only to us as co- editors but also to many volume editors. Holger Rossow is now, with this volume, withdrawing from the editorial team with whom he has shaped and maintained *anglistik & englischunterricht* for fifteen years. We are grateful for his long-term contribution and wish him the best of luck for his life 'post-*a & e*'.

Holger Rossow will be succeeded by Nicole Maruo-Schröder as a member of the editorial team. She works as professor of cultural studies in the English and American Studies Department at the University of Koblenz. In addition to her experience with (journal) editing, she will bring her teaching and research interests in the fields of gender, visual culture, American literature and culture to the editorial team. She is looking forward to working with Gabriele Linke and Merle Tönnies on continuing *a & e*.

Contents

Marie Hologa and Sophia Lange
Introduction: Romantic Ethics and the 'Woke' Romantics   9

Monika Lee
Shelley's *The Cenci* and Discourses of Sexual Violence   23

Katie Smith
Childlessness: Uncovering Abortion in Mary Wollstonecraft's
Maria and the Wrongs of Woman (1798)   45

Maria Juko
'Woke' Wollstonecraft? Mary Wollstonecraft's Adventurous
Wives in the Classroom   67

Md. Monirul Islam
Teaching Romanticism in the Indian Classroom: Culture of
Conformity and Pedagogies of Dissent   93

Sérgio Das Neves
Novalis and the Alchemical Expansion of Consciousness   117

Lorenz A. Hindrichsen
Erasing Intersectionality: Silencing Female Black Voices
in English Romantic Texts   137

Theadora Jean
"My Beloved Race": Mary Shelley, Racial Politics and
Romanticism   167

Paul Almonte
"How Did Such an Age Come About?": The Anti-Woke
Romanticism of Yukio Mishima   189

List of Contributors   211

Marie Hologa
Sophia Lange

Romantic Ethics and the 'Woke' Romantics

Introduction

It is certainly not an exaggeration that the field of Romantic studies has currently experienced an unprecedented revival due to its sometimes-uncanny reverberations into our present. For roughly the last decade, there have been parallel social formations and political movements which seem to echo concerns of late eighteenth- and early nineteenth-century Western thought. Feminist movements (e.g. #MeToo), Black Lives Matter (BLM), a global pandemic, and the return to Cold War oppositions contain a similar spirit of the political activism that drove Romantic writers. Several ideas propagated in these movements have emerged in socio-political debates and texts of the time. In recent years, various works have been published which sought to highlight the continuous importance of precisely those discourses popularised by Romantic writers. Those discussions range from the writers' striking awareness of environmental crises and climate change, over their reaction to and reworking of global pandemics, most notably illustrated in Mary Shelley's *The Last Man*, to queerness and gender fluidity in Gothic Romances.[1]

Currently, canonical texts are being re-read, such as the richly annotated new edition of Jane Austen's *Pride and Prejudice* by Robert P. Irvine (Broadview Press, 2020), Sharon Ruston's *The Science of Life and Death in Frankenstein* (Bodleian Library Press, 2021), or Omar F. Miranda's didactic version of Shelley's *The Last Man* (Romantic Circles, 2022).[2] At the same time, we have seen a (re-)discovery of formerly marginalised Romantic texts such as the anonymous *The Woman of Colour* (Dominique (ed.), Broadview Press, 2007) or Olaudah Equiano's *The Interesting Narrative* (Carey (ed.), Oxford University Press, 2018), and letter correspondences of lesser-known Romantic authors (see Callaghan and Howe).[3] We would like to acknowledge the important contributions made by those works in their highlighting of Romantic

9

echoes into the present, which may help to cement Romanticism's relevance for a deeper understanding of contemporary discourses and their origins. In the words of Peter Kitson,

> Romantic period studies is a vibrant and developing field of enquiry which is constantly moving in new directions, employing new approaches and discussing areas of concern for the present day [...]. As well as the production of new texts and the rediscovery of neglected writers, the current critical landscape shows an increasing concern with a Transatlantic and a Global Romanticism, intrigued by the period's perceptions and understandings of other peoples and cultures of the world, especially in terms of religion, and the creative but also troubled relationship between East and West.[4]

It is of course uncontested that a clear demarcation, both temporally and thematically, of Romanticism is not viable due to its often overlapping and intersecting discourses catalysed in this Age of Revolutions. The circle of Romantic writers, and in fact all those who had a public voice at the time, can, by definition, never have been a homogenous or univocal group. Based on their competing perspectives on matters of class, race, gender, and beyond, hybrid and sometimes contradictory formations emerged, which challenges scholars and teachers of Romanticism alike to conceptualise this highly complex period. However,

> [t]his is not to say that Romanticism lacks defining characteristics or that we cannot apply these characteristics with some certainty to the period's various literary achievements. But it is to say that one of these defining features is the fact that these features frequently contradict one another, and so paint the picture of a period often distinctly at odds with itself and its own desires, potentials and aims.[5]

The fact that works by Romantic authors are still celebrated globally and have become core constituents of curricula worldwide should not, however, lull us into an unreflecting acceptance of their writers' agenda, but instead prompt teachers and instructors worldwide to meet such texts with informed criticism to inspire discussions and reflections amongst students. *Bitch Magazine*'s Li Sian Goh calls for a re-evaluation of beloved classics to unpack their multi-layered web of meaning and avoid a pretentious 'woke' reading taste, which would only be "another form of social capital to be accumulated by white Twitter users, who will dutifully read books by minority writers to be seen as antiracist".[6] Naturally, as white, middle-class, cis female scholars working in eighteenth- and nineteenth-century literature and culture, we as editors cannot possibly exclude ourselves from those whom Goh accuses of armchair activism and performative wokeness. Instead of involuntarily contributing to this issue by simply praising canonical works for their auguring insight into contemporary matters, the present volume proposes to re-evaluate Romantic texts through the lens of cultural studies as they invoke the ambiguity that the concept of wokeness contains.

The term 'woke' derives from 'to be awake' and, in its original form, can loosely be defined as "a state of being aware, especially of social problems such as racism and inequality".[7] The idea of wokeness, i.e. an awareness of social issues, first gained mainstream popularity in 2008, when US-American R&B singer-songwriter Erykah Badu released her song "Master Teacher", prominently featuring the phrase "I stay woke" in its refrain.[8] In the context of the corresponding album *New Amerykah Part One (4th World War)*, which unsparingly highlights institutionalised racism as experienced by African Americans, the wokeness alluded to in "Master Teacher" calls on African Americans to challenge racialised marginalisation despite and because of the aversions they are met with in their day-to-day lives.

Badu was by far not the first one to employ the concept of wokeness to define a special recognition of inequalities. As early as the 1930s and 1940s, African American songwriters coined the term to shed light on the vulnerable position of Black Americans and to alert the public to hate crimes. As the term entered mainstream use over the course of the twentieht century, African Americans consequentially spoke out against the appropriation of the word by white musicians, which removed 'wokeness' from its original meaning and offered a broader definition as an awareness of social injustice.[9] In the context of the BLM movement, the term and corresponding hashtag #StayWoke were popularised further, with the hashtag having already been successfully employed in the activism against the imprisonment of Pussy Riot members in 2012.[10] Given the varying context in which the term and its derivations have been used in recent years, it becomes apparent that 'woke' has become a synonym for a democratic, left-leaning political ideology encompassing discourses such as climate change, trans rights, critical race theory, classism, or feminism.

Alongside its appropriation by various subcultural formations, removing the term from its origins in the exposing of racial inequalities, 'wokeness' has not only been increasingly criticised by right-wing politicians and conservatives who fear unstoppable waves of alleged 'cancel culture' inspired by young voters' growing awareness of inequalities, but the term has also acquired a rather derogatory second meaning, defining it as "self-righteousness masquerading as enlightenment", closely connected with performative wokeness, i.e. the preference of self-promotion through pretend-wokeness over actual activism.[11]

The inherent double-edgedness of the term is precisely why we have chosen it as a focal point for our present volume. While many Romantic authors, similar to those activists describing themselves as woke today, utilised their texts to shed light on topics such as slavery and colonialism, education and pedagogics, inequalities of the sexes, crime and punishment, or human perfectibility, it cannot be overlooked that they were also writing from the privileged position of wealth, education, whiteness and/or male subject position that most moral instructors and visionary idealists enjoyed. On the other hand, there were just as many conservative writers and thinkers (sometimes even formerly radical activists shifting over the course of their productive biographies)[12] promoting the status quo and the ancien régime in what is very much an anti-woke struggle against social reform. Edmund Burke, for example, wrote of a "savage atrocity" (424)[13] that had infected the minds of French revolutionaries, but he remained certain that "[t]he people of England will not ape the fashions they have never tried" (299).[14]

We therefore see a significant parallel between the literary activism of Romantic writers and the wokeness of activists in Western contemporary cultures, especially given the criticism surrounding their works which either celebrates their progressive impetus or unveils the underlying shortcomings of their performative activism and intrinsic close-mindedness.[15] However, it still appears that Romantic ideas echo into contemporary controversies surrounding questions of white privilege, gender and sexual inequalities, human rights, and the increasing marginalisation of vulnerable groups in the face of global crises. In "A Short History of Wokeness", *Sp!ked Magazine*'s Kevin Baldeosingh understands Romanticism's assumed "rejection of reason" as having "sowed the seeds of today's woke movement".[16] While there is much to unpack in this statement, it does strike a chord when Baldeosingh quotes Colin Campbell's influential *The Romantic Ethic and the Spirit of Modern Consumerism* (1987) to highlight that in Romanticism's inward turn, performed to scrutinise the self and safeguard the same from intrusive forces of enlightened capitalist devaluation, eighteenth- and nineteenth-century thinkers detached themselves from dissatisfactory reality and escaped into utopian dreams of democratised futures (n.pag.). If indeed an inward turn in Romantic writers can be identified (which might as well just be one of the clichés circulating about Romanticism),[17] it is not up to us to judge this in any way. Instead, it must be viewed as a response to the dominant ideologies threatening collective and individual identities. Consequentially, we are inviting the readers of this volume to re-consider Romantic writers and their texts as reflective of their historical and social contingencies and at the same time as shaping those realities through the works that they produce. By definition, our contemporary Romantic canon can only be a residual and reductive version of the period, which, in retrospect, allows only a very limited and privileged perspective on 'the past as it really was'. As relayed by Simon Kövesi,

> [i]f you think a work of literature should *always* be regarded as a classic, as essential reading, then actually you are loosening your argument from any sense of history, any understanding of the evolution and development of taste, value, ethics, and art. [...] We might therefore regard the canon with at least a degree of suspicion because it suggests fixity where there is none, an eternal pre-determination of literary quality where the goalposts and measures of such qualities in fact shift and merge, disappear and re-appear.[18]

It is therefore essential to de-colonise and break the canon as well as re-consider those works that do make up the canon. Naturally, as we attempt to intervene in canonical selections and readings in this very volume, we are also speaking from a position of privilege, perhaps best illustrated as a form of isolation, or insular echo chamber which alienates the privileged from other forms of knowledge. While such notions have the potential to contribute to a further marginalisation of the Other, the positive notion of wokeness alluded to here implies the attempt to recognise this limitation and possibly resolve it – if not in an actively political way, then at least for the sake of knowledge. This might be achieved by critically reconsidering one's 'truths', attitudes and stereotypes and finding out about how and where they emerged from.

Those benefitting from hegemonic discourse should become aware of their privileged position and try to de-familiarise their social reality. For that matter, it can never suffice to justify one's insularity or ignorance in the line of rejection of those other forms of knowledge, e.g. apologetically: "As a white/cis/able/young/middle-class/Western person, I cannot speak for the respective subaltern 'other'." Spivak's influential notion of 'un-learning' must be invoked here, as it calls on us to "work[...] critically back through one's history, prejudices, and learned, but now seemingly instinctual, responses".[19] By confronting the canonical works of Romantic authors through a woke engaging with their socio-political criticisms as well as their inherent, if perhaps involuntary, reproduction of privilege, we seek to unlearn presupposed notions to counter "a closing down of creative possibility, a loss of other options, other knowledge".[20] In line with the ambivalence of wokeness, Spivak's idea can be followed further as she proposes to not simply unlearn one's privilege per se to achieve multiperspectivity and the recognition of hierarchies, but to "unlearn[...] one's privilege as one's loss".[21] This notion is pivotal if we speak about ethics and wokeness, as it involves a recognition of our very own social circumstances that may have inhibited us from obtaining the necessary "knowledge of the others who occupy those spaces most closed to our privileged view".[22]

By relating these insights to our field of research, namely *Romantic Ethics and the Woke Romantics*, we invite our readers to enter a meta-level here: It is not necessarily the privileged position of the Romantic writers that will be questioned here, but rather the canonical status of their writings, which more often than not may inhibit critical reading and an unprejudiced approach to the text, especially in didactic settings. The idea to un-learn the canonicity of Romantic texts and their dominant interpretations will not gloss over their immense contribution to individualism, democratic political participation, or gender equality, but rather enable a re-configuration of such texts as rhizomatic structures, allowing for multiple entry points and equally multifaceted, critical interpretations. As uncanny parallels unfold between issues addressed in Romantic texts and contemporary civil movements, readers and learners must be encouraged to re-evaluate their own privileged readings of such texts, as well as the authors' very own positions of privilege which originally facilitated their artistic creations, to unveil the uncontested relevance Romantic texts still hold in the 21st century. By perceiving the ways in which authors like Mary Wollstonecraft, her son-in-law Percy Shelley, or first-generation Romantic author William Blake have already highlighted shortcomings of patriarchal societies in their disregard of female rights, Black rights, and body rights in the Long Eighteenth Century, contemporary readers may develop newfound appreciation for these canonical works – especially if analysed through the lens of double-edged wokeness.

Given that many of the primary works investigated here still feature prominently in high school and university settings alike (such as Mary Shelley's *Frankenstein* or William Blake's poetry), this volume also seeks to offer ideas for didactic approaches to Romantic texts in the contemporary classroom. The selected essays offer striking insight into the discursive potentials of approaching Romantic discourses through their intersection with present-day movements such as BLM or #MeToo. Thus, this volume caters to scholars of Romanticism as well as those involved in teacher training, higher education, and secondary schools due to the broad range of texts and cultural formations discussed, which may support lecturers and teachers in mapping new approaches to Romanticism and revising their syllabi.

In her article, Monika Lee reconsiders an overlooked and critically misrepresented character of Percy Shelley's *The Cenci* (1819) in the figure of Lucretia by drawing our attention to her role in opposing and resisting the violent, sexual transgressions of a patriarch. By re-reading Shelley's work in the context of contemporary feminist movements and debates on consent and domestic rape, Lee unveils the progressive undertones of *The Cenci* as a republican drama, as well as its author's deep investment in the nuances of sexual permissiveness, which anticipates current questions of victim-blaming and jurisdiction in sex offender cases.

In a similar vein, Katie Smith highlights the injustice faced by female victims of sexual transgression in coping with illegitimate pregnancies by way of abortion or suicide in Mary Wollstonecraft's *Maria, or The Wrongs of Woman* (1798). Her focus is on Wollstonecraft's case for the need of female solidarity across social classes in opposition to male exploitation, which "anticipates 21st-century wokeness by considering inequality as a spectrum which all women experience in varying degrees".[23]

With a different approach to the proto-feminist writer, Maria Juko promotes including Wollstonecraft's progressive views on education and equality of the sexes in German EFL curricula in order to fill the gaps in literary periodisation (between Renaissance and Postmodernity) and female activism. By considering modern representations of Wollstonecraft and her impact, Juko shows how the author and the long history of feminism can be rendered more didactically tangible for students in our day and age.

In his contribution on "Teaching Romanticism in the Indian Classroom", Monirul Islam takes this pedagogic intervention in conservative teachings of the Romantic canon a step further by calling for freedom in the selection of syllabi in Indian higher education. His key idea is to reveal the potential for political activism in Romantic texts and channel this into political dissent from 21st-century hegemonic power structures.

Sérgio Das Neves invites his readers on a transcendental journey into the convoluted realms of alchemical allegories in German Romanticism and their alignments of natural science and poetry as means to improve the world. Conceptualised as the search for the Philosopher's Stone, a metaphor for moral perfection, Novalis' *Heinrich von Ofterdingen* (1802) is presented as similar to Wordsworth's idea of the poet as moral and creative guide for common people. This finds its modern-day expression in the striving for imaginative freedom and appreciation of artistic quality in the face of neoliberal dictates of efficiency and quantifiable value.

Very much in contrast to Das Neves' focus on the writer as moral guide, Lorenz A. Hindrichsen's "Erasing Intersectionality: Silencing Female Black Voices in English Romantic Texts" draws attention to the deliberate absence or cultural appropriation of marginalised intersectional subjects like the female Creature in Mary Shelley's *Frankenstein* (1818), William Blake's chimney sweepers and the black enslaved Joanna/ Giovanna, or Samuel Taylor Coleridge's Abyssinian Maid. In pointing to the performative activism inherent in such works, Hindrichsen's contribution "[r]ecognis[es] the privileged stance of Romantic writers and their tendency to replicate vestiges of privilege in their writing"[24] as well as the fetishised reception and sometimes even haptic consumption of racialised bodies.

Theadora Jean then calls for a re-reading of two of the most canonical texts of the Romantic period, namely Shelley's *Frankenstein* and *The Last*

Man (1826), resulting in the painful acknowledgement of racial and colonial anti-wokeness by "accept[ing] the flaws and prejudices of our most beloved writers, especially when it comes to literary critique and academic pedagogy".[25]

Moving beyond the Romantic era, Paul Almonte widens the scope of Romantic legacies towards cross-cultural repercussion in Mishima's tetralogy *Sea of Fertility* (1965-1970), in which he shows the author's ambivalence between woke empathy and conservative idealism as anti-woke anxiety of national decline in twentieth-century Japan. Conceptions of beauty and immortality based on Romantic aesthetics set the ground for expanding the canon to include a non-Western perspective.

We hope that our volume of *anglistik & englischunterricht* can offer a glimpse into the variety of scholarship and didactic impulses concerned with a re-reading of (canonical) Romantic texts to cater to the multifacetedness of the period with its often-intersecting and contra-dictory discourses on issues such as race, class, gender, or agency. In bringing together the scholarly and didactic approaches to Romantic works and reviewing their authors' ethical concerns, our contributors allow for a fresh outlook on the lasting impact of eighteenth- and nineteenth-century literature and culture. For scholars and teachers alike, our collection is proof that "despite the singular noun used to describe it, Romanticism should more properly be recognized as Romanticisms".[26] Moving away from a notion of Romantic studies as a normative discipline, we desire to encourage an expansion of curricula, syllabi, and research as well a modification of questions posed to a supposedly over-researched canon.

Notes

[1]   Higgins, David (2017). *British Romanticism, Climate Change, and the Anthropocene. Writing Tambora*. London: Palgrave Macmillan; Hunt, Eileen M. (2020). "Mary Shelley Created 'Frankenstein,' and Then a Pandemic." *The New York Times*, 13 Mar. 2020, n.pag. Web. 17 September 2021. https://www.nytimes.com/2020/03/13/opinion/mary-shelley-sc-fi-pandemic-novel.html.; O'Rourke, Michael and David Collings (eds.) (2004). "Introduction: Queer Romanticisms: Past, Present, and Future." *Romanticism on the Net: Special Edition on Queer Romanticism* 36-37, n.pag. Web. 19 May 2022. https://www.erudit.org/en/journals/ron/2004-n36-37ron947/011132ar/.

2　Austen, Jane (2020 [1813]). *Pride and Prejudice*. Ed. Robert P. Irvine. Peterborough, Ontario: Broadview Press; Ruston, Sharon (2021). *The Science of Life and Death in Frankenstein*. Oxford: Bodleian Library Press; Shelley, Mary (2022 [1826]). *The Last Man*. Abridged Version. Ed. Omar F. Miranda. *Romantic Circles*. Web. 20 March 2022. http://romantic-circles.org/romantic-circles.org/scholarlyresources/226786.

3　Anonymous (2007 [1808]). *The Woman of Colour*. Ed. Lyndon J. Dominique. Peterborough, Ontario: Broadview Press; Equiano, Olaudah (2018 [1789]). *The Interesting Narrative*. Ed. Brycchan Carey. Oxford: Oxford University Press; Callaghan, Madeleine and Anthony Howe (2020). *Romanticism and the Letter*. London: Palgrave Macmillan.

4　Kitson, Peter (2011). "Mapping the Current Critical Landscape." *The Romanticism Handbook*. Eds. Sue Chaplin and Joel Faflak. London: Continuum, 185-199, 198.

5　Chaplin, Sue and Joel Faflak (eds.) (2011). "Introduction and Timeline." *The Romanticism Handbook*. London: Continuum, xiii-xxxiii, xiv.

6　Goh, Li Sian (2017). "Degrees of Wokeness. Race and Otherness in *Jane Eyre*." *Bitch* 75, 29-32, 31.

7　"wokeness." *Cambridge Advanced Learner's Dictionary & Thesaurus*, Cambridge: Cambridge University Press. 2021. n.pag. Web. 17 September 2021. https://dictionary.cambridge.org/us/dictionary/english/wokeness.

8　Badu, Erykah (2008). "Master Teacher." *New Amerykah Part One (4th World War)*. Universal Motown.

9　Baisya, Pramila (2021). "The Appropriation of Wokeness." *Her Campus*. n.pag. Web. 18 May 2022. https://www.hercampus.com/school/new-school/appropriation-wokeness/.

10　Wynter, Kevin (2022). *Critical Race Theory and Jordan Peele's Get Out*. London: Bloomsbury Academic.

11　"wokeness." (2019) *Urban Dictionary*, top definition by Fata Morgana, 15 May 2019. Web. 17 September 2021. https://www.urbandictionary.com/define.php?term=wokeness.

12　See Almonte in this volume, 188-189.

13　Burke, Edmund (1897). *Reflections on the Revolution in France*. London: George Bell and Sons., 424.

14　*Ibid*., 299.

15　Jacobs, Alan (2017). "Wokeness and Myth on Campus." *The New Atlantis* 53, 33-44, 35.

16　Baldeosingh, Kevin (2019). "A Short History of Wokeness." *Sp!ked*, n.pag. Web. 17 September 2021. https://www.spiked-online.com/2019/08/05/a-short-history-of-wokeness/.

17 Esterhammer, Angela (2020). *Print and Performance in the 1820s. Improvisation, Speculation, Identity.* Cambridge: Cambridge University Press.
18 Kövesi, Simon (2011). "Canonicity." *The Romanticism Handbook.* Eds. Sue Chaplin and Joel Faflak. London: Continuum, 141-157, 152.
19 Landry, Donna and Gerald MacLean (1996). *The Spivak Reader.* New York and London: Routledge, 4.
20 *Ibid.*
21 Spivak, G.C. (1990). *The Post-Colonial Critic: Interviews, Strategies, Dialogues.* New York: Psychology Press, 14.
22 *Ibid.*, 4-5.
23 See Smith in this volume, 45.
24 See Hindrichsen in this volume, 157.
25 See Jean in this volume, 183.
26 Ruston, Sharon (2013). *Creating Romanticism. Case Studies in the Literature, Science and Medicine of the 1790s.* London: Palgrave Macmillan, 175.

Bibliography

Anonymous (2007 [1808]). *The Woman of Colour.* Ed. Lyndon J. Dominique. Peterborough, Ontario: Broadview Press.
Austen, Jane (2020 [1813]). *Pride and Prejudice.* Ed. Robert P. Irvine. Peterborough, Ontario: Broadview Press.
Badu, Erykah. "Master Teacher." *New Amerykah Part One (4th World War).* Universal Motown. 2008. CD.
Baisya, Pramila (2021). "The Appropriation of Wokeness." *Her Campus*, n.pag. Web. 18 May 2022. https://www.hercampus.com/school/new-school/appropriation-wokeness/.
Baldeosingh, Kevin (2019). "A Short History of Wokeness." *Sp!ked*, n.pag. Web. 17 September 2021. https://www.spiked-online.com/2019/08/05/a-short-history-of-wokeness/.
Burke, Edmund (1897). *Reflections on the Revolution in France.* London: George Bell and Sons.
Callaghan, Madeleine and Anthony Howe (2020). *Romanticism and the Letter.* London: Palgrave Macmillan.
Chaplin, Sue and Joel Faflak (eds.) (2011). *The Romanticism Handbook.* London: Continuum.

Esterhammer, Angela (2020). *Print and Performance in the 1820s. Improvisation, Speculation, Identity*. Cambridge: Cambridge University Press.

Equiano, Olaudah (2018 [1789]). *The Interesting Narrative*. Ed. Brycchan Carey. Oxford: Oxford University Press.

Goh, Li Sian (2017). "Degrees of Wokeness. Race and Otherness in *Jane Eyre*." *Bitch* 75, 29-32.

Higgins, David (2017). *British Romanticism, Climate Change, and the Anthropocene. Writing Tambora*. London: Palgrave Macmillan.

Hunt, Eileen M (2020). "Mary Shelley Created 'Frankenstein,' and Then a Pandemic." *The New York Times*, 13 Mar. 2020, n.pag. Web. 17 September 2021. https://www.nytimes.com/2020/03/13/opinion/mary-shelley-sc-fi-pandemic-novel.html.

Jacobs, Alan (2017). "Wokeness and Myth on Campus." *The New Atlantis* 53, 33-44.

Kitson, Peter (2011). "Mapping the Current Critical Landscape." *The Romanticism Handbook*. Eds. Sue Chaplin and Joel Faflak. London: Continuum, 185-199.

Kövesi, Simon (2011). "Canonicity." *The Romanticism Handbook*. Eds. Sue Chaplin and Joel Faflak. London: Continuum, 141-157.

Landry, Donna and Gerald MacLean (1996). *The Spivak Reader*. New York and London: Routledge.

O'Rourke, Michael and David Collings (eds.) (2004). "Introduction: Queer Romanticisms: Past, Present, and Future." *Romanticism on the Net: Special Edition on Queer Romanticism* 36-37, n.pag. Web. 19 May 2022. https://www.erudit.org/en/journals/ron/2004-n36-37-ron947/011132ar/.

Ruston, Sharon (2013). *Creating Romanticism. Case Studies in the Literature, Science and Medicine of the 1790s*. London: Palgrave Macmillan.

---. (2021). *The Science of Life and Death in Frankenstein*. Oxford: Bodleian Library Press.

Shelley, Mary (2022 [1826]). *The Last Man*. Abridged Version. Ed. Omar F. Miranda. *Romantic Circles*. Web. 20 March 2022. http://romantic-circles.org/romantic-circles.org/scholarlyresources/226786.

Spivak, G.C. (1990). *The Post-Colonial Critic: Interviews, Strategies, Dialogues*. New York: Psychology Press.

"wokeness." *Cambridge Advanced Learner's Dictionary & Thesaurus*, Cambridge: Cambridge University Press. 17 September 2021. https://dictionary.cambridge.org/us/dictionary/english/wokeness.

"wokeness." (2019) *Urban Dictionary*, top definition by Fata Morgana, 15 May 2019. Web. 17 September 2021. https://www.urbandictionary.com/define.php?term=wokeness.

Wynter, Kevin (2022). *Critical Race Theory and Jordan Peele's Get Out*. London: Bloomsbury Academic.

Monika Lee

Shelley's *The Cenci* and Discourses of Sexual Violence

1. Introduction

Although twentieth-century critics often read Percy Bysshe Shelley's *The Cenci: A Tragedy in Five Acts* as unsuited to the stage,[1] this play has been highly regarded since its 1819 publication. Henry Crabb Robinson records that "Wordsworth spoke of it as the greatest tragedy of the age".[2] For Mary Shelley, "[t]he Fifth Act is a masterpiece. It is the finest thing he ever wrote, and may claim proud comparison not only with any contemporary, but preceding, poet".[3] Lord Byron, Thomas Love Peacock, George Bernard Shaw, and Oscar Wilde all praised the play.[4] Despite their assessments, the first public performance occurred many decades later in Paris in 1891, although Shaw informs us that an 1886 London production, while not licenced because of censorship laws, was private in only a "technical" sense; the first official public English performance took more than a century (1922) to manifest.[5]

Not surprisingly, critical commentary has vastly outpaced performance, yet the time when the drama could successfully be embraced by the theatrical world has surely come. Shelley's play was deemed unperformable in 1819 and the subsequent century, not because of irremediable faults in its dramatic integrity or audience appeal but because of subject matter, its two central actions being incestual rape and parricide, and possibly also because of its anti-clerical, anti-aristocratic, and anti-monarchist tendencies.[6] *The Cenci* expresses a modern sensitivity to and awareness of sexual assault and domestic violence. Shelley's explicit and nuanced exploration of power dynamics and consent foreshadow the ongoing ethical reckoning of the #MeToo movement. This paper will examine discourses of sexual violence as they intersect with both historical and contemporary conceptions, laws, and linguistic paradigms, and thereby revise some major critical debates which have informed understanding of the text and its ethics.

Canonical critical debate about *The Cenci* takes as its launching point the ambivalent "Preface" in which Shelley raises the moral issue of whether or not Beatrice Cenci is justified in planning the assassination of Count Cenci.[7] Although this moral conundrum is indeed present in both preface and poetry, its dominance in critical discussion suggests that the crime of parricide is the play's central concern, and thereby has the effect of deflecting readerly attention from other crimes central to the action, particularly those enacted by Count Cenci himself. Worse still, focusing on crimes against Count Cenci minimises Beatrice Cenci's lived experiences, which are the heart of Shelley's drama. What makes Beatrice Cenci a superb character and *The Cenci* an important and powerful play is not whether she did right or wrong but the wrongs she suffers, not her guilt or guiltlessness but what she experiences and how she experiences it, not her choices but what she says and how. These elements derive from the play's poignant, moving, and accurate contextualisation of sexual and domestic violence. This paper explores four broad areas of analysis whose relevance to the discourse of sexual violence persists in our own time and substantiates a progressivist, or 'woke', perspective on cultural misogyny: first, bystander disbelief; secondly, Shelley's explicit thematisation of consent; thirdly, the domestic abuse (of Beatrice's stepmother Lucretia); and finally, rape and its suppressive effects on discourse. Aspects of woke social justice clearly look back to English Romanticism for antecedents.

2. Bystander Disbelief

Act I prepares the audience for the catastrophe by establishing the incredulity of family and friends; bystander disbelief and inaction are the context for the tragic action. Therefore, even before the drama validates women's experiences of sexual and domestic violence, the audience becomes aware of widespread social scepticism surrounding these facts, especially when the allegations are against a man as powerful and wealthy as Count Cenci. *The Cenci* opens with a conversation between the aristocratic antagonist and Cardinal Camillo during which the Count brags about his sadistic delights. Camillo responds with lukewarm admonitions before saying, "I thank my God that I believe you not" (I.1.120). Hence, in the opening scene of the play, Shelley exhibits how a well-meaning and benevolently disposed individual psychologically protects himself by not crediting what he does not want to think or believe. Furthermore, later in the same Act, Orsino converses with Beatrice, and afterward, in a soliloquy, he says, "Then as to what she suffers from her father, / In all this there is much exaggeration" (I.2.72-73). Subsequently, Orsino asserts that ordinary drinking, losing one's temper, and adultery are called "foul tyranny" by "Daughters and wives" (I.2.78). Notably, Orsino, Beatrice's friend and not her father's, claims to be in love with her, yet he does not believe she endures what she indeed suffers. Why then does Orsino disbelieve wives and daughters? The question arises logically from the circumstance of Orsino taking the side of the father against the daughter, who is both his friend and former lover.

Two men disbelieving Cenci's depravity, one benevolent (Camillo) and one corrupt (Orsino), might suffice to indicate that women encounter persistent incredulity, especially by men,[8] but Shelley underscores the point at a banquet in the third scene where Count Cenci exhorts his friends and extended family not to credit gossip and rumours about him. The reply of the "First Guest" reads: "In truth, my Lord, you seem too light of heart, / Too sprightly and companionable a man, / To act the deeds that rumour pins on you" (I.3.14-16). The guest then turns and repeats this view to a companion who invites Count Cenci to share his good news. When Count Cenci joyfully announces the murders of two of his own sons, an event for which he has longed and news of which causes Lucretia to faint, the declaration of Cenci's heartlessness prompts a "Third Guest" to respond, "I do believe it is some jest; [...] / stay! stay! / I see 'tis only raillery by his smile" (I.3.71-76). Count Cenci continues to invite his guests to drink to his triumph, before one lone guest denounces him, at which point Cardinal Camillo attributes Cenci's behaviour to madness ("You are insane" [I.3.93]). When several of the guests are leaving, Beatrice makes an eloquent plea for protection: "Shall we therefore find / No refuge in this merciless wide world?" (I.3.106-107). She explains that Lucretia and she fear dying soon, presumably at the hands of her murderous father: "His wife remains and I, whom if you save not, / Ye may soon share such merriment again / As fathers make over their children's graves" (I.3.122-125). This request is both direct and specific in how protection may be afforded – "Take us away!" (I.3.129) – yet no one will even look at Beatrice as they ignore her plea. When Beatrice wishes that she were dead, Cardinal Camillo is touched and asks Colonna, "Can we do nothing?" and Colonna answers, "Nothing that I see. / Count

Cenci were a dangerous enemy" (I.3.142-143). Cenci also receives pardons from the Pope who, according to Camillo, considers it a "most dangerous example / In aught to weaken the paternal power, / Being, as 't were, the shadow of his own" (II.2.54-56). While Count Cenci bids his guests farewell, he defuses the tension by attributing madness to Beatrice ("that insane girl", I.3.160) and uttering the sentence: "I will not make you longer / Spectators of our dull domestic quarrels" (I.3.162-163). The words "dull", "quarrels", and "domestic" trivialise Beatrice's accusations and assert the family's privacy as a defence against any interference, thereby neutralising what is dangerous, indeed life-threatening for Beatrice and Lucretia. Hence, Act I emphasises the essential social preconditions of sexual assault by establishing both disbelief and inaction as the context for the tragic action.[9]

3. Consent and Consensus

Anna Clark notes that in England during the eighteenth century, consent was implied by a woman's status rather than whether she agreed to sexual intercourse: "In practice, British judges and juries refused to take rape victims seriously; they almost never regarded the rape of an adult woman as a punishable offense".[10] Pamela Haag elucidates the extent to which "consent" gradually became part of the legal understanding of rape or seduction after the 1840s in the United States, but the actual legal history indicates that consent was deemed irrelevant ("judges unabashedly maintained the irrelevance of consent to seduction"): "She could not dispose of what was not hers in the first place – her labor, chastity, body, and character".[11] Susan S.M. Edwards documents that in Britain too, female chastity became a key consideration in case law, beginning with landmark case precedents established in 1811 and 1817.[12] Prior to these, the complainant's and the accused's social class were the dominant factors in British rape convictions. Against this legal context, Shelley's explicit focus on consent in 1819 is progressive.

The verb "consent" appears in the play's opening sentence, when Camillo tells Count Cenci, "That matter of the murder is hushed up / If you consent to yield his Holiness your fief that lies beyond the Pincian gate.—" (I.1.1-3). In other words, Pope Clement VIII will forgive Count Cenci his crime of murder if he gives roughly a third of his holdings

(I.1.15) to the Vatican.[13] This introduction of "consent" showcases a paradigm of a power imbalance with the dominant individual, the Pope, taking something away from the less potent person, Count Cenci. The second occurrence of the word "consent" is in an intriguing allusion to the biblical account of Judas' kiss of betrayal. In Act III, after Beatrice and Lucretia, along with Orsino, envision a plan to assassinate the Count, the sister asks for her brother Giacomo's "consent" to the plan: "[Y]et kiss me; I shall know / That then thou hast consented to his death" (III.1.385-386). This second example of "consent" represents a more equal and mutual form of agreement. These two examples establish differing understandings of the word, Camillo's operating in the context of a power imbalance and Beatrice's representing mutuality.

The theme of consent resonates with contemporary discussions of sexual violence in Act IV which opens with a soliloquy by Count Cenci in which he says he can force his will on Beatrice through torments and torture, but that he wants to corrupt her will as well as her body: "No, 'tis her stubborn will, / Which, by its own consent, shall stoop as low / As that which drags it down" (IV.2.10-12). Cenci's aim is Beatrice's 'consent' which he believes would make her more guilty, miserable, and abject than assault can render her. Lest we mistake Cenci's motive, Shelley repeats it after Beatrice refuses to come, and Cenci orders Lucretia:

> Go thou quick, Lucretia,
> Tell her to come; yet let her understand
> Her coming is consent, moreover,
> That if she come not I will curse her. (IV.1.100-104)

Cenci's conception of consent is warped and inaccurate, his demands backed by implicit and explicit threats. Even if consent were valid under such coercive circumstances,[14] Beatrice refuses to grant it (Lucretia: "She said, 'I cannot come'; Go tell my father that I see a torrent / Of his own blood raging between us", IV.1.113-115). After numerous threats and curses, followed by Lucretia conveying Beatrice's second refusal to obey, Cenci interrupts and says, "'Tis well, I can do both: first take what I demand, / And then extort concession" (IV.1.169-171). Etymologically derived from the Latin *concessiō,* "concession" refers to the "action of yielding or giving way, grant, permission, (in rhetoric) admission of guilt, conceding of a point".[15] Presumably, voluntary concession then, like consent, cannot be extorted.

Stuart M. Sperry's "The Ethical Politics of Shelley's *The Cenci*" argues that Shelley's awareness of an unbridgeable rift between custom and morality was longstanding by the time he composed *The Cenci*. Sperry's carefully researched study of the play is among the finest available; nevertheless, the claim that Beatrice's tragic flaw is her idealisation of her virginity reflects a mistaken and sexist misunderstanding of how victims experience rape.[16] *The Cenci* situates the rape of Beatrice in what is closer to a feminist and contemporary ethics than the legal and historical context in which Shelley lived. The historical material, "Relation of the Death of the Family of the Cenci", which Mary Shelley scrupulously translated from the Italian, and to which Shelley largely adhered, nowhere suggests that Beatrice Cenci, having a possible lover, a young and handsome Guido Guerra, was a virgin at the time of her molestation by Count Cenci.[17] The name of a different historical lover was Olimpio Calvetti, about whom the Shelleys may have known.[18] In addition, the words, "virgin", "virginity", "chaste", or "chastity" do not appear anywhere in the text. The words "pure" and "purity" occur five times in describing Beatrice, all of them after the violation. In other Shelley poems, explicitly sexual heroines are sometimes described as "pure", and sexual passion is associated with purity throughout Shelley's oeuvre. The descriptor "pure" applies to the sexual heroine, Cythna, and even to the incestuous passion between brother and sister which develops to a crisis in *Laon and Cythna*, Canto 6, Stanzas 23-42: "To the pure all things are pure!" (6.33).[19] We find the same identification of purity with sexual passion in *Queen Mab* (8.202; 9.202) and in *Epipsychidion* (565-569). Therefore, when Shelley has Cardinal Camillo say that Beatrice is "as pure as speechless infancy" (V.2.70) after the rape, Camillo employs a Shelleyan idiom in which female purity belies chastity or virginity. Beatrice seems to be referring to herself as someone who hypothetically "was the most pure and innocent on earth" (V.2.139), and Giacomo vindicates this self-identification when he calls her "the one thing innocent and pure" (V.3.101), while Bernardo praises his sister as "[t]hat perfect mirror of pure innocence" (V.4.130).

Shelley's rhetoric of female sexuality exposes a prevalent misinterpretation in literary criticism of Beatrice's emotions and experiences. Congruent with an understanding of consent, especially "affirmative consent", as the cornerstone of emerging contemporary understandings of rape,[20] Shelley's Beatrice shows us that consent is far more important to the drama's ethics than is chastity. Beatrice is traumatised because of violence and assault, not because of sexual activity or the loss of virginity. The history of Shelley's attribution of purity to his most sexual heroines and even to sexual passion itself renders her alleged virginity not just uncertain but irrelevant. Moreover, Count Cenci's crime, which we are led to understand constitutes the worst kind of brutality, effects Beatrice's desperation. Whatever occurs off-stage between Act II and Act III is too horrible for an already much abused daughter to fathom or articulate, ghastly enough to precipitate madness. Mary Shelley omits the relevant passages from her translation of "Relation of the Death of the Family of the Cenci" in a footnote asserting "*The details here are horrible, and unfit for publication" after the words: "[Count Cenci] often endeavoured, by force and threats, to debauch his daughter Beatrice, who was now grown up, and exceedingly beautiful – *" (297).

4. Domestic Abuse

Act II focuses on Count Cenci's abuse of his wife, Beatrice's stepmother, Lucretia, a character criticized when not overlooked in literary criticism. Act II opens with Lucretia reacting to her husband hitting her. The dialogue begins with Lucretia's attempt to soothe her son, Bernardo: "Weep not, my gentle boy; he struck but me / Who have borne deeper wrongs. In truth, if he / Had killed me, he had done a kinder deed" (II.1.1-3). Lucretia has many of the traits of what is called either 'abused spouse syndrome', 'battered wife syndrome', or 'abused partner syndrome'.[21] Lucretia experiences "[h]yperarousal and high levels of anxiety", "[a]voidance behaviour and emotional numbing usually expressed as depression, dissociation, minimization, repression, and denial", "negative alterations in mood and cognition," and "somatic or physical complaints".[22] Moreover, she expresses "learned helplessness", has a death wish, and is more concerned for others, in this instance her son, than herself. At times she is worried about her abuser and tries to save him. Like many victims of interpersonal violence (IPV), Lucretia clings to false hopes that Cenci will repent and reform. Shelley's Lucretia thus fulfils many diagnostic criteria, not formulated in 1819, for the effects of subjection to intimate partner violence.

Just as today there is widespread condemnation and judgment of female victims of interpersonal violence,[23] so too contemporary literary critics, when they write about Lucretia at all, often blame, shame, or disparage her. Rebecca Nesvet writes, "Lucretia's cowardly enabling of tyranny exacerbates her children's misery" (141).[24] Lucretia's efforts to reduce her children's suffering, in addition to her suicidality and despair, appear not only unsympathetic but also as blameworthy in Nesvet's account. Parker Reeve likewise deflects some of Count Cenci's guilt onto Lucretia: "Lucretia's timid attempts to mollify Cenci in his outrages against Beatrice ring with a collaborator's idiom ('Oh husband! Pray forgive poor Beatrice, / She meant not any ill' (ii.i.129-30)", and although he goes on to offer a sophisticated analysis of her role in establishing moral ambiguity and mirroring, he persists in engaging in a post-Freudian pathologising of "smother" love, unwarranted by Lucretia's goodness and her children's devotion to her.[25] Jeffrey N. Cox identifies Lucretia as "wholly ineffectual" because of her naïve religious faith.[26] Stuart Curran's assessment is more comprehensive, when he writes that "only on those occasions when Shelley can exploit Lucretia as a mother does her language possess vitality", but otherwise he laments her "frigid rhetoric", noting that "weakness is her only pronounced characteristic". He concludes that "Lucretia is not a compelling figure, and hardly a deep one".[27] The list of critics who disparage Lucretia is a long one.[28]

A handful of critics attempt to do justice to Lucretia's virtue and intentions. Donna Richardson singles her out as alone representing the virtues of "humility, mercy, and love" and also observes that Lucretia repeats the moral of Shelley's Preface, that "one cannot be morally degraded by another's act (III.i.119-122)": "Lucretia retains enough love and self-esteem to tell Beatrice the one truth that would have saved her: 'Whate'er you may have suffered, you have done / No evil' (III.i.121-122)".[29] Young-Ok An considers Lucretia only briefly but does understand the importance of the relationship between the two female characters: "The encoded bonding between them symbolically prefigures a restorability after violation, or, a radically different female desire that is yet to be realized".[30] Leila Walker analyses the figurative role of hair in *The Cenci* as a marker of Beatrice's and Lucretia's "loving relationship".[31] Stuart Peterfreund integrates Lucretia into his analysis of metonymy in *The Cenci*, noting that both she and Beatrice step onto the scaffold together to become literary history and "an oft-told 'tale for distant years'".[32] Dozens of other commentaries on *The Cenci* mention Lucretia only in delineating or summarising plot.

Contrary to a pervasive avoidance of or distaste for Lucretia in criticism, Shelley emphasises the sweetness of her disposition ("that gentle lady" [I.2.17]) and her protection of her stepchildren from their father (I.2.89-93). Modern studies of battered or abused women suggest Lucretia's passivity, of which some critics complain, is a result not of innate character but of long-term violent spousal abuse, a learned behaviour which develops even in strong women responding to a life permeated by fear.[33] When Beatrice champions Lucretia against her abuser, she therefore requites the stepmother credited with saving her and Bernard from murder in childhood, a predicament with biographical resonance for Mary Shelley, whose mother Mary Wollstonecraft played this protective role in relation to her father's violence toward her own mother.[34]

The current laws of many Western democracies afford Lucretia an exculpation which many critics have denied her. A plea of self-defence against a charge of murder could work in Lucretia's case with expert testimony that she suffers from "Battered Wife Syndrome".[35] To support the argument of self-defence, a defence attorney would need to prove that the accused realistically feared murder at the hands of her husband. Shelley establishes the plausibility of the murder of Lucretia by Cenci. Cenci himself suggests he would like to see Lucretia and Bernardo both dead when he speaks, in their absence, to Cardinal Camillo, "Bernardo and my wife could not be worse / If dead and damned" (I.1.135-136). Finally, the Count also directly threatens her with murder: "If you dare speak that wicked lie again / I'll kill you" (II.1.150-151), and "But I will take you where you may persuade / The stones you tread on to deliver you" (II.1.163-164). That Lucretia realistically expects to be murdered is decisively and repeatedly corroborated in the dialogue.

A second pillar of the defence would show that the accused has sought and not found protection. Beatrice and Lucretia make multiple attempts to seek help from the church, from the law, and from their friends and relatives. In Act I, scene 2, Beatrice sends a petition to the Pope through Orsino. Lucretia signals her despair, when the petition is returned unopened: "So, daughter, our last hope has failed" (I.2.28). In Act I, scene 3, Beatrice pleads with a powerful relative, Prince Colonna, Cardinal Camillo, and indeed anyone else at the banquet who is willing, to "[t]ake us away!" (I.3.129), yet no one replies. Although Orsino fails to deliver Beatrice's petition, Cardinal Camillo unsuccessfully seeks aid from the Pope (II.2.28-40), while Giacomo pleads for his siblings, "shall they have no protection?" (II.2.51). Later, after the murder of Cenci, Beatrice reproaches the Pope's Legate, Savella, and the law-keepers for failing her, "What! will human laws, / Rather will ye who are their ministers, / Bar all access to retribution first" (IV.4.117-119), and then for abandoning the victims of crime, when the ministers of the law are culpable ("'Tis ye are culprits", IV.4.124). Beatrice interprets the failure of "the ministers of the law" as guilt; she thereby gives voice to Shelley's lifelong belief that law, and justice are often opposed ("What is called justice civilly or politically is often opposed to" actual justice).[36]

In summary of Lucretia's case, because of the combination of the realistic threat of being murdered and the lack of redress or protection, the wife learns that the only escape from the violence and the threat of murder is either her own death or the death of her spouse, a situation Lucretia enunciates clearly to Beatrice: "We know that death alone can make us free; / His death or ours" (III.1.78-79). In the case of intimate partner violence, the plea of self-defence works as follows: when the threat of murder and the sought but unavailable protection from the law are established, the charge is not thereby lessened from first degree murder to any other lesser charge but is dropped altogether; the accused who killed her husband is considered altogether innocent.[37] Under current Canadian law, therefore, Lucretia would be acquitted.

5. Rape

This word is never mentioned in the play, and no synonyms or other explanations of rape occur; yet readers, audiences, and literary critics accept it. Even now rape is notoriously difficult to prosecute and prove in a court of law,[38] yet we know that Count Cenci's rape of Beatrice occurs off-stage between Act II and Act III, partly because written records have established the repeated incestual rape of Beatrice as historical fact but also because of Shelley's literary dexterity. There are multiple reasons why nothing is said explicitly in *The Cenci* to convey the crime of rape, a word that carries its own violence, insofar as it creates prejudice against and stigma for its victims. Before Beatrice's violation, Lucretia asks her "what can have thus subdued" (II.1.50) Beatrice's hitherto "firm mind" (II.1.48). After Lucretia begs again for an explanation of Beatrice's distress, with the stage direction "(speaking very slowly with a forced calmness)," Beatrice replies, "It was one word, Mother, one little word" (II.1.63). The smallest of the options in 1819 was rape.[39]

Moreover, Beatrice's stepmother's name, Lucretia, cannot help but remind the prospective nineteenth-century audience of the "one little word" which Beatrice refuses to utter and Shelley omits, because the ancient Roman Lucretia, wife of a Roman senator, was the victim of possibly the most famous sexual assault in Western European history. Her violation by the son of an Etruscan king *circa* 508 B.C.E. was immortalised throughout Western art in numerous paintings titled "The Rape of Lucretia", including one by Titian which the Shelleys would have seen in Venice, as well as paintings of Lucretia by Shelley's two favourite painters, Raphael and Guido Reni, and the poem "The Rape of Lucrece" by Shelley's favourite English poet, Shakespeare. Enthusiastic republicans, the Shelleys would also have been aware that the rape of the Roman Lucretia and her subsequent suicide on the steps of the Roman Senate were said to be the direct cause of the founding of a Roman Republic.[40] The death wish of Shelley's Lucretia needs to be understood in the context of the other idealised, abused, and suicidal Lucretia, and, at the very least, the text alludes to her through the unspoken word, "rape". The presence of a suicidal Roman Lucretia in *The Cenci* acts as a subtext of Beatrice's "one little word" and a gloss on Beatrice's logophobia.

When Beatrice introduces her father's issued threat, the "one little word" is a menace, not yet enacted but terrifying enough to bring on Beatrice's first fit of madness. Nowhere in the play is Beatrice able or willing to say this word or any words denoting the crime aloud. Why? William Brewer, in an essay about logophobia in Mary Shelley, succinctly summarises P.B. Shelley's scepticism and frustration with words across his prose and poetic texts.[41] Avoidance of naming "rape" in *The Cenci*, therefore, instantiates Shelley's broader distrust of language.

However, Beatrice's refusal to name the crime also has reasons which feed into but individuate her logophobia in the context of discourses of sexual violence, past and present.[42] Her first reason is to protect the woman she loves, Lucretia, whom she considers her mother:

> Ah! No, 'tis nothing new.
> The sufferings we all share have made me wild;
> He only struck and cursed me as he passed;
> He said, he looked, he did;—nothing at all
> Beyond his wont, yet it disordered me.
> Alas! I am forgetful of my duty,
> I should preserve my senses for your sake. (II.1.73-79)

This victim psychology has also been vindicated in studies of why women do not report rape. The desire to protect loved ones from knowledge, [43] when added to bystander disbelief and the lack of legal redress, then as now, are compelling reasons for silence. Even beyond this astute psychological realism, the post-traumatic repression of mentioning "rape" illustrates her logophobia: Beatrice fears the word and understands its danger. Beatrice explains her refusal to name the deed as a lack of words which could ever do it justice:

> What are the words which you would have me speak?
> I, who can feign no image in my mind
> Of that which has transformed me. [...]
>   Of all words,
> That minister to mortal intercourse,
> Which woulds't thou hear? (III.1.107-113)

Her refusal to speak any word or words to express the event is asserted as a permanent decision, one that she intends to keep until death, and, one that she attributes to an imagined comrade in suffering; she implies that any other woman would keep such a vow of silence, "if another ever knew / Aught like to it, she died as I will die, / And left it, as I must, without a name" (III.1.114-116). A third reason Beatrice gives for refusing to utter the word or make the accusation is that doing so will tarnish her future reputation:

> If I could find a word that might make known
> The crime of my destroyer; and that done
> My tongue should like a knife tear out the secret
> Which cankers my heart's core; aye, lay all bare
> So that my unpolluted fame should be
> With vilest gossips a stale mouthed story;
> A mock, a bye-word, and astonishment:— (III.1.154-160).

Such is her reply to Orsino's "Accuse him of the deed, and let the law / Avenge thee" (III.1.152-153). She then expresses her disbelief in any legal recourse, ending sarcastically with "Oh, most assured redress!" (III.1.166). Moreover, we learn that Count Cenci's intention in committing the crime is in large part to sully her name, "She shall stand shelterless in the broad noon / Of public scorn, for acts blazoned abroad, [...] / Her name shall be the terror of the earth" (IV.1.82-92). He and Beatrice both understand that a declaration of this particular crime has potential to stigmatise its survivor more than its perpetrator.[44]

6. Conclusion

P.B. Shelley opposed nineteenth-century English laws[45] which gave fathers sovereignty over and ownership of children and wives until 1839.[46] *The Cenci* was ahead of its time in discussing credibly and with sensitivity the reality of sexual violence and domestic abuse: including bystander disbelief of victims, a lack of legal redress, the importance of consent (what it is and is not), domestic abuse and its psychological consequences, and, finally, the crime that Beatrice refuses to name for good reasons. Through proto-feminist lenses, Shelley's play reads as a potent critique of Church, State, and society for their shared failure to protect women from domestic abuse and sexual violence.[47] *The Cenci*'s attacks on religion, the aristocracy, wealth, law, and the hierarchical structure of the family form an uncompromising examination of power and violence, whose controversial influence is also evident in the history of the play's production and reception. We should therefore re-read Shelley's *The Cenci* in the context of Romantic ethics and 'wokeness' relevant to the #MeToo movement, and we must also critique the drama's reception history as a longstanding suppression of the work's progressive and indeed activist themes. This text is less about parricide than about the physical and emotional experiences of Beatrice and her other persecuted family members, especially Lucretia. The ethical dilemma of Beatrice's supposed guilt is less central than the social and political structures which foster violence and injustice, and a reading must acknowledge that psychological truths and political subversions are the source of the tragedy's pathos and power, and make it as relevant today as it was during the Romantic Age.

Acknowledgements

I acknowledge with gratitude major contributions to this essay by my thorough and dedicated research assistant, Shelly Harder.

Notes

[1] Mulhallen, Jacqueline (2010). *The Theatre of Shelley*. Cambridge: Open Book Publishers, 1-2.

[2] Robinson, Henry Crabb (1938). *Henry Crabb Robinson on Books and Their Writers*. Ed. Edith J. Morley. Vol. 1. London: J.M. Dent and Sons, 409.

[3] Shelley, Mary (1839). "Note on *The Cenci*." *The Poetical Works of Percy Bysshe Shelley*. Vol. 2. London: Edward Moxon, Dover Street, 279.

[4] Byron, George Gordon (1982). *Selected Letters and Journals*. Ed. Leslie A. Marchand. London: John Murray, 254; Peacock, Thomas Love (1860). "Memoirs of Percy Bysshe Shelley: Part II." *Fraser's Magazine for Town and Country, 1830-1869* 61, 105; Shaw, George Bernard (1972). "'Art Corner' [A Review of *The Cenci*]." *The Shaw Review* 15.1, 37; Wilde, Oscar (2013). *The Complete Works of Oscar Wilde*. Eds. John Stokes and Mark W. Turner. Vol. 6. Oxford: Oxford University Press, 78.

[5] For details about these and other productions see Cameron, Kenneth N. and Horst Frenz (1945). "The Stage History of Shelley's *The Cenci*." *PMLA* 60.4, 1080-1105, 1086.

[6] See Stephens, John Russell (1980). *The Censorship of English Drama, 1824-1901*. Cambridge: Cambridge University Press, 11, 38.

[7] Shelley, Percy Bysshe (2002 [1819]). *The Cenci: A Tragedy in Five Acts. Shelley's Poetry and Prose*. Eds. Donald H. Reiman and Neil Fraistat. New York: Norton, 142. Further references to this edition will be included in the text.

[8] Gender still plays this role in whether people believe accounts of the abuse and assault of women by men: "Men are less punitive toward the perpetrator and assign more blame to the victim than do women (Bell et al., 1994; Langley *et al.*, 1991; McDonald & Kline, 2004; Pollard, 1992; Ryckman, Graham, Thornton, Gold, & Lindner, 1998)" (Black and Gold, 116).

[9] Contemporary research confirms that similar biases in "perceptions of culpability" influence jurors in rape trials still (Pica, 3965-3967).

[10] Clark, Anna (1987). *Women's Silence, Men's Violence: Sexual Assault in England, 1770-1845*. London: Pandora, 58.

[11] Haag, Pamela (1999). *Consent: Sexual Rights and the Transformation of American Liberalism.* Ithaca: Cornell University Press, 5; "Seduction was initially deliberated in civil suits in which the violation of a daughter/servant's chastity was taken to be a violation of the father/master's 'private' rights to her labor and services. The civil suit, while it did not disappear, was eclipsed in the 1840s by successful feminist campaigns to *criminalize* seduction as an offense against 'public' purity" (3).

[12] Edwards, Susan S.M. (1979). *Female Sexuality, the Law, and Society: Changing Socio-legal Conceptions of the Rape Victim in Britain since 1800.* University of Manchester, Dissertation, 173-74. Case law established key precedents for the consideration of chastity in rape trials in 1811 and 1817.

[13] The crime for which Cenci was put on trial and required to pay large fines was sodomy (Ricci, Vol. 1, 49; Bertolotti, 26). Truman Steffan notes that "Shelley substituted murder for atheism and sadistic promiscuity for sodomy" (606).

[14] Under Canadian law, "no consent is obtained if [...] the accused induces the complainant to engage in the activity by abusing a position of trust, power or authority" (CC § 273.1 (3)), such that "situations of forced submission [...] do not constitute consent" (Gotell, 868). Furthermore, in the case of R. v. Ewanchuk, "[t]he Court unanimously found that there is no defense of 'implied consent' in Canadian law" and that "silence and ambiguous conduct do not constitute consent" (Gotell, 869). Within this legal context, Cenci's statement that Beatrice's "coming is consent" (IV.1.102) would not constitute a legitimate defence.

[15] "concession, n." *OED Online*, Oxford University Press, September 2021, Web. 14 March 2022. www.oed.com/view/Entry/38189.

[16] Sperry, Stuart M. (1986). "The Ethical Politics of Shelley's *The Cenci*." *Studies in Romanticism* 25.3, 411-427, 420.

[17] Shelley, Mary (2016). *Mary Shelley's Literary Lives and Other Writings. Volume 4, 'Life of William Godwin': Poems, Uncollected Prose, Translations, Part-authored and Attributed Writings*, Eds. Pamela Clemit and A.A. Markley, London: Routledge, 298.

[18] For identification of Olimpio as Beatrice's lover and Beatrice's not being "chaste", see Ernest Sutherland Bates (1908). *A Study of Shelley's Drama 'The Cenci'.* New York: Columbia University Press, 33.

[19] "The positioning of the consummation of Laon and Cythna's love as its central episode enforces the status of the incest as both controlling symbol and thematic reference point for the whole" (Donovan 1987, 57).

[20] Graham, Laurie M., *et al.* (2017). "Sexual Assault Policies and Consent Definitions: A Nationally Representative Investigation of U.S. Colleges and Universities." *Journal of School Violence* 16.3, 243-258, 244.

[21] The category of "battered wife syndrome," as it was first named, although still controversial, was created in the late 1970s with contributions from both psychologists and sociologists. In a review of the existing studies by Kuhl and Satagun, "the battered woman can thus be described as someone who: is significantly depressed, has minimal ego boundaries and coping skills, and has a high tolerance for frustration" (100).

[22] Walker, Lenore E. (2016). *The Battered Woman Syndrome.* 4th ed. New York: Springer Publishing Company, 50.

[23] "Although public awareness of the effects of IPV has shifted over the past 40+ years, misconceptions about IPV are still quite prevalent. A study by Ewing and Aubrey (1987) found that both men and women in the general public agreed with several myths related to BWS, specifically that a battered woman could 'simply leave.' With regard to jury selection, one particularly relevant finding of their study was that many female research participants believed battered women were masochistic, emotionally disturbed, and partially responsible for the abuse (Ewing & Aubrey, 1987)" (Paradis *et al.* 2020, 368).

[24] Nesvet, Rebecca (2017). "'The Scene Itself': Rousseauvian Drama and Roman Space in Shelley's *The Cenci.*" *Jean-Jacques Rousseau and British Romanticism: Gender and Selfhood, Politics and Nation.* Eds. Russell Goulbourne and David Higgins. New York: Bloomsbury, 131-149.

[25] Parker, Reeve (2011). *Romantic Tragedies: The Dark Employments of Wordsworth, Coleridge, and Shelley.* Cambridge: Cambridge University Press, 195, 197.

[26] Cox, Jeffrey N. (1987). *In the Shadows of Romance: Romantic Tragic Drama in Germany, England, and France.* Athens: Ohio University Press, 144.

[27] Curran, Stuart (1970). *Shelley's Cenci: Scorpions Ringed with Fire.* Princeton: Princeton University Press, 58, 65.

[28] Watson, Melvin R. (1958). "Shelley and Tragedy: The Case of Beatrice Cenci." *Keats-Shelley Journal* 7, 13-21, 18; Bates, Ernest Sutherland (1908). *A Study of Shelley's Drama 'The Cenci'.* New York: Columbia University Press, 77.

[29] Richardson, Donna (1995). "The *Harmartia* of Imagination in Shelley's *The Cenci.*" *Keats-Shelley Journal* 44, 230-234.

[30] An, Young-Ok (1996). "Beatrice's Gaze Revisited: Anatomizing *The Cenci.*" *Criticism* 38.1, 27-68, 59.

[31] Walker, Leila (2013). "Percy Bysshe Shelley and the Ekphrasis of Hair." *European Romantic Review* 24.2, 231-250, 244.

[32] Peterfreund, Stuart (2002). *Shelley Among the Others: The Play of the Intertext and the Idea of Language.* Baltimore: Johns Hopkins University Press, 264.

[33] Meier and Seligman were the first to coin the phrase "learned helplessness" and describe this psychological phenomenon, which has since gained widespread acceptance and applicability, but Launius and Lindquist showed the extent to which the apparent passivity of battered spouses was in no way innate but altogether a learned behaviour.

[34] "The quickness of her father's temper led him sometimes to menace similar violence to his wife. When that was the case, Mary would often throw herself between the despot and his victim, with the purpose to receive upon her own person, the blows that might be directed against her mother. She has even laid whole nights at their chamber-door, when, mistakenly, or with reason, she apprehended that her father might break out into paroxysms of violence" (Godwin 1798, 9-10).

[35] "The admission of BWS evidence in Canada is not unique. Similar developments can be cited for Australia, Britain, and New Zealand (Seddon, 1993; Sheehy, Stubbs, & Tolmie, 1992)" (Tang, 618).

[36] Shelley, Percy Bysshe (1965). *The Complete Works of Shelley: Prose VII.* Eds. Roger Ingpen, Walter E. Peck and Richard Garnett. New York: Gordian Press, 272.

[37] Charles Patrick Ewing, in his ground-breaking study of abused wives who kill their partners, writes "a legal judgment that a battered woman killed her batterer in self-defense means that she is completely exonerated" (1987, 47).

[38] "For example, the International Violence Against Women Survey found that victimized women in the 11 countries surveyed most often reported the incident if the violence was considered serious or life-threatening (Johnson, Ollus and Nevala 2008). Additionally, victims reporting the incident were often met with scepticism and suspicion on the part of police and prosecutors, which resulted in a substantial number of cases being unfounded – that is, categorized as false, baseless or 'no-crimed' – as well as low arrest rates and shockingly low rates of prosecution and conviction" (Spohn 2020, 89).

[39] The word "sex" was not used as it is now to signify sexual intercourse. The word "incest" did not carry the same negative connotations for Romantic writers that it does now. However, although the word "incest" is not as little, it is a plausible option.

[40] Livy (1960). *The Early History of Rome: Books I-V of The History of Rome from Its Foundations.* Trans. Aubrey De Sélincourt. London: Penguin Books, 103-104.

[41] Brewer, William D. (1994). "Mary Shelley on the Therapeutic Value of Language." *Papers on Language and Literature* 30.4, 387-407, 388.

[42] That modern women are also reluctant to report rape is well established by the research. See Whiting *et al.* (2021, 751) for a summary of findings.

[43] Ullman writes, "[s]ome survivors felt that their disclosure would feel like a 'burden' on the family and could not imagine placing that onto loved ones" (2020, 844).

[44] "Others fear retaliation or being judged by family and community, which is particularly relevant for those who are harmed by well-known or powerful people (Adefolalu 2014)" (Whiting *et al.* 2021, 751).

[45] See Nathaniel Brown (1979). *Feminism and Sexuality in Shelley*. Cambridge, Mass: Harvard University Press, 99.

[46] See Trev Lynn Broughton, and Helen Rogers (2007). *Gender and Fatherhood in the Nineteenth Century*. Basingstoke: Palgrave Macmillan, 9.

[47] Kristine Johanson (2007) provides an excellent feminist understanding of women as property in *The Cenci* from a feminist and Wollstonecraftian perspective.

Bibliography

An, Young-Ok (1996). "Beatrice's Gaze Revisited: Anatomizing *The Cenci.*" *Criticism* 38.1, 27-68.

Bates, Ernest Sutherland (1908). *A Study of Shelley's Drama 'The Cenci'*. New York: Columbia University Press.

Bertolotti, A. (1877). *Francesco Cenci e la sua Famiglia: Notizie e Documenti*. Florence: Tipografia Della Gazzetta d'Italia.

Black, Katherine A. and David J. Gold (2008). "Gender Differences and Socioeconomic Status Biases in Judgments About Blame in Date Rape Scenarios." *Violence and Victims* 23.1, 115-128.

Brewer, William D. (1994). "Mary Shelley on the Therapeutic Value of Language." *Papers on Language and Literature* 30.4, 387-407.

Broughton, Trev Lynn and Helen Rogers (2007). *Gender and Fatherhood in the Nineteenth Century*. Basingstoke: Palgrave Macmillan.

Brown, Nathaniel (1979). *Feminism and Sexuality in Shelley*. Cambridge, Mass: Harvard University Press.

Byron, George Gordon (1982). *Selected Letters and Journals*. Ed. Leslie A. Marchand. London: John Murray.

Cameron, Kenneth N. and Horst Frenz (1945). "The Stage History of Shelley's *The Cenci.*" *PMLA* 60.4, 1080-1105.

Clark, Anna (1987). *Women's Silence, Men's Violence: Sexual Assault in England, 1770-1845*. London: Pandora.

"concession, n." *OED Online*, Oxford University Press, September 2021, Web. 14 March 2022. www.oed.com/view/Entry/38189.

Cox, Jeffrey N. (1987). *In the Shadows of Romance: Romantic Tragic Drama in Germany, England, and France*. Athens: Ohio University Press.

Curran, Stuart (1970). *Shelley's Cenci: Scorpions Ringed with Fire*. Princeton: Princeton University Press.

Donohue, Joseph W. (1970). *Dramatic Character in The English Romantic Age*. Princeton: Princeton University Press.

Donovan, John (1987). "Incest in *Laon and Cythna*: Nature, Custom, Desire." *Keats-Shelley Review* 2.1, 49-90.

Edwards, Susan S.M. (1979). *Female Sexuality, the Law and Society: Changing Socio-Legal Conceptions of the Rape Victim in Britain since 1800*. Diss. University of Manchester.

Ewing, Charles Patrick (1987). *Battered Women Who Kill: Psychological Self-Defense as a Legal Justification*. Lexington: Lexington Books.

Godwin, William (1798). *Memoirs of the Author of A Vindication of the Rights of Woman*. 2nd ed. London: J. Johnson.

Gotell, Lise (2008). "Rethinking Affirmative Consent in Canadian Sexual Assault Law: Neoliberal Sexual Subjects and Risky Women." *Akron Law Review* 41.4, 865-898.

Graham, Laurie M., et al. (2017). "Sexual Assault Policies and Consent Definitions: A Nationally Representative Investigation of U.S. Colleges and Universities." *Journal of School Violence* 16.3, 243-258.

Haag, Pamela (1999). *Consent: Sexual Rights and the Transformation of American Liberalism*. Ithaca: Cornell University Press.

Johanson, Kristine (2007). "'Every Holy and Unstained': Illuminating the Feminist *Cenci* Through Mary Wollstonecraft and Shakespeare's *Titus Andronicus*." *"Divining Thoughts": Future Directions in Shakespeare Studies*. Ed. Peter Orford. Newcastle: Cambridge Scholars Publishing, 98-105.

Kuhl, Anna F. and Inger Sagatun (1987). "Emergence of the Battered Woman Syndrome: The Impact Upon the Legal System." *American Journal of Criminal Justice* 11.1, 94-114.

Launius, Margaret H. and Carol Ummel Lindquist (1988). "Learned Helplessness, External Locus of Control, and Passivity in Battered Women." *Journal of Interpersonal Violence* 3.3, 307-318.

Livy (1960). *The Early History of Rome: Books 1-V of The History of Rome from Its Foundations*. Trans. Aubrey De Sélincourt. London: Penguin Books.

Meier, Steven F. and Martin Seligman (1976). "Learned Helplessness: Theory and Evidence." *Journal of Experimental Psychology: General* 105.1, 3-46.

Mulhallen, Jacqueline (2010). *The Theatre of Shelley*. Cambridge: Open Book Publishers.

Nesvet, Rebecca (2017). "'The Scene Itself': Rousseauvian Drama and Roman Space in Shelley's *The Cenci*." *Jean-Jacques Rousseau and British Romanticism: Gender and Selfhood, Politics and Nation*. Eds. Russell Goulbourne and David Higgins. New York: Bloomsbury, 131-149.

Paradis, Cheryl, Monique Bowen and Gene McCullough (2020). "Intimate Partner Violence: Psychological Effects and Legal Defenses." *Assessing Trauma in Forensic Contexts*. Eds. Rafael Art Javier, Elizabeth A. Owen and Jemour A. Maddux. Cham: Springer, 351-378.

Parker, Reeve (2011). *Romantic Tragedies: The Dark Employments of Wordsworth, Coleridge, and Shelley*. Cambridge: Cambridge University Press.

Peacock, Thomas Love (1860). "Memoirs of Percy Bysshe Shelley: Part II." *Fraser's Magazine for Town and Country, 1830-1869* 61, 92-109.

Peterfreund, Stuart (2002). *Shelley Among the Others: The Play of the Intertext and the Idea of Language*. Baltimore: Johns Hopkins University Press.

Pica, Emily, Chelsea Sheahan and Joanna Pozzulo (2020). "'But He's a Star Football Player!': How Social Status Influences Mock Jurors' Perceptions in a Sexual Assault Case." *Journal of Interpersonal Violence* 35.19-20, 3963-3985.

Ricci, Corrado (1926). *Beatrice Cenci*. Trans. Morris Bishop and Henry Longan Stuart. 2 Vols. London: William Heinemann.

Richardson, Donna (1995). "The *Harmartia* of Imagination in Shelley's *The Cenci*." *Keats-Shelley Journal* 44, 216-239.

Robinson, Henry Crabb (1938). *Henry Crabb Robinson on Books and Their Writers*. Ed. Edith J. Morley. Vol. 1. London: J.M. Dent and Sons.

Shaw, George Bernard (1972). "'Art Corner' [A Review of *The Cenci*]." *The Shaw Review* 15.1, 35-38.

Shelley, Mary (2016). *Mary Shelley's Literary Lives and Other Writings. Volume 4, 'Life of William Godwin': Poems, Uncollected Prose, Translations, Part-authored and Attributed Writings*, Eds. Pamela Clemit and A.A. Markley, London: Routledge.

---. (1839). "Note on *The Cenci*." *The Poetical Works of Percy Bysshe Shelley*. Vol. 2. London: Edward Moxon, Dover Street, 272-280.

Shelley, Percy Bysshe (2002 [1819]). *The Cenci: A Tragedy in Five Acts. Shelley's Poetry and Prose*. Eds. Donald H. Reiman and Neil Fraistat. New York: Norton, 138-201.

---. *Epipsychidion. Shelley's Poetry and Prose*. Eds. Donald H. Reiman and Neil Fraistat. New York: Norton, 390-407.

--- (2012). *Laon and Cythna. The Complete Poetry of Percy Bysshe Shelley*. Eds. Donald H. Reiman, Neil Fraistat and Nora Crook. Vol. 3. Baltimore: Johns Hopkins University Press, 109-320.

--- (2002 [1819]). *Queen Mab. Shelley's Poetry and Prose*. Eds. Donald H. Reiman and Neil Fraistat. New York: Norton, 15-71.

--- (1965). *The Complete Works of Shelley: Prose VII*. Eds. Roger Ingpen, Walter E. Peck and Richard Garnett. New York: Gordian Press.

Simpson, Michael (1998). *Closet Performances: Political Exhibition and Prohibition in the Dramas of Byron and Shelley*. Stanford: Stanford University Press.

Sperry, Stuart M. (1986). "The Ethical Politics of Shelley's *The Cenci*." *Studies in Romanticism* 25.3, 411-427.

Spohn, Cassia (2020). "Sexual Assault Case Processing: The More Things Change, the More They Stay the Same." *International Journal for Crime, Justice and Social Democracy* 9.1, 86-94.

Steffan, Truman (1969). "Seven Accounts of the Cenci and Shelley's Drama." *Studies in English Literature, 1500-1900* 9.4, 601-618.

Stephens, John Russell (1980). *The Censorship of English Drama, 1824-1901*. Cambridge: Cambridge University Press.

Tang, Kwong-leung (2003). "Battered Woman Syndrome Testimony in Canada: Its Development and Lingering Issues." *International Journal of Offender Therapy and Comparative Criminology* 47.6, 618-629.

Ullman, Sarah E. *et al.* (2020). "Reasons for and Experiences of Sexual Assault Nondisclosure in a Diverse Community Sample." *Journal of Family Violence* 35.8, 839-851.

Walker, Lenore E. (2016). *The Battered Woman Syndrome.* 4th ed. New York: Springer Publishing Company.

Walker, Leila (2013). "Percy Bysshe Shelley and the Ekphrasis of Hair." *European Romantic Review* 24.2, 231-250.

Watson, Melvin R. (1958). "Shelley and Tragedy: The Case of Beatrice Cenci." *Keats-Shelley Journal* 7, 13-21.

Whiting, Jason B. *et al.* (2021). "Trauma, Social Media, and #WhyIDidntReport: An Analysis of Twitter Posts about Reluctance to Report Sexual Assault." *Journal of Marital and Family Therapy* 47.3, 749-766.

Wilde, Oscar (2013). *The Complete Works of Oscar Wilde.* Eds. John Stokes and Mark W. Turner. Vol. 6. Oxford: Oxford University Press.

Katie Smith

Childlessness: Uncovering Abortion in Mary Wollstonecraft's *Maria and the Wrongs of Woman* (1798)

1. Introduction

Mary Wollstonecraft's focus on abortion in *Maria* may initially seem to contradict her emphasis on motherhood as the most important female role. However, by including abortion in this text, whose heroine is "tortured by maternal apprehension",[1] Wollstonecraft treats nurturing and terminating a pregnancy as interconnected experiences by which women can relate to each other.[2] That Wollstonecraft's two major female characters, Jemima and Maria, both undergo abortions marks the author's attempt to illustrate a common thread of oppression across class boundaries – an early foray into intersectionality. This expansion into working-class experience is accompanied by a shift in Wollstonecraft's attitude to abortion. Contrary to her earlier assertion that abortion served only to veil female promiscuity, Wollstonecraft explores the pressing financial and social threats awaiting unmarried pregnant women. In doing so, Wollstonecraft recentres female lived experience in contemporary abortion discourse and emphasises lived experience of womanhood across classes in a way that anticipates wokeness in 21st-century discourses.

In *Maria*, Wollstonecraft dramatises the awful possibilities an unwed mother-to-be faced to avoid social disgrace, including abortion and suicide. Redirecting abortion discourse away from male social commentary, Wollstonecraft creates a space in which to consider experiences outside of society's default view of women as chaste wives and mothers such as those of the illegitimate, childless ex-prostitute Jemima. This refocusing neither privileges Maria's middle-class voice nor presents hers and Jemima's experience as identical. While Jemima recounts her abortion with brutal realism, Maria's laudanum overdose – an act which ends her pregnancy – employs tropes common in sentimental

45

fiction, evoking *Clarissa* in Wollstonecraft's presentation of Maria's moral victory in death.[3] Mary Poovey's observation that sentimental fiction provided a platform to re-emphasise bourgeois morality but also to garner support for humanitarian causes (such as abolition) suggests that middle-class readers were primed to expect moral instruction in such novels.[4] By embedding Jemima's narrative into a novel that apes sentimental style – and whose heroine, Poovey notes, holds the same idealistic attitudes to marriage that sentimental novels reinforced – Wollstonecraft injects the experience of working-class women into a middle-class structure to cultivate cross-class empathy in her readership.[5] Having introduced this possibility, Wollstonecraft considers how cross-class camaraderie might provide an alternative to the societal model in which women survive by exploiting each other to gain men's favour.

Eighteenth-century abortion discourse was limited and male-dominated, attracting prolific commentators including Jean-Jacques Rousseau and the Marquis de Sade. Both commentators neglect the personal impact of abortion on women. While Rousseau condemned "secret abortions" as a means for women to "cheat nature"[6] and de Sade valued them for this same reason, these two prominent intellectuals offer limited insight into what should be done regarding the illegitimate children whose birth abortion prevents – a topic on which Wollstonecraft, the mother of an illegitimate daughter, is uniquely qualified to comment.[7] Furthermore, Wollstonecraft's abortion discourse is deeply gynocentric even in her chosen format. Poovey suggests that the sentimental genre provided its mainly female readers with an opportunity for controlled rebellion, wherein they could indulge in transgressive fantasies without real-life consequences.[8] By discussing abortion in this genre, Wollstonecraft uses a format that would primarily allow for discourse between women on a topic that affects women, rather than amplifying male voices. This issue has proved persistent in 21st-century discourse, for example in Texas governor Greg Abbott's flippant assertion that an abortion can easily be arranged before the sixth week of pregnancy despite the fact that pregnancy is not always detected within this timeframe.[9] In this article, I will explore how Wollstonecraft challenges existing eighteenth-century abortion debates by redirecting attention from detached male sociological theory to women's lived experiences and the personal impact of terminating a pregnancy in a way that anticipates the 21st-century woke emphasis on lived experience.

Angus McLaren notes that the stigma surrounding abortion makes it difficult to quantify the practice historically, though France's comparatively low birth rate in the early 1800s suggests greater prevalence there than elsewhere.[10] While the 1791 French Penal code cited no punishment for a woman who had her pregnancy terminated, strengthening the possibility that abortion was common,[11] this was also the case in English law, which only punished infanticide or "concealment" of stillbirth.[12] Wollstonecraft's engagement with abortion in *Maria* suggests her heightened interest in the topic after publishing *A Vindication of the Rights of Woman* (1792), wherein she criticised women who "destroy the embryo in the womb".[13] Though there is nothing to indicate that Wollstonecraft wished or attempted to procure abortion for herself, she would likely have known about the practice in France and contrasted its prevalence there with its apparent rarity in England.

Due to the assumed regularity of abortion in France, I have chosen to contrast Wollstonecraft with two prominent French commentators on abortion: Jean-Jacques Rousseau and the Marquis de Sade. Wollstonecraft often analysed Rousseau's ideas, commenting in *Vindication* that, despite "admir[ing] [his] genius", she considered his female character Sophie "grossly unnatural" (17-18). Wollstonecraft's initial resistance to abortion as enabling promiscuity coincides with Rousseau's prim disavowal of abortion, indicating that Wollstonecraft knew his anti-abortion stance prior to depicting abortion in *Maria*. Though Wollstonecraft is not engaging so directly with de Sade, they are writing with wildly different approaches in the same timeframe with a shared interest in abortion and women's suffering. Moreover, de Sade's *Philosophie de la Boudoir* anticipates many modern pro-choice arguments, including the assertion that a foetus has no independent personhood entitling it to life.[14] While de Sade cannot be said to have been as representative of his time as Rousseau, his anticipation of modern attitudes merits attention, and the contrast clarifies several nuances in Wollstonecraft's stance.[15]

When reading Wollstonecraft's depiction of abortion, it is essential to understand the procedure as her contemporaries would have known it. Before modern pregnancy tests, physicians recognised that "suppression of the *menses*" (emphasis added) indicated pregnancy.[16] Culturally, however, great emphasis was given to the state of having 'quickened' which indicates the moment the woman first feels her foetus moving. Wollstonecraft's letters to Gilbert Imlay indicate that she herself took quickening as the first confirmation that she was pregnant: "gentle twitches [...] make me *begin to think, that I am nourishing a creature*" (emphasis added).[17] Her phrasing suggests she began to think about her foetus as a separate "creature" and herself a mother-to-be at this moment. Likewise, Hugh Lenox Hodge notes in his lecture *On Criminal Abortion* that, historically, a quickened foetus had a soul whereas an unquickened one did not.[18] That this distinction was codified into English law only five years after *Maria*'s publication suggests that the general public still accepted quickening as the point at which a foetus became a baby.

Unlike modern usage, the eighteenth-century term 'abortion' did not solely describe deliberate terminations. In his lecture *An Introduction to the Practice of Midwifery*, the physician Thomas Denman uses "abortion" and "miscarriage" interchangeably (369). The French language similarly lacked this distinction: a contemporary French-English dictionary translates "avorter" as either "to miscarry" *or* "to prove abortive".[19] Though this oversight makes it difficult to trace abortion historically, it also indicates that English law did not distinguish women who deliberately aborted their pregnancies from women who miscarried. Furthermore, the few criminal cases around abortion in the Old Bailey archives imply a general disinterest in prosecuting women for having abortions: normally, abortionists ended up in court because their patient either had testified against them or died.[20] Consequently, an eighteenth-century Englishwoman could reasonably expect not to be prosecuted for seeking abortion and, prior to quickening, may not have even viewed her foetus as a separate being. Therefore, Wollstonecraft's unambiguous description in *Maria* of Jemima's "sensations of new-born life" (98) shows how essential she considered abortion, and specifically of a quickened foetus, to her discussion of women's experience: Jemima acknowledges her pregnancy as a baby, has already begun bonding with it, and still has an abortion she does not want because the patriarchal society she inhabits leaves her without a better option. This choice to have Jemima's abortion occur late enough that she considers her foetus a baby allows the novel to retain relevance in the face of the Texas Heartbeat Act (2021), named so because it grants a foetus legal protection once its heartbeat is detectable.[21] The question for Wollstonecraft, however, is not whether the foetus is alive, but whether its life matters more than its mother's.

2. "This Infernal Potion": Accounts of Abortion

Wollstonecraft's use of first-person perspective gives nuance to the pre-existing connotation between abortion and hypocrisy, namely the claim that women "cheat nature" to hide their sexual indiscretions.[22] After commenting that a Methodist meeting provides opportunity for Jemima's employer to rape her, Wollstonecraft compounds this irony through the character's comment that she submits to avoid her "mistress's fury".[23] The implication that Jemima fears her rape being discovered more than the rape itself highlights how precarious her situation is. Here Wollstonecraft deconstructs Rousseau's assertion that hypocrisy causes women to abort: Jemima seeks to pretend to retain her virginity and thus to maintain her reputation from economic necessity, and her abortion is arranged by her employer to conceal *his* sexual transgression, not hers.[24]

Having destabilised the idea that only licentious women sought abortions, Wollstonecraft begins dissecting the extent to which abortion actually helps impregnated women. By noting that Jemima's rapist arranges the abortion to protect his reputation, and that he provides the abortifacient without Jemima asking for or wanting it, Wollstonecraft narratively echoes but implicitly critiques male-dominated abortion discourse, in which even pro-abortion stances enabled the mistreatment of women.[25] For example, A.D. Farr observes that de Sade recognises abortion as a necessary means to the end of unbridled freedom, explaining that, for de Sade, a woman's right to abortion is essential to allow her to conceal and thus continue her sexual transgressions.[26] While Farr notes that de Sade's argument anticipates modern pro-choice attitudes, it is worth considering how de Sade's advocacy of abortion stems partly from his assertion that women exist to be men's playthings – a stance that goes as far as deeming chaste women "useless and therefore contemptible".[27] While de Sade's advocacy of state-sanctioned brothels for male and female use suggests some interest in egalitarianism, his writing suggests no interest in empowering women like the sentimental serial monogamist Maria or sex-hating Jemima,[28] whose "horror of men" reads to a modern eye as sexual trauma.[29] As a working-class woman, Jemima can only take back control of her fertility because a corrupt male gives her the option; however, without male corruption, she would not be pregnant at all. Jemima's "rage giving place to despair" during her abortion suggests a latent understanding of how her socio-economic circumstances have obstructed her bodily autonomy (98). Jemima's body is not her own even in the moment she aborts, and the abortion is both traumatic and unable to protect her socially. On the contrary, it is only *after* the abortion that Jemima becomes a prostitute (98). Abortion does not save women from consequence, Wollstonecraft suggests, but perpetuates the brutality to which women are subjected.

Wollstonecraft further challenges de Sade's view of the abortion as an easy solution for corrupt women by detailing Jemima's "mental anguish" during the "approaching dissolution" of her pregnancy and, potentially, her own life (98). Wollstonecraft's decision to delay the abortion in Jemima's narrative highlights the depth of Jemima's reluctance to end her pregnancy. Only *after* being raped again, "scratched, kicked", "pushed out of door" and insulted by her rapist as having "disturbed the peace of the family" does Jemima feel demoralised enough to use the abortifacient, a set of events through which Wollstonecraft again contradicts the idea that abortion unproblematically allows women to conceal sexual incontinence (97-98). On the contrary, Wollstonecraft stresses that Jemima is *not* naturally lascivious through the character's own quite cynical comment that she "had not even the pleasure of being enticed into vice" (98). Power, not pleasure, takes the forefront in Jemima's descriptions of having to "submit" sexually (96) or be "abused" (98); it is noticeable that she feels guilt not for having seduced the tradesman, but for how she used her sexual power at another woman's expense (104). By showing Jemima engaged in consensual sex only after her abortion, Wollstonecraft destabilises the notion that abortion allows a woman to conceal her existing corruption. Instead, the abortion serves as a kind of social suicide through which Jemima rejects the society which has failed her; the image of her having "crawled" out of her sickbed is reminiscent of an infant's crawling, symbolising her 'rebirth' into the corruption into which circumstances have forced her (98).

Jemima's distress when undergoing her abortion further challenges male commentators' view of abortion as unproblematic. Though de Sade's analogy that aborting a foetus is essentially the same as evacuating one's bowels is more flippant and more performative in its insensitivity than Rousseau's assertions; both neglect the physical and emotional cost of abortion to the woman seeking it.[30] By comparing abortion to an unavoidable bodily function, de Sade overlooks the risk that a woman might die from her abortion – a point Wollstonecraft makes emphatically clear by describing Jemima's intense physical reaction to the abortifacient, which leaves her "confined to [her] bed for several days." (98) Jemima's reaction is consistent with having taken savin (juniper), an effective but dangerous emmenagogue.[31] Jemima's account also matches a young woman's testimony in 1834 that taking savin as an abortifacient left her bedridden and "ill in every way [...] for fourteen days."[32] Jemima's hope in *Maria* that the abortion might "destroy [her] at the same time" as her foetus is not an hyperbolic desire but an unsettling, quite realistic possibility, to the point that Jemima's initial impression of abortion is to equate it with "killing [her]self" (96).

3. "Better to Die with Me": Suicide as Abortion

Wollstonecraft repeatedly connects abortion to suicide, presenting both sympathetically in Jemima's narrative, which opens with Jemima's mother attempting to "famish herself" into a miscarriage (92).[33] In Jemima's comment that her mother lacked "resolution" to kill herself, Wollstonecraft presents suicide as an act of will. Wollstonecraft repeats this pattern when describing a pregnant girl thrown out by her tradesman lover at Jemima's request (104). The suicide is described in painstaking detail: "approaching a tub where horses were watered, she sat down in it [...] with desperate resolution [...] – till resolution was no longer necessary!" (104). By emphasising the woman's "resolution", Wollstonecraft draws a subtle parallel between the girl and Jemima's mother, another pregnant woman deceived in "the fervour of seduction" (92). The dashes and exclamation points in Jemima's syntax, reserved for moments of particular distress, hint at Jemima's own lack of resolution as she pleads with Maria to "wonder not that [she] became a wolf!" – a metaphor that highlights Jemima's predatory action as contrary to human nature (104). Jemima's apparent respect for the girl's "resolution" and her desire for death during her own abortion suggests equivalency between the two acts as a desperate woman's last resorts.

Wollstonecraft sharpens her focus on similarities between abortion and suicide through the most finished version of the novel's ending, in which Maria overdoses on laudanum with the intention of killing herself and, by extension, becoming "the tomb" of her foetus by Darnford (176). While Wollstonecraft does not explicitly frame this scene as an abortion, she stages it similarly to Jemima's termination. Maria's assertion that "it is better [for the foetus] to die with [her]" (176) mirrors Jemima's desire "that [the abortion] might destroy [her], at the same time that it stopped the sensations of new-born life" (98). Wollstonecraft also employs similar structures to both scenes: both women drink an abortifacient, suffer anguish, fall ill, then ultimately survive while their pregnancies end (98). As with Jemima's abortion, Wollstonecraft makes her condonement of Maria's actions abundantly clear:

> Her murdered child again appeared […], [Maria was] mourning for the babe of which she was the tomb. – "And could it have a nobler? – Surely it is better to die with me […] I cannot live! – but could I have deserted my child the moment it was born?" (167)

The exclamation that Maria "cannot live" mitigates the heroine's decision by suggesting her lack of options, as does the subtlety with which Wollstonecraft depicts the loss of Maria's pregnancy. Although Maria's suicide adheres to a pattern in sentimental novels where the heroine, wronged by her lover, commits suicide, the *deus ex machina* of Jemima's reappearance distracts the reader from the detail that Maria's overdose terminates her pregnancy.[34] In doing so, Wollstonecraft downplays Maria's miscarriage, by focusing the reader's attention on Maria's reasons behind the overdose instead emphasising the tragedy of her initial situation and the intensity of her joy at being reunited with her first child.[35]

The swerve from tragic suicide to happy reunion occurs within three short sentences: "'Behold your child' exclaimed Jemima. Maria started off the bed and fainted. – Violent vomiting ensued." (177) By placing the "violent vomiting" as the subject in this short sentence, Wollstonecraft presents the act of vomiting as an uncontrollable physical reaction which externalises Maria's terror at losing her child, further empowering the character's maternal instinct so that the mere sight of her first child prompts Maria's body to reject the overdose, symbolically purifying her from her attempted suicide/abortion. This idea that maternal instinct can supersede the character's own choices and biology suggests an implicit distinction between the born and unborn child. While Maria recognises her pregnancy as an independent creature and feels enough duty towards it that she refuses to leave it "without a mother's care", her body refuses to let her die once she realises her daughter by Venables is alive, overriding her previous assertion that she "cannot live" (176). Only Maria's declaration that she "will live for her child!" – rather than her "children" – reveals that she has miscarried as a result of her overdose (177). By only offering this slight insinuation, Wollstonecraft downplays Maria's abortion, instead emphasising her relationship with her living child and, to a lesser extent, her camaraderie with Jemima.

Inasmuch as suicide was prevalent in sentimental fiction – a choice which re-emphasises Maria's middle-class credentials – Maria's choice to overdose while pregnant would likely have been more controversial judging from William Hunter's impassioned defence of women who pursued "an end to a life which is become insupportable".[36] Hunter's argument that suicide while pregnant in "a frenzy of despair" is not "more offensive [...] than under a frenzy from [...] lunacy" (8) was originally written in 1773 and still reprinted posthumously in 1818, suggesting that pregnant women's suicide was a longstanding point of contention. By subverting a typically sentimental suicide, Wollstonecraft affirms Maria's choice to commit suicide rather than give birth to a child she believes she cannot support. By having the unborn child's death coincide with the first child's reappearance, when Maria believed her first child dead, Wollstonecraft symbolically rewards Maria for refusing to bring a baby into a society that would mistreat it by restoring her 'dead' daughter by Venables to her in place of the pregnancy she has terminated.

4. "Her Protector – and Eternal Friend" – Absent Fathers and Illegitimate Children

Wollstonecraft's notes indicate that at least one undeveloped ending involves Maria either miscarrying or aborting and then committing suicide after Darnford abandons her.[37] Darnford's mysterious absence in the most developed ending similarly implies that Wollstonecraft planned this version wherein Darnford abandons his lover and unborn child. Through this implied abandonment, Wollstonecraft provides a critique of sexual irresponsibility not articulated elsewhere in abortion discourse, namely the double standard which treated only women's sexual transgressions as unethical while permitting male promiscuity. Maria's attempt to escape a socially unacceptable pregnancy through suicide illustrates how seriously sexual double standards can harm even middle-class women who value marriage and monogamy, particularly given that several of the unmarried women who become pregnant in the novel have been promised marriage.

Men's role in creating illegitimate children is a significant omission in Rousseau's writing in light of his choice to relinquish all five of his own to a foundling hospital.[38] Given his previously discussed unwillingness to encourage this behaviour for others, this is a convenient blind spot in Rousseau's philosophy. Rather than specifically condemning abortion,

Rousseau attacks the "Laws of Continence and Honour" which he claims "multiply" terminations by creating an incentive to conceal sexual transgression, extending this idea to other "shameful methods"[39] such as infanticide, masturbation, and anal sex, apparently advocating for both sexes' unrestrained fertility without exploring or even acknowledging the stigma illegitimate children endured. By having Darnford display unrestrained sexuality through his pursuit of a married woman and prior involvement with prostitutes, then detailing Maria's suicide after he abandons her, Wollstonecraft draws attention to the havoc men's sexual incontinence wreaks on women (86).

While Wollstonecraft's comment that Maria views Darnford "as her husband" (165) supports Poovey's argument that Maria considers marriage a solution rather than a problem, it also sanctions Maria's adulterous union as equal to her marriage to Venables, creating a cognitive dissonance between Maria's moral status as a woman in a happy if transgressive 'marriage' and her legal status as a runaway wife held captive in a madhouse. Put simply, Wollstonecraft uses the sentimental genre's pro-marriage sentiments to make Maria's relationship with Darnford palatable to the reader, undermining Maria's legal marriage in the process. Given that this occurs after the revelation of Venables's failed attempt at "bartering [Maria's] person", Wollstonecraft invites the reader to treat the two "husbands" as having equal rights to Maria.[40] That this is a major point in Maria's defence of Darnford in the latter's adultery trial implies an attempt by Wollstonecraft to present chastity as a virtue regardless of gender. Fundamentally, Maria's argument is grounded in the fact that Venables, by attempting to engage her in prostitution, had willingly rescinded his right to an exclusive sexual union, leaving no marital exclusivity upon which Darnford could intrude.

Most damning for men like Venables in Wollstonecraft's novel is how their conduct of sexual incontinence makes abortion the most viable recourse available to their impregnated lovers, who cannot rely on them to become responsible fathers. Within the three scenes of attempted suicide or abortion, Wollstonecraft draws attention to the respective paternal absences. Immediately prior to taking the abortifacient, Jemima recalls not only that she "had no claim" to "her father's roof" but that she "shrunk back as from death [from her] father's execrations"; seeking instead the father of her child, she immediately receives the curses she hoped to avoid: "he 'damned me for a bastard'" (97). Having "no claim" to her "father's roof" has similarly tragic consequences for the tradesman's cast-off lover, who cannot face her parents after her baby's father has cast her aside. Even the middle-class Maria fares poorly on this front, crying out, "may I find a father where I am going!" (176) Wollstonecraft's use of the word "father" in an appeal to God immediately before a miraculous rescue intensifies the absence of a human male saviour. By repeatedly highlighting male inaction during instances of both intentional and incidental abortion, Wollstonecraft draws attention to the omission of male responsibility in eighteenth-century abortion discourse. While Rousseau primarily blames women, and de Sade encourages them, neither seriously considers men's responsibilities towards their children.

Wollstonecraft's critique of paternal irresponsibility is accentuated by her use of the traditionally moralistic sentimental genre. By using a genre that typically reinforces marriage's importance, Wollstonecraft extends the genre's emphasis on husbands to fathers, illustrating how male sexual incontinence damages not only the women they impregnate but also the children they sire. In light of new, Romantic ideas about children as "nature's priests", the re-evaluation of children not as untamed adults but pure beings capable of morally guiding adults came with the implication that men should naturally want to be around their children.

Wollstonecraft's discourse is rare in that it considers men's personal responsibility to their illegitimate children whereas both Rousseau and de Sade treat illegitimate children as an abstract social problem. Rousseau's admission that he abandoned his own children in *Confessions* suggests that illegitimate children's treatment is a point of contention for him. Contrary to his own abandonment of his offspring, Rousseau seems to take issue with the idea that society as a whole should shoulder the responsibility for illegitimate children, judging from his reluctance to "expose any young people who may read [him] to the same error".[41] Aside from "lack of means to bring them up", Rousseau's comment that he "was acting as a citizen and [...] as a member of Plato's Republic [wherein children are raised without knowledge of their parentage]" suggests an ideological motivation to abandon the children (333). For de Sade, the political impact of illegitimate children on a republic similarly trumps the personal. Monarchy, he argues, relies on a high birth rate as a king needs subjects; in a republic, that same "abundant population" and the "individual commiseration" at losing such children become a "vice".[42]

That de Sade considers illegitimate children superfluous insofar as that advanced civilizations empower monarchy and advocate abortion or even infanticide as justifiable to preserve a republic – rather than a question of personal morality and lived reality – suggests a wider apathy towards the treatment of illegitimate children. Wollstonecraft examines that political importance from a separate stance than her male counterparts: rather than abortion being an important means to revolutionary ends, the greater equality promised by a republic matters because it allows for a world in which women can either access abortions or have no need for them. This focus on the hypocrisy by which women were subjugated even after the revolution is presented by Wollstonecraft in a microcosm when Jemima seeks aid from her libertine friend on the grounds that he had decried "the evils which arise in society from the despotism of rank and riches."[43] In his patronising reply that Jemima should "exert her powers" to fix her own situation,[44] Wollstonecraft succinctly critiques her fellow republicans' complacency when presented with women's struggles, highlighting the same lack of sympathy and in fact powerlessness which her novel attempts to bridge.

While Wollstonecraft also addresses Rousseau and de Sade's concern that restricting abortion access results in illegitimate children, her portrayal is unusually empathic. When depicting Venables's illegitimate daughter, Wollstonecraft's language evokes pity for the "sallow" child "scarcely able to support her own weight" (132) – a description that echoes Jemima's account of herself as "a weak and rickety babe" (92). That the incident occurs after Jemima's narrative accentuates the cruelty of Venables's annoyance at being expected to pay "a little physic" for the dying child (132) – a bitterly ironic reaction given Maria's recollection that she originally fell in love with her husband because he donated "a guinea" to Peggy's children to appear generous (120). Maria's knee-jerk reaction to the sight of the "squalid" child and anguish at her husband's "inhuman" attitude challenges the apathy towards illegitimate children; Maria's feelings are so natural that they need no explanation.

5."Why Must I Call her Woman?" Female Antipathy and Solidarity in Pregnancy

By presenting Maria's generosity as the natural reaction to a pitiful child, Wollstonecraft subtly critiques women who limit their desire to nurture to their biological children by contrasting the mistreatment Jemima endured as an illegitimate child (132).[45] That it is not her abortion but the pregnant girl's suicide that provides a measure of Jemima's corruption – the only act for which Jemima fears losing Maria's "esteem" (104) – suggests that women's corruption stems from their security being dependent on "fostering of libertinism in men" (122). Jemima's use of sexual power to the pregnant girl's detriment is the only act for which she calls herself "a wolf", a metaphor by which Wollstonecraft implies that women's exploitation of other women is inherently dehumanising.[46] By contrasting Jemima's recollections of women harming women with the camaraderie that emerges between Maria and her keeper after Jemima confesses her abortion, Wollstonecraft impresses upon her readers the importance of maternal feeling as an experience through which women can understand and develop sympathy for each other, having already underscored the empathetic bond possible but often denied between women subjected to male sexual caprice. Notably, Wollstonecraft does not restrict the desire to nurture a child to biological mothers, instead presenting it as an inherently understood part of womanhood or even humanity in general: while the childless Jemima is willing to listen to Maria's sorrows, it is only when Maria reveals her child was seized while she was breast-feeding that "the woman [awakes] in a bosom long estranged from feminine emotions".[47] That Wollstonecraft describes Jemima's sympathy as *reawakened* at this moment rather than initially created insinuates an inherent sympathy between the two women which, though numbed by the necessities of a sexist society, can be reawakened to the benefit of both Jemima and Maria.

Showcasing Jemima and Maria's newfound solidarity, Wollstonecraft narratively prioritises the shared experience of pregnancy and maternal love across classes, contrasted with the ruthlessness shown to Jemima's mother, whose "virtuous mistress had forced her [...] in the very pangs of labour" to a "wretched garret" and "felt no sympathy" (92). That Wollstonecraft gives such attention to the hypocrisy of a mistress who has children but lacks compassion for a pregnant servant suggests an interest in inter-class issues at odds with her intention in *Vindication* to give priority "to the middle class, because they appear to be in the most natural state" (4). In *Maria*, the class issues to which Wollstonecraft vaguely alludes in *Vindication* are developed more fully by the author's use of a destabilising setting. Maria's middle-class status, which would normally allow her some superiority over Jemima, is undercut by her circumstances as an inmate in the asylum where Jemima works, a situation which makes Maria reliant on the working-class woman for her physical, intellectual and emotional needs.[48] This destabilisation of class boundaries runs down to the very language Jemima uses to tell her story, most notable in Jemima's explanation that her "sentiments and language" were acquired at the "very dear rate" of becoming a libertine's mistress (99). Here, Wollstonecraft ironises her own assertion in *Vindication* about the more "natural state" (4) of the middle class: Jemima's seemingly respectable "sentiments and languages" (99) are not only *un*natural but a result of her corruption.

The implication that each class has different natural "sentiments", though problematic to a modern reader, is somewhat eclipsed by Wollstonecraft's focus on maternal feeling (rather than the actual state of maternity) as an experience through which women of different classes can understand each other and bond over their shared desire to nurture. Maria's offer to "teach [her daughter] to consider [Jemima] a second mother" – as opposed to a nanny or servant – exemplifies Wollstonecraft's prioritisation of the desire to nurture children as a virtue over conventionally sentimental, bourgeois values (108). That Jemima's sexual transgressions do not bar her from being fit for motherhood provides an alternative to the social emphasis on chastity which, Wollstonecraft observes, deems a woman "honourable" when she is actually just monogamous.[49] Wollstonecraft substitutes maternal kindness for chastity as the inherently feminine virtue, as suggested by Maria's "maternal benediction" to Jemima – a phrase that elevates motherly tenderness to the level of a blessing (109). This emphasis on cross-class compassion between women marks a shift away from Wollstonecraft's stated goal in *Vindication* of "taking a separate view of the different ranks of society, and of the moral character of women in each" (4). While her initial plan in *Vindication* aims to avoid giving instruction exclusively "applicable to *ladies*" (emphasis in the text) rather than "women", hinting at an understanding of class issues if not a particular interest, Wollstonecraft's contrast between the well-to-do Maria Venables and the illegitimate ex-prostitute Jemima develops this in a direction that conflicts with Wollstonecraft's distinctions between women's "moral character" in different social classes (3-4). Furthermore, Jemima's role in reuniting Maria with her daughter suggests that Wollstonecraft fully intended for Maria to make Jemima the child's "second mother", an act which would symbolically present the two characters as equals through their shared love of Maria's child (108). Despite her belief that working-class women are morally different from middle-class ones, Wollstonecraft presents the possibility that women can bond through their natural desire to nurture, a state which makes them vulnerable to the same risks but also provides grounds on which to understand, sympathise with and help each other.

While Wollstonecraft's most developed ending continues to develop the possibility of inter-class cooperation between women, an endeavour which shows the Romantic novelist's 'woke' sentiments, this is not to say that Wollstonecraft's exploration of class boundaries is untroubled. Poovey argues that Wollstonecraft snips the most radical aspects of her depiction of cross-class cooperation before fully exploring them, citing in particular Jemima's request to become Maria's housekeeper rather than a "second mother" as a return to the middle-class sensibilities of the sentimental genre.[50] While Poovey is correct in noting that this choice undermines the equality between the two women, Maria's offer of a co-parenting situation still merits consideration, while Jemima's "insisting" on "being considered as [Maria's] housekeeper" adjusts her expectations to the society they are re-entering (167). Jemima's request for "the customary stipend" (167) signals her continued protectiveness around her "independence" (98) – a reasonable concern given that she will presumably be dismissed for aiding Maria's escape.

Additionally, Wollstonecraft's choice to include this discussion as reported speech (rather than the direct speech used to accentuate Maria's sincerity as she implores Jemima to "read [her] soul" (108)) subtly signals an ironic loss of freedom as the two women leave the madhouse. While Maria's class status was obscured by her incarceration, the two women enjoyed a more equal dynamic than they could when free, adding credence to Maria's view of "the world [as] a vast prison" (73). Ironically, the madhouse grants the women freedom to transgress class boundaries. The society they are re-entering is so perverse that Jemima expects to lose Maria's "esteem" specifically because she has proved worthy of it, stifling the positive value of female solidarity with the rigid sexual conventions against which both Jemima and Maria have transgressed (104). This irony emphasises the inherent flaw in these social conventions that value an absence of sexual transgression over any maternal virtue, the exact issue which eventually leads to Jemima's abortion and Maria's overdose.

That Wollstonecraft's radical acceptance of abortion has been largely overlooked even in contemporary scholarship suggests a continued reluctance to consider abortion rights as a central feminist issue, particularly given the wealth of material on Wollstonecraft's writing and her inclusion of abortion in a sentimental novel – a genre historically understood to have significant moral value for its primarily female readership.[51] This gap in analysis becomes even more conspicuous given that Wollstonecraft fell pregnant in France, a country with a suggestively low birth rate at the time.[52] Yet Wollstonecraft's contribution is an essential one when considering how attitudes to abortion have changed, not only because she provides a female voice but because she brings the debate into the realm of the practical and the personal. While Rousseau is vocal on the problem of abortion, he has little to say on the solution, dismissing contraception, notions of sexual honour and even illegitimate children themselves.[53] De Sade's abortion discourse is perhaps more straightforward and modern, but similarly neglects the needs of the exact people most affected by abortion or its absence – namely women and illegitimate children. By contrast, Wollstonecraft's empathetic portrayals of desperate women explore much of the nuance her male contemporaries neglect. By reconciling a supposedly immoral act with its impact on women from varied walks of life, Wollstonecraft attempts a more holistic consideration of the problems women face within a patriarchal society that encourages male sexuality while punishing women for the same behaviour. By bringing male fault to the forefront in a genre that typically reinforced marriage and catered to a female readership, Wollstonecraft begins a conversation among women about how they could and should be treated, building a case for increased female solidarity based on the shared experience of maternity. It is perhaps the emphasis on male fault that made male reviewers so intensely touchy. The mud-slinging around Wollstonecraft's recently published biography infected nearly all of initial reviews and is perhaps best captured in the *Anti-Jacobin Review*'s index: "prostitution – see Mary Wollstonecraft".[54]

Wollstonecraft's attempt to address abortion commentators' unwillingness to consider women's experiences, particularly in addressing the treatment of working-class women, anticipates 21st-century wokeness by considering inequality as a spectrum which all women experience in varying degrees. Though Poovey rightly asserts that Wollstonecraft's relationship with class is a troubled one, this is not to say that Wollstonecraft's interest is insincere or performative. By attempting to address abortion as an issue which all women face, Wollstonecraft attempts something akin to wokeness in the canon by addressing the uncomfortable truth that systematic oppression forces the oppressed to participate in their own and others' mistreatment. Jemima's abortion and her conduct towards the pregnant girl exemplify this dilemma. While both situations are caused by male profligacy, it is the women who must endure the consequences, ending their pregnancies and enduring the aftermath. By using abortion as a way to promote empathy between women, Wollstonecraft has created a novel which remains relevant not only for its discussion of abortion, but its emphasis on an empathic, personal approach to abortion rather than a detached, ideological one. Instead of focusing inwards at the expense of detaching from reality, Wollstonecraft draws her experiences outwards and connects them to similar issues faced by other women to create empathy. While Wollstonecraft's place in the canon relies on her relative privilege, her advocacy for women who aborted disrupts a discourse which ignored women's experiences completely.

Notes

1   Wollstonecraft, Mary (2009 [1798]). *Maria and The Wrongs of Woman.* Oxford: Oxford University Press, 69.
2   Wollstonecraft, Mary (2004 [1792]). *A Vindication of the Rights of Woman.* London: Penguin Books, 6.
3   Daiches, David (1979). *A Critical History of English Literature: The Restoration to 1800, Volume 3.* New Delhi: Allied Publishers Private, 710.
4   Poovey, Mary (1982). "Mary Wollstonecraft: The Gender of Genres in Late Eighteenth-Century England." *NOVEL: A Forum on Fiction* 15.2, 111-117.
5   *Ibid.* 114.
6   Rousseau, J.J. (1761). *A Discourse Upon the Origin and Foundation of the Inequality Among Mankind.* London: R. and J. Dodsley, 211.
7   Gordon, Lyndall (2005). *Mary Wollstonecraft. A New Genus.* Boston, Mass: Little Brown, 329. Gilbert Imlay arranged for Wollstonecraft to be certified as his wife in 1793 during the Reign of Terror in France, granting her American nationality, which protected her from arrest (see 212).
8   Poovey (1982), 116.
9   Yang, Maya (2021). "AOC on Texas Governor's 'Disgusting' Abortion Remarks: 'He is not familiar with a female body.'" *The Guardian.* Web. 8 September 2021. https://www.theguardian.com/world/2021/sep/08/alexandria-ocasio-cortez-greg-abbott-texas-abortion-ban.
10   McLaren, Angus (1978). "Abortion in France: Women and the Regulation of Family Size 1800-1914." *French Historical Studies* 10.3, 461.
11   National Constituent Assembly (1791). *French Penal Code.* Web. 18 September 2022. http://ledroitcriminel.fr/la_legislation_criminelle/anciens_textes/code_penal_25_09_1791.htm. Article 17 cites a punishment of "twenty years in chains" [translation by the author] for abortionists but no punishment is cited for women undergoing abortion.
12   King James I (1623). *An Act to Prevent the Destroying and Murdering of Bastard Children.* Web. 18 September 2022. https://statutes.org.uk/site/the-statutes/seventeenth-century/1623-21-james-1-c-27-to-prevent-the-destroying-and-murthering-of-bastard-children/. Similarly, William Hunter's lecture *On the Uncertainty of the Signs of Murder in the Case of Bastard Children* does not acknowledge deliberate abortion.

[13] Wollstonecraft (2004 [1792]), 87.

[14] Farr, A.D. (1980). "The Marquis de Sade and Induced Abortion." *Journal of Medical Ethics* 6. 1, 9. Neither de Sade nor Rousseau makes a moral distinction between abortion and infanticide.

[15] Rousseau's writings are generally accepted to have influenced Maximilien Robespierre and other major figures in the French Revolution. De Sade, though a figure of interest, was infamous more for his sexual exploits. De Sade's work was deeply controversial due to its pornographic content, which later led to Napoleon ordering his arrest.

[16] Denman, Thomas (1825). *An Introduction to the Practice of Midwifery*. New York: E. Bliss and E. White, 162. This guide appears to have been widely read; new editions were still being published in 1832.

[17] Wollstonecraft, Mary (1879). *Mary Wollstonecraft: Letters to Imlay*. Ed. Charles Keegan Paul. London: C. Kegan Paul & Co., 10.

[18] Hodge, Hugh Lenox (1854). *On Criminal Abortion. A Lecture Introductory to the Course on Obstetrics, and Diseases of Women and Children*. Philadelphia: T. K. and P. G. Collins, 12. Though writing significantly after Wollstonecraft's death, Hodge similarly emphasises quickening's longstanding cultural importance by citing the Malicious Stabbing and Shooting Act 1803, which made quickening the deciding detail when charging an abortionist: legally, a post-quickening abortion was murder (14).

[19] Boyer, Abel (1793). *Boyer's Royal Dictionary Abridged. In Two Parts, 1. French and English, 2. English and French*. Dublin: James Moore, 32.

[20] Old Bailey (1829). "Trial of Charlotte Inman and John McFeydon." *Old Bailey Proceedings Online*, 2011. Web. 27 August 2021. https://www.oldbaileyonline.org/browse.jsp?id=t18290409-234-defend2182&div=t18290409-234#highlight. --- (1834). "Trial of William Childs." *Old Bailey Proceedings Online*, 2011. Web. 27 August 2021. https://www.oldbaileyonline.org/browse.jsp?id=t18340515-47-person510&div=t18340515-47#highlight. --- (1856). "Trial of William Gayloe." *Old Bailey Proceedings Online*, 2011. Web. 27 August 2021. https://www.oldbaileyonline.org/browse.jsp?id=def1-1003-18561027&div=t18561027-1003#highlight.
The records on illegal abortion are sparse but suggest a general unwillingness to prosecute women for aborting their foetuses. Notably, William Childs's trial includes a witness testimony from a young woman to whom the defendant administered savin. Her decision to testify suggests that she was unafraid of being charged herself.

[21] Texas State. (2021). *The Texas Heartbeat Act*. Web. 18 September 2022. https://capitol.texas.gov/tlodocs/87R/billtext/html/HB01515I.htm.

[22] Rousseau (1761), 211. Rousseau does not single out abortion as more immoral than the other "shameful methods" of concealing sexuality, implicitly presenting unmitigated fertility as a natural and desirable state. Please note

that the preceding quote in the chapter title refers to Wollstonecraft (2009 [1798]), 96.

[23] Wollstonecraft (2009 [1798]), 96.

[24] Wollstonecraft treats it as obvious that Jemima could not report her rape to the police. The Old Bailey archives record only seven rape trials in 1793.

[25] See Wollstonecraft (2009 [1798]), 96.

[26] Farr (1980), 8.

[27] de Sade, Donatien Alphonse François (1794). *Justine ou les Malheurs de la Vertu: Volume 1*. 3rd edition. France: La Bordonnaye, 67, translation by the author.

[28] Steintrager, James A. (2016). *The Autonomy of Pleasure: Libertines, License, and Sexual Revolution*. New York: Columbia University Press, 122.

[29] Wollstonecraft (2009 [1798]), 99.

[30] Farr (1980), 9.

[31] Gradwohl, Alex (2013). "Herbal Abortifacients and their Classical Heritage in Tudor England." *Penn History Review* 10.1, 58-59.

[32] Old Bailey (1834). "Trial of William Childs." The "several days" Jemima spends in bed in comparison to the "two weeks" stated in this trial suggests that Jemima may be downplaying her illness after the abortion or was thrown out of her lodgings before she had entirely recovered.

[33] Please note that the preceding quote in the chapter title refers to Wollstonecraft (2009 [1798]), 176.

[34] Dow, Gillian (2019). "Sentiment from Abroad: French Novels after 1748." *The Sentimental Novel in the Eighteenth Century*. Ed. Alfred J. Rivero. Cambridge: Cambridge University Press, 97.

[35] This ending does not specify whether Maria's pregnancy has quickened.

[36] Hunter, William (1818). *On the Uncertainty of the Signs of Murder in the Case of Bastard Children*. London: J. Callow, 7.

[37] *Ibid.*, 176. Please note that the preceding quote in the chapter title refers to Wollstonecraft (2009 [1798]), 165.

[38] Rousseau (1971 [1789]), 333.

[39] Rousseau (1761), 211-212.

[40] Wollstonecraft (2009 [1798]), 171.

[41] Rousseau (1971 [1789]), 333.

[42] de Sade, Donatien Alphonse François (1891). *La Philosophie de la Boudoir*. Bruxelles: Chez les Marchands de Nouveautés, 223, translation by the author.

[43] Wollstonecraft (2009 [1798]), 102.

[44] *Ibid.*

[45] Please note that the preceding quote in the chapter title refers to Wollstonecraft (2009 [1798]), 101.

[46] *Ibid.*, 122.

[47] *Ibid.*, 73.

[48] In addition to enabling the affair with Darnford (90), Jemima provides Maria with food (71) and entertainment (84). Wollstonecraft's comment that Jemima might have never assisted Maria "[had] her master trusted her" (72) hints at the issue of female credibility being underestimated.

[49] Wollstonecraft (2004 [1792]), 84.

[50] Poovey (1982), 119.

[51] *Ibid.*, 215.

[52] Gordon (2005), 213.

[53] Rousseau (1761), 86.

[54] *The Anti-Jacobin Review and Magazine, Issues 1-6* (1799). London: J. Whittle.

Bibliography

Anti-Jacobin Review and Magazine, Issues 1-6 (1799). London: J. Whittle.

Boyer, Abel (1793). *Boyer's Royal Dictionary Abridged*. In Two Parts, 1. French and English, 2. English and French. Dublin: James Moore.

Daiches, David (1979). *A Critical History of English Literature: The Restoration to 1800*, Volume 3. New Delhi: Allied Publishers Private.

de Sade, Donatien Alphonse François (1794). *Justine ou les Malheurs de la Vertu:* Volume 1. 3rd edition. Paris: La Bordonnaye.

--- (1891). *La Philosophie de la Boudoir*. Bruxelles: Chez les Marchands de Nouveautés.

Denman, Thomas (1825). *An Introduction to the Practice of Midwifery*. New York: E. Bliss and E. White.

Department of Health and Social Care (2021). "Abortion Statistics, England and Wales: 2020." *National Statistics*. Web. 6 August 2021. https://www.gov.uk/government/statistics/abortion-statistics-for-england-and-wales-2020/abortion-statistics-england-and-wales-2020.

Dow, Gillian (2019). "Sentiment from Abroad: French Novels after 1748." *The Sentimental Novel in the Eighteenth Century*. Ed. Alfred J. Rivero. Cambridge: Cambridge University Press, 87-106.

Farr, A.D (1980). "The Marquis de Sade and Induced Abortion." *Journal of Medical Ethics* 6.1, 7-10.

Gordon, Lyndall (2005). *Mary Wollstonecraft: A New Genus*. Boston, Mass: Little Brown.

Gradwohl, Alex (2013). "Herbal Abortifacients and their Classical Heritage in Tudor England." *Penn History Review* 10.1, 44-71.

Hodge, Hugh Lenox (1854). *On Criminal Abortion. A Lecture Introductory to the Course on Obstetrics, and Diseases of Women and Children.* Philadelphia: T. K. and P. G. Collins.

Hunter, William (1818). *On the Uncertainty of the Signs of Murder in the Case of Bastard Children.* London: J. Callow.

King James I (1623). *An Act to Prevent the Destroying and Murdering of Bastard Children.* Web. 18 September 2022. https://statutes.org.uk/site/the-statutes/seventeenth-century/1623-21-james-1-c-27-to-prevent-the-destroying-and-murthering-of-bastard-children/.

Lord Ellenbrough (1803). *The Malicious Shooting or Stabbing Act.* Web. 18 September 2022. https://statutes.org.uk/site/the-statutes/nineteenth-century/43-geo-3-c-58-lord-ellenboroughs-act-1803/.

McLaren, Angus (1978). "Abortion in France: Women and the Regulation of Family Size 1800-1914." *French Historical Studies* 10.3, 461-485.

National Constituent Assembly (1791). *French Penal Code.* Web. 18 September 2022. http://ledroitcriminel.fr/la_legislation_criminelle/anciens_textes/code_penal_25_09_1791.htm.

Old Bailey (1829). "Trial of Charlotte Inman and John McFeydon." *Old Bailey Proceedings Online*, 2011. Web. 27 August 2021. https://www.oldbaileyonline.org/browse.jsp?id=t18290409-234-defend2182&div=t18290409-234#highlight.

--- (1834). "Trial of William Childs." *Old Bailey Proceedings Online*, 2011. Web. 27 August 2021. https://www.oldbaileyonline.org/browse.jsp?id=t18340515-47-person510&div=t18340515-47#highlight.

--- (1856). "Trial of William Gayloe." *Old Bailey Proceedings Online*, 2011. Web. 27 August 2021. https://www.oldbaileyonline.org/browse.jsp?id=def1-1003-18561027&div=t18561027-1003#highlight.

Poovey, Mary (1982). "Mary Wollstonecraft: The Gender of Genres in Late Eighteenth-Century England." *NOVEL: A Forum on Fiction* 15.2, 111-126.

Rousseau, Jean Jacques (1761). *A Discourse Upon the Origin and Foundation of the Inequality Among Mankind.* London: R. and J. Dodsley.

--- (1971 [1789]). *The Confessions*. Ed. J.M. Cohen. London: Penguin Books.

Steintrager, James A (2016). *The Autonomy of Pleasure: Libertines, License, and Sexual Revolution*. New York: Columbia University Press.

Texas State. (2021). *The Texas Heartbeat Act*. Web. 18 September 2022. https://capitol.texas.gov/tlodocs/87R/billtext/html/HB01515I.htm.

Wollstonecraft, Mary (1879). *Mary Wollstonecraft: Letters to Imlay*. Edited by Charles Keegan Paul. London: C. Kegan Paul & Co.

--- (2004 [1792]). *A Vindication of the Rights of Woman*. London: Penguin Books.

--- (2009 [1798]). *Maria and The Wrongs of Woman*. Ed. Gary Kelly. Oxford: Oxford University Press.

Yang, Maya (2021). "AOC on Texas Governor's 'Disgusting' Abortion Remarks: 'He is not familiar with a female body.'" *The Guardian*. Web. 8 September 2021. https://www.theguardian.com/world/2021/sep/08/alexandria-ocasio-cortez-greg-abbott-texas-abortion-ban.

Maria Juko

'Woke' Wollstonecraft? Mary Wollstonecraft's Adventurous Wives in the Classroom

1. Introduction

Mary Wollstonecraft's conduct-book-like *A Vindication of the Rights of Woman* (1792) challenged eighteenth-century ideals of femininity. Complementing her early feminist agenda, in her novella *Mary* (1788) and her unfinished novel *Maria, or The Wrongs of Woman* (published posthumously in 1798) the author narrates the lives of wives trapped in matrimony but fighting for their liberation.

"An icon of the Anglo-Saxon feminist movement", Wollstonecraft's life and her works can function as a vantage point for an introduction to a history of gender equality in the Anglophone world for the English curriculum in German schools.[1] My ensuing commentary will focus on Hamburg's curriculum for the "gymnasiale Oberstufe", grades eleven and twelve (German equivalents of year five and six of grammar school). The English curriculum for Hamburg's schools allows for a stronger inclusion of gender discourses. Although Wollstonecraft as a subject for study has been explored by Wendy Gunther-Canada (1997), and Wollstonecraft's pedagogy by Mitzi Myers (1989) and more recently Kirstin Collins Hanley (2013), so far Mary Wollstonecraft has not been considered a topic for the EFL classroom, a critical lacuna I would like to address here.[2]

Wollstonecraft's call for independence, I argue, can be linked to the ongoing fight for gender equality, and as such the author's texts provide a starting point for women's movements, continued by early feminists such as US-American Susan B. Anthony and British suffragettes. Agreeing with Hanley, I recognise "Wollstonecraft's instructional literature as an innovative educative force working within and alongside the powerful cultural imperative for the improvement of self and others in the late eighteenth century".[3] My paper supports an inclusion to the EFL classroom of authors such as Wollstonecraft, who has been dubbed 'the mother of feminism'.[4] While author William Shakespeare features in

67

Hamburg's English curriculum and even appears in the official list of possible topics, women authors can be included if individual teachers decide to do so.[5] Evidently, works by 'the Bard' have become a staple of English lessons, in Germany and elsewhere. Eighteenth- and nineteenth-century writers, and particularly women writers, such as Mary Wollstonecraft, can present alternatives or additions for an understanding of an Anglophone culture and history, without, however, implying that the EFL classroom needs an overview of the history of English or American literature. Rather than calling for an overhaul of the English curriculum altogether, I therefore suggest including segments and extracts from eighteenth- and nineteenth-century literature (Wollstonecraft, or Hays, Radcliffe, Austen, Brontë) to counter the usual length of the works, and to engender analysis of them. As always, the works need to be embedded and explained in their given socio-cultural context. In the following, I will first consider the English curriculum at Hamburg's high schools and sketch the trajectory of conduct literature with its distinct instructional character. I will suggest points of analysis of Wollstonecraft's biography and graphic novels about her life and work as points of entry thereof. Indeed, the "alert to [...] social discrimination and injustice" that she highlights in her works, signalling her attacks on the establishment, contributes to Wollstonecraft's 'wokeness'.[6] Her *Vindication* and her two novels *Mary* and *Maria, or The Wrongs of Woman* in which she appropriated the genre of the conduct book for her own proto-feminist purposes, I argue, could be drawn on to illustrate to students a long history of feminism and evaluate contemporary society.

2. Hamburg's EFL Framework and Wollstonecraft

Despite 21st-century interventions of gender equality campaigns and programmes, texts by women writers are still not featured in Hamburg's English curriculum. Hamburg's framework for its foreign languages for grades eleven and twelve (students would typically be sixteen to eighteen years old) includes five different fields and provides an example for corresponding topics:

> 1) current political and social topics, such as genetic engineering, 2) universal human topics, such as visions of the future, 3) development and

identity, such as American identities, 4) multicultural and intercultural relationships, such as domination, integration, assimilation: Hispanics in the USA, 5) art, culture, media: acquire, understand, enjoy, such as works by Shakespeare (on screen).[7]

While politics, and particularly racial injustice, has become an important topic in the EFL classroom, gender studies and the history of feminism have not been mentioned explicitly. However, the category "current political and social topics" allows for a discussion of gender equality and the inclusion of women writers arguing on the issue.[8] Because environment, society, and culture are always attached to questions of gender, individuals are directly affected by changes to and within these areas of life. Historically, particularly women have been restricted in their rights to move within but also contribute to these fields. Wollstonecraft attacks women's lacking involvement in society, further underlining her woke character through her "alert to [...] social discrimination and injustice".[9] As intersectional analysis has entered academic conventions, I suggest that the same approach should be implemented in schools for a more complex and wide-ranging analysis and understanding of women's roles in society. Intersectional inquiries indeed correspond to Hamburg's demand that students are familiar with

> current political and social topics; topics of universal relevance such as identity, love, future, death; national developments in relation to Germany and Europe; the multitudinous entanglements within English-speaking cultures; examples of cultural products such as arts, literature and media, including two literary texts, one from the last 20 years, one poem, short story, and essay each, and otherwise cultural productions such as films.[10]

This in turn should help to

> communicate with native speakers, compare relations between English-speaking countries and Germany to position themselves, share, discuss and problematise aspects of their own experiences with native speakers' ones, observe similarities and contrasts between the different value systems, identify cliches and prejudices and gauge their own cultural understanding with others, analyse this understanding within literature or films and relate them to their own life.[11]

An introduction to Mary Wollstonecraft's life and works promises a combination of multiple requirements and pedagogical objectives. Wollstonecraft's novels and texts allow for a critical literary analysis and cover political and social issues that concern society, class, and gender. More so, the eighteenth-century writer asked how to change society to become more egalitarian – a crucial question still. Echoing the key principle inherent in wokeness, Wollstonecraft is "aware, especially of social problems".[12] Wollstonecraft's texts are easily accessible, and with enough material about her, a study of her life and works can help instigate a discussion of whether and how contemporary society has changed in regard to women's rights and oppression by patriarchal forces.[13]

3. Conduct Books and Wokeness

Whilst conduct books were primarily concerned with teaching a socially acceptable behaviour, some conduct books writers used their texts as (political) platforms to instigate reform and spread scepticism among their mostly young readers, targeting a similar age group as German eleventh and twelfth graders. Romantic writers, particularly from the radical camp, questioned the status quo and challenged misbalances in society.[14] Similarly, Mary Wollstonecraft used the mode of the conduct book for her own feminist purposes. Romanticism, defined by Morse Peckham,

> [w]hether philosophic, theologic, or aesthetic, [...] is the revolution in the European mind against thinking in terms of static mechanism and the redirection of the mind to thinking in terms of dynamic organicism. Its values are change, imperfection, growth, diversity, the creative imagination, the unconscious.[15]

Wollstonecraft attempted to improve women's condition in society via her advice literature. She could be called a 'woke' writer, as the *OED* defines 'woke' as "[o]riginally: well-informed, up-to-date. Now chiefly: alert to racial or social discrimination and injustice".[16] Using this rhetoric, pupils could be able to grasp her importance. Via her texts and biography, students could debate and discuss implications of 'wokeness' in its more problematic meanings but also employ it for a critique of 21st-century society.

On a formal level, conduct books established social boundaries and gender roles. Vivien Jones defines the conduct book as a

> sub-genre among the hundreds of books and periodicals […] which offered instruction in all areas of social, domestic, and professional behaviour […] [As such,] they were powerfully instrumental in defining an ideological identity for the emergent middle class.[17]

Hence, on a class dimension, conduct books manifested class belonging and addressed the hegemonic mainstream, i.e., the emerging middle class. In her influential *Desire and Domestic Fiction*, Nancy Armstrong goes so far as to suggest that the genre of the conduct book helped to establish the idea of the middle class as a separate socio-political group.[18] Countering Mary Poovey's thesis that "conduct books present a popularized, and sometimes frankly secularized, version of the ideas more rigorously set out in sermons",[19] I would argue that (women) writers demonstrated a need for reform of women's education and appropriated the popular genre of advice literature for their own purposes. Jones claims that Poovey's and Armstrong's understanding of conduct literature denies it wider political power.[20] For Jones, the conduct book could not just teach adequate behaviour to its reader but also "(self-) improvement" in terms of intellectual growth, countering ideas of women's inferiority.[21] On the surface, conduct books play into patriarchal ideals but underneath they have the potential to convey a critique of society and by extension incite a reflection on women's roles in society.[22] As Wendy Gunther-Canada argues, since

> throughout the ages [women] have been almost entirely absented from the political realm, it has often been assumed that women did not write political theory. What this assumption presupposes is that if women had written about politics, in numbers and forms like men, then political theory written by women would be included in the canon of political thought.[23]

Conduct books were therefore platforms with political potential to impact social discourse on women's roles by women writers, establishing and continuing a history of feminism in Britain and beyond.

Mary Wollstonecraft is one of the trailblazers of feminist movements, who appropriated the popular genre of advice literature to influence her readers and instigate a social reform regarding women's rights. Her agenda is the "female mental improvement as a means of escape from fashionable uselessness".[24] Wollstonecraft's texts influenced and inspired subsequent generations of early feminists and helped generate discourses on women's roles in society, a valuable insight for pupils.

4. Introducing Mary Wollstonecraft

Biographical accounts and material on Mary Wollstonecraft help to establish an understanding of her importance for British culture and the onset of feminist movements for pupils. What may be of key interest for younger learners is that Mary Wollstonecraft's biography is filled with struggles: Born in 1759 in Spitalfields in England, she was a member of what we would now deem the middle class. As Gordon notes, Wollstonecraft's biography is "the story of an independent and compassionate woman who devised a blueprint for human change, [...] a new kind of creature who found her voice in a brief moment of historical optimism".[25] Her parents favoured their firstborn, Mary Wollstonecraft's oldest brother. As soon as she was of an age to leave the household, she traded the relative comfort of her childhood home for a position as a lady's maid and so began her life as a working woman throughout which she continued to support her family. Together with her close friend Fanny Blood she opened a boarding school in Newington Green in London. However, Fanny soon left England for her husband who lived in Portugal. Together with her younger sisters Wollstonecraft tried to manage the school but the three failed when Mary left to help Fanny, who fell ill and eventually died after pregnancy. Wollstonecraft herself had two children by two different men, one of them while unmarried – a scandal in the late eighteenth century.[26]

Professionally, Wollstonecraft was an aspirational and visionary woman. As a governess and teacher, Wollstonecraft was confronted with the task to instruct her (mostly female) students. Quickly, however, she realised she wanted to make a name for herself as a writer. Despite her struggles, Mary Wollstonecraft believed in the Enlightenment power of self-improvement and "a female genius in particular [that] needs to educate herself".[27] Under the wing of Joseph Johnson, she managed to read and discuss almost every important work of social commentary in the late eighteenth century. When offered to pick up the pen herself, she decided to begin with a conduct book *Thoughts on the Education of Daughters* (1787), followed by a children's book *Original Stories from Real Life* (1788) with a "pronounced disciplinary character" and *The Female Reader* (1789).[28] These texts are revolutionary because they present a woman's perspective on women's education and situation in society for women, thereby challenging male authorial voices. As Todd notes,

> [d]idactic fiction of the early nineteenth century showed the moral value of paid employment for females, but this was not so when Mary was growing up, and the novelists of her day routinely portrayed the horror of ladies earning bread outside the family.[29]

Wollstonecraft used the genre's popularity for economic reasons despite personal reservations.[30] Wollstonecraft published more political texts such as *A Vindication of the Rights of Men* (1790), and *A Vindication of the Rights of Woman* (1792), as well as a response to Edmund Burke's work on the French Revolution, *An Historical and Moral View of the French Revolution; and the Effect It Has produced in Europe* (1794). Staying true to her Romantic roots, she wrote about her travels in *Letters Written in Sweden, Norway, and Denmark* (1796), based on her letters to her lover Gilbert Imlay. After her death, her husband, William Godwin's *Memoirs of the Author of A Vindication of the Rights of Woman* (1798) unwittingly revealed Wollstonecraft's scandalous biography and ruined her reputation for a considerable amount of time. Confronting students with Wollstonecraft's biography helps to establish her revolutionary character.

Although it is fair to assume that few students in Germany have heard of Mary Wollstonecraft, her life is an exceptional story of perseverance and self-confidence that pupils can also garner from creative interpretations of Wollstonecraft's life. To better capture the attention of pupils, one can refer to graphic novels that focus on Wollstonecraft's life, such as Martha Mackay's *Mary Wollstonecraft: A Life in Pictures* (2021) and a chapter dedicated to Wollstonecraft in Lauren Burke, Hannah K. Chapman, and Kaley Bales's *Why She Wrote: A Graphic History of the Lives, Inspiration, and Influence Behind the Pens of Classic Women Writers* (2021).[31] Burke, Chapman and Bales's chapter focuses on Wollstonecraft's time in France, her encounter with Imlay, and her subsequent commentary on the French Revolution. Poignantly, Burke, Chapman and Bales's Wollstonecraft summarises that the "revolution is imperfect, but it is also extraordinary. Perhaps future generations will look upon this and learn".[32] Likewise, Mackay notes "[w]hether people know who Mary is or not, everyone's lives have been shaped by the actions and words of this remarkable woman".[33]

Figure 1 Mary Wollstonecraft on the cover of Mackay's graphic novel. © Martha Mackay, produced by New Unity. Newington Green Meeting House, People's History Museum, Wollstonecraft Society, 2021. With permission from the Wollstonecraft Society and New Unity.

The cover of Mackay's short graphic novel already offers points for analysis. Pupils could first try to describe the cover of the graphic novel and could then be allowed to research symbols online, as well as consult an additional biographical handout on the writer. The following elements are linked to feminism and Wollstonecraft's biography and could be noted by students: She stands in front of a writing desk, representing her profession as a writer; pens and paper complement that impression. A bookshelf holds a copy of a work by William Godwin, Mary Wollstonecraft's husband, and the symbol on the spine signifies his pro-anarchist attitude. Ship and painting indicate Wollstonecraft's extensive travels in Scandinavia. The handshake symbolises Wollstonecraft's call for a united and reformed society. A small French flag is reminiscent of Wollstonecraft's time in France during the French Revolution. Women's fights for autonomy are also worked into the cover: first, the teacup presents two interlocking female symbols, perhaps hinting at Wollstonecraft's relationships with women, and the broken chain as well as the ball and chain stand for women's fights for freedom in a patriarchal society. What pupils could take away is that both graphic narratives position 'woke' Wollstonecraft as a historical figure and radical Romantic who understood, anticipated, and participated in the reformation of, encouraging a more egalitarian one. Pupils can compare the comics with Wollstonecraft's biography and work out differences and similarities in the modes of (visual) representation. The style of the graphic novels can also be compared to gauge the different visualisations of Wollstonecraft and the effect the style has on one's reception of her.

In the image printed above, Wollstonecraft's window looks out into a garden with the newly erected statue of herself, but she cannot see the statue from this perspective. The statue itself is another aspect that works towards a better understanding and gauging of the eighteenth-century writer's significance. The statue, designed by Maggi Hambling and revealed to the public in late 2020, triggered a critical response. A series of articles on the statue spawned a discussion about representations of women artists as naked and sexualised.[34] Despite the criticism, the sculptural artwork intends to underline Wollstonecraft's confident and forward-thinking nature. Wollstonecraft's catch phrase "I do not wish [women] to have power over men; but over themselves" is inscribed in the statue.[35] Hambling defended the statue by stating that "[she] wanted to capture the spirit of Mary Wollstonecraft and the struggle for the rights of women. It's a struggle that goes on – and so the figure is a challenge to our world".[36] Resonating with Burke, Chapman, Bales and Mackay, Hambling supports the idea that Wollstonecraft's works have a lasting impact on generations of women and on those fighting for gender equality. In a classroom setting, teachers could either introduce the statue at the beginning of the unit and collect pupils' associations, or, for a more extensive discussion, have them argue for and against the aesthetic concept of the statue after having received a biographical input. In addition, teachers could also show other shortlisted submissions for the design of the statue and have pupils vote for their favourite. Time and classroom setting permitting, pupils could also be tasked to design a statue themselves. Via these representations students could assess and appreciate Wollstonecraft's lasting impact on 21st-century feminist debates.

5. *A Vindication of the Rights of Woman* in the EFL Classroom

Wollstonecraft has penned numerous works, but none has been as politically provoking as *A Vindication of the Rights of Woman* (1792). It is this work in particular that positions Wollstonecraft as fighting for a more egalitarian society and thus has become one of the most fundamental texts in the history of women's rights during the French Revolution. Indeed, while the *Vindication* functions as an instructive text on how to change society, Wollstonecraft also considers individual behaviour and its influence on society at large, creating a reciprocal relationship between individual and community. Analysing the *Vindication* demonstrates to students a long history of fights for women's rights by women writers and reveals the Romantic writer's wokeness. This again could alert students to social injustices and activate their own wokeness by relating Wollstonecraft's texts to contemporary debates of feminist movements in the twenty-first century, such as #MeToo, as well as an ongoing gender inequality – of course, it should be noted that Wollstonecraft's deliberations are limited to a white privileged point of view.[37] In the EFL classroom setting, one may approach the *Vindication* with two group puzzles. In the first group puzzle, the class could be divided into at least four groups, assigning to them the title, chapter titles, and some quotes to identify the possible focus of the *Vindication*. In a second step, with different combinations of pupils, the new groups will be given the intro and passages from the text. Pupils should summarise the passages and work out what Wollstonecraft criticised about society (women's education, women's inferiority, marriage). The following section provides

76

further background knowledge and suggests passages for suitable reading on the part of the teachers.

Considering late eighteenth-century society, Karen O'Brien stresses that the British Enlightenment believed "that there is such a thing as society, that humans are principally intelligible as social beings, and that society itself is subject to change".[38] Likewise, women at that time were regarded

> as distinct and influential social members [...][,] as both subjects and authors of works of social enquiry in the light of the Enlightenment idea that society can progress by its own endeavour, not only economically but also in its moral relations, education and culture.[39]

As such, "the status and educational level of women in a given society were important indicators of its degree of historical progress".[40] Considering Wollstonecraft's deliberations on women's conditions and status in society as an indicator of society's need for reforms, Sapiro refers to the *Vindication* "as the first major work of feminist political theory" but refrains from calling Wollstonecraft "a feminist [as] [t]here was no such social movement in her time".[41]

In addressing the *Vindication* to the French diplomat Charles-Maurice de Talleyrand-Périgord, Wollstonecraft posits that

> Sir, Having read with great pleasure a pamphlet which you have lately published, I dedicate this volume to you; to induce you to reconsider the subject and maturely weigh what I have advanced respecting the rights of woman and national education: and I call with the firm tone of humanity; for my arguments, Sir, are dictated by a disinterested spirit – I plead for my sex – not for myself. Independence I have long considered as the grand blessing of life, the basis of every virtue – and independence I will ever secure by contracting my wants, though I were to live on a barren heath.[42]

Students could research the context online that Talleyrand published a report on public education in 1791 in which he suggested a free public education for boys and men up until university level. His neglect of girls and women in that report is what drives Wollstonecraft to ask him "to reconsider the subject"; that is, to include women in his treatise.[43] Her response, however, is no mere request but an elaborated series of essays, "arguments [...] dictated by a disinterested spirit".[44] Wollstonecraft does

77

not ask to benefit herself from these reforms, she only "plead[s] for [her] sex".[45] Alan Richardson has argued that women writers of the late eighteenth century aimed to reframe the restrictive domestic role of women that was largely enforced in the realm of education.[46] Remarkably, Wollstonecraft clearly demonstrates her personal contribution to the request: her use of the first-person pronoun positions Wollstonecraft not just as the author of the pamphlet but more so stresses a woman's voice. It is woman who is neglected and therefore woman must speak up to change woman's situation. As Hanley notes, the *Vindication* "draws upon the female-centered pedagogic tradition […] in which young women learn from one another's virtues and faults through the careful supervision of a rational mentor or mother figure". [47]

And Wollstonecraft's goal is women's independence. "[T]he rights of woman and national education" are intertwined: if women's education improves, then women will be closer to liberation.[48] Independence is so vital to Wollstonecraft that she reduces her needs even if it means living with barely anything, symbolised by the image of the "barren heath", an infertile piece of land, perhaps signalling a refusal to reproduce.[49] Siding with women's needs in society, Wollstonecraft appropriates the genre of the conduct book to inspire change, not just for herself, but for all women. Indeed, the "I" becomes replaced by the female reader through the act of reading, the act of self-education. Although Wollstonecraft's theory has been called a "feminist misogyny" by Sandra Gubar, her argument intended to improve women's conditions.[50] Gubar's criticism ties Wollstonecraft's wokeness to a "self-righteousness masquerading as enlightenment" – Wollstonecraft is not proposing radical means to remove patriarchal forces.[51] This engenders a discussion of how radically feminist Wollstonecraft's text really is. Students could thus relate her *Vindication* to women's situation in the 21st century, particularly with regard to the stronghold of *coverture*, for this I would watch a video explaining the legal term.[52] Further, pupils could rewrite the paragraph for a contemporary audience with contemporary concerns regarding gender (in)equality.

The *Vindication* is an instructive text that seeks to change women's situation in society as Wollstonecraft "wish[es] to see woman placed in a station in which she would advance, instead of retarding, the progress of those glorious principles that give a substance to morality".[53] By taking issue with fellow male authors, Wollstonecraft clearly counters the process of *coverture*, and as such Blackstone's argument in *Commentaries on the Laws of England* (1765-1769) that "by marriage, the husband and wife are one person in law".[54] While Wollstonecraft admired Rousseau's writings, she contests his ideas of the ideal woman, as man's education "make[s] a man and his wife *one*".[55] She condemns that "Rousseau declares that a woman should never, for a moment, feel herself independent, that she should be governed by fear to exercise her natural cunning [...]. What nonsense!"[56] And so, Wollstonecraft sets out her agenda, as

> [c]ontending for the rights of woman, [her] main argument is built on the simple principle, that if she be not prepared by education to become the companion of man, she will stop the progress of knowledge and virtue; for truth must be common to all, or it will be inefficacious with respect to its influence on general practice.[57]

And, Wollstonecraft asks, "how can woman be expected to co-operate unless she know why she ought to be virtuous?"[58] According to Sutherland, "[f]or Wollstonecraft, the blame for a degraded femininity lies [...] with its instrument, education".[59] Wollstonecraft's ensuing advice does not always contradict eighteenth-century ideals of femininity, but she wishes to elevate women's position to one of equal partner in a relationship that upholds morality.

Women's oppression at the hands of their fathers, husbands and brothers is Wollstonecraft's major concern in the *Vindication*. Explicitly, Wollstonecraft attacks the relegation of women into the status of "convenient slaves" but notes that "slavery will have its constant effect, degrading the master and the abject dependent".[60] However, "[i]f women are to be excluded, without having a voice, from a participation of the natural rights of mankind", so long "man must, in some shape, act like a tyrant, and tyranny, in whatever part of society it rears its brazen front, will ever undermine morality".[61] At various points she emphasises that men's behaviour towards women in fact risks the moral status of society at large. In a later passage Wollstonecraft argues that "[t]here must be more equality established in society, or morality will never gain ground", yet "if one half of mankind be chained to its bottom by fate, [...] they will be continually undermining it through ignorance or pride".[62] She suggests that "the most perfect education, [...] is such an exercise of the understanding as is best calculated to strengthen the body and form the heart".[63] The similarity of the *Vindication* to conduct books of its time is evident as Wollstonecraft is clearly setting out to build an idealised middle-class woman, as well as man, after her fashion. She guides her reader in different areas of life – education, finding a partner, marriage – seeking to teach a 'correct' character. But, more so, Wollstonecraft appropriates the genre to reform society and improve women's conditions in it.

Collecting Wollstonecraft's different concerns regarding women in eighteenth-century society helps learners to understand why the text is considered one of the first feminist works and to reflect on current social issues and the global question of gender equality. In a final step, pupils could be tasked to create a book cover for the *Vindication*, which they would present and explain in a gallery walk to transfer their knowledge to a creative product.

6. Mary and Maria as Critics of Patriarchal Systems

Wollstonecraft's novels complement her radical political essays, *Mary* and *Maria, or The Wrongs of Woman*, serve as instructive texts that demonstrate women's oppression in society. Instead of reading the entirety of the two texts, learners should focus on the context attached to them to understand Wollstonecraft's concerns. Her direct address to the reader, her inclusion of working-class women, and women's destiny and role in society are embedded in her instructional texts that challenge the patriarchal society of late eighteenth-century Britain.

As a didactic activity, the class could again be divided into groups and be given four to six different short passages from the two texts. In their groups, pupils could collect the different topics and issues that Wollstonecraft addresses in her fiction: female protagonists that are usually expected to remain without aspirations (in the prefaces), divorce and (the double standard in) marriage in Maria's hearing (and perhaps Mary's recount of her forced marriage), or working-class women's miserable situation in Jemima's account. Pupils could then receive the titles of the two works and be asked for their expectations (by now they should have noted Wollstonecraft's more explicit critique of society) and then they could be provided with short summaries of the two texts. The following notes can help teachers to understand some selected abstracts in more detail.

Johnson calls *Mary* "a bold and suggestive novel that addresses the fundamental relationship of gender to the novel as a genre".[64] Mary is daughter to parents who neglect her only for her to become "heiress" to her parents' fortune after her older brother dies from a "violent fever".[65] After her brother's death, "her mother began to think her of consequence, and did not call her *the child*" (14). To satisfy a neighbour that helps the family financially, her parents marry her off to the debtor's son. Because of her autodidactic nature and her strong religious faith, as well as an alternative grand tour to Lisbon, Mary finds her own voice. Eventually, however, she is forced to return to her husband.

Wollstonecraft anticipates criticism for her more radical early feminist protagonist in her first novella *Mary,* "a tutee in progress".[66] However, she justifies and legitimises her character in her preface, stating that "in a fiction, such a being may be allowed to exist; whose grandeur is derived from the operations of its own faculties, not subjugated to opinion; but drawn by the individual from the original source" (3). Reckoning with her fellow writers and critics, she positions herself as writing against the stereotypical depictions of women in fiction, for

> [i]n delineating the Heroine of this Fiction, the Author attempts to develop a character different from those generally portrayed. This woman is neither a Clarissa, a Lady G –, nor a Sophie. – It would be vain to mention the various modifications of these models, as it would to remark, how widely artists wander from nature, when they copy the originals of great masters. They catch the gross parts; but the subtle spirit evaporates; and not having the just ties, affectation disgusts, when grace was expected to charm. (3)

Wollstonecraft attacks models relied upon by Samuel Richardson for his Clarissa, as well as Jean-Jacques Rousseau's Sophie and Héloïse. Female characters created by these male writers deny women the autonomy to choose their own destiny in life, replicating patriarchal logic of the ideal woman. Wollstonecraft tries to escape this notion in her fiction.[67] As a fictionalised conduct book, Wollstonecraft's text conforms to Armstrong's thesis that "[b]ecause [conduct books] appeared to have no political bias, [...] they presented – in actuality, still present – readers with ideology in its most powerful form".[68] Wollstonecraft positions herself against the status quo and questions conventional ideas of femininity in her instructive tale.

Wollstonecraft continues challenging society's idea of femininity in her last novel, *Maria, or The Wrongs of Woman*. Beginning *in medias res*, the reader encounters Maria, who has been committed to a private asylum by her husband, George Venables. After having tempted Maria into marriage for financial motifs, she was forced to endure George's tyrannical behaviour. Her attempt to escape the marriage was thwarted and she is then drugged and separated from her child, after having been "hunted, like an infected beast, from three different apartments" (157). In the asylum, Maria is seduced by Henry Darnford, whom she is in love with. Her ward Jemima, whom she grows close to, aids her with her second escape, but she is found again and asked to testify in court on account of her seduction by Darnford.

Maria, or The Wrongs of Woman opens in a similar fashion as *Mary*, with a preface legitimising her re-working of the female protagonist, as

> [i]n many works of this species, the hero is allowed to be mortal, and to become wise and virtuous as well as happy, by a train of events and circumstances. The heroines, on the contrary, are to be born immaculate; and to act like goddesses of wisdom, just come forth highly finished Minervas from the head of Jove. (67)

Again, Wollstonecraft posits herself as challenging male writers who condemn female protagonists as inferior to their male counterparts even if presented as "immaculate" (67) heroines. As Hanley notes, *Wrongs* is "a fiction dedicated to exposing the wrongs inflicted on women through unjust and oppressive social and legal institutions".[69]

Extending her usual scope of upper-middle-class female characters, Wollstonecraft includes working-class Jemima and allows her to recount her own biography that demonstrates that woman's disastrous situation in society is reduced to terrible circumstances.[70] Coinciding with Sutherland's estimation of conduct books that "[c]oherent identity is a limiting and impossible fiction", Wollstonecraft contrasts Maria's demise, who was admitted to a private asylum by her husband, with Jemima's socio-economic situation as "a slave, a bastard, a common property" (98).[71] Rostek argues that "Jemima's suffering as a *feme sole* is but the mirror-opposite of the oppression of a *feme covert*: the patriarchal economy by default forces women, whether married or unmarried, to pay an unreasonably high price for ensuring their survival and material provisioning".[72] Jemima considers herself an "outcast from society" (73), "born a slave, and chained by infamy to slavery during the whole of existence" (95). Indeed, Jemima wants to pursue a path of self-improvement. Pointing towards class limitations, Jemima argues that

> prejudices [...] are obstinately maintained by the poor, to the exclusion of improvement; they have not time to reason or reflect to any extent, or minds sufficiently exercised to adopt the principles of action, which form perhaps the only basis of contentment in every station. (102-103)

Jemima, as an illegitimate daughter and member of the labouring poor, is not the typical subject of conduct books and thus also demonstrates the critical neglect of women who do not belong to the upper echelons of society in the trajectory of advice literature.

Maria is confronted with a tyrannic husband in the narrative. Particularly, the divorce scene in Maria's narrative takes issue with the idea of *coverture*. Consider the first sentence of Maria's defence in which she explains that she was "[m]arried when scarcely able to distinguish the nature of the engagement, [...] yet [she] submitted to the rigid laws which enslave women, and obeyed the man whom [she] could no longer love" (171). Maria clearly demonstrates that she continued to follow eighteenth-century ideals of femininity and expectations of woman's role in society but by virtue of being a woman she becomes "enslave[d]" (171) on the day of her marriage. Bearing her feelings in front of an audience of male jurors and judges in the form of a letter that is read out by Darnford's lawyer, Wollstonecraft evokes the sentimental genre through Maria's confession of her deepest thoughts. Maria continues that "[w]hether the duties of the state are reciprocal, I mean not to discuss; but I can prove repeated infidelities which I overlooked or pardoned" (171). Divorces were handled as a "private Act of Parliament" and were thus pricey affairs, and because of the double standard in eighteenth-century society, women could only seek a separation on the grounds of adultery and "compounded by other offences, such as incest or bigamy", whereas a man could ask for a separation on the grounds of an extramarital affair.[73] Maria then argues that "education and circumstances lead men to think and act with less delicacy, than the preservation of order in society demands from women" (171), clearly attacking not just the double standard but all education of boys and girls and particularly advice literature that does not prepare women enough for marriage and at the same time convinces them to accept a man's behaviour. After recounting the unfortunate events that led to her "imprison[ment]" (172) at the "private mad-house" (172) to which she was committed by her husband, she closes her remarks with a rhetorical question addressed to the judges and jury: "If I am unfortunately united to an unprincipled man, am I for ever to be shut out from fulfilling the duties of a wife and mother?" (173) Through Maria, Wollstonecraft cleverly uses the idea of woman's mission as wife and mother to her advantage, claiming that a conspicuously irreverent husband endangers woman's role in society. Returning to the nature of conduct (and attacking conservative conduct literature), Maria demands that "I wish my country to approve of my conduct", meaning her leaving her tyrannical husband, "but, if laws exist, made by the strong to oppress the weak, I appeal to my own sense of justice, and declare that I will not live with the individual, who has violated every moral obligation which binds man to man" (173). Maria clearly attacks the law "made by the strong to oppress the weak" (173) but also demonstrates her independent mind that allows her to see the faults and flaws not just in her betrothed's behaviour towards her but in the legal and the underlying patriarchal system at large.

Mary and Maria are both women that are encouraged to think for themselves and consider their best options in life. Despite this, they are both forced to live with husbands others chose for them and to cater to upper-middle-class expectations of femininity. As Hanley argues, "[r]egardless of their oppressive circumstances, Wollstonecraft demonstrates that rationally educated women can triumph over the most egregious of wrongs through their utter refusal to act wrongly in return".[74] Wollstonecraft attacks advice literature of the day via her female characters that recognise a disadvantage in society as well as the faults of their own education and the limits to their body and mind due to laws of the day. Students engaging with these texts will recognise women's disadvantageous position within society in the eighteenth century and can form comparisons to 21st-century women's rights. The unit could conclude in a classroom debate in which pupils discuss the extent of women's marginalisation in society.

7. Conclusion

Working with these passages allows pupils to understand the pressing issues of Wollstonecraft's time with regard to women's roles that she addressed in her fiction and non-fiction. Wollstonecraft's early feminism was particularly interested in middle-class women, even if in her last novel she also considered the plight of working-class and deserted women in the narrative of Jemima. However, her feminist agenda encouraged and challenged society to recognise the oppression of women. I concur with Hanley who argues that

> [t]he personal history of every-woman, no matter how fallen, is the basis for self-improvement and social reform. The success of this paradigm is, of course, contingent on the female reader's own judgment and willingness to forgive (while critically reflecting on) the faults of others in order to correct her own.[75]

Wollstonecraft's women-centred attack on the misogynist society speaks for her revolutionary vision of the future.

As a starting point for a critical study of gender and gender equality, Wollstonecraft's texts and her life story, that of a 'woke' and radical Romantic, offer points of entry to a women's movement that wanted to reform society from the eighteenth century until the present. The feminist movement did not exist in the form that pupils are familiar with today, but we find traces of these philosophies of equality in the writings of eighteenth-century women writers already. These texts are valuable additions to the EFL classroom and illustrate efforts at challenging patriarchal dictate by a Romantic woman writer in the Anglophone sphere.

Notes

[1] Bahar, Saba (2002). *Mary Wollstonecraft's Social and Aesthetic Philosophy: 'An Eve to Please Me'.* Houndmills: Basingstoke, 1.

[2] See Gunther-Canada, Wendy (1997). "Teaching Mary Wollstonecraft: Women and the Canonical Conversation of Political Thought." *Feminist Teacher* 11.1, 20-29. Myers, Mitzi (1989). "Pedagogy as Self-Expression in Mary Wollstonecraft. Exorcising the Past, Finding a Voice. " *Jump* 2, 76-91.

Collins Hanley, Kirstin (2013). *Mary Wollstonecraft, Pedagogy, and the Practice of Feminism*. Abingdon: Routledge.

[3] Hanley (2013), 5.

[4] *The Guardian* headline reads "Mary Wollstonecraft Statue: 'Mother of Feminism' Sculpture Provokes Backlash". Anonymous, 10 Nov 2020. Web. 30 August 2021. https://www.bbc.com/news/uk-england-london-54886813.

[5] Landesinstitut für Lehrerbildung und Schulentwicklung (2009). *Bildungsplan gymnasiale Oberstufe. Neuere Fremdsprachen*. Freie und Hansestadt Hamburg. Behörde für Schule und Berufsbildung, 32.

[6] "woke." *Oxford English Dictionary*. Oxford University Press. Web. 29 August 2021. www.oed.com/view/Entry/58068747.

[7] Landesinstitut (2009), 32. (translation by the author)

[8] *Ibid.*

[9] "woke." *Oxford English Dictionary*. Web. 29 August 2021.

[10] Landesinstitut (2009), 29. (translation by the author)

[11] *Ibid.*, 30. (translation by the author)

[12] "wokeness." *Cambridge Dictionary*. Web. 20 December 2021. https://dictionary.cambridge.org/us/dictionary/english/wokeness.

[13] For intersectional feminist analysis it is necessary to include examples of non-white feminists in the classroom too, for example Sojourner Turner or Audre Lorde.

[14] Cladis, Mark (2014). "Radical Romanticism: Democracy, Religion, and the Environmental Imagination." *Soundings: An Interdisciplinary Journal* 97.1, 21-49, 30-31.

[15] Peckham, Morse (1951). "Toward a Theory of Romanticism." *PMLA* 66.2, 5-23, 14.

[16] "woke. " *Oxford English Dictionary*. Web 29 August 2021.

[17] Jones, Vivien (1990). *Women in the Eighteenth Century. Constructions of Femininity*. London and New York: Routledge, 14.

[18] Armstrong, Nancy (1987). *Desire and Domestic Fiction. A Political History of the Novel*. New York and Oxford: Oxford University Press, 66.

[19] Poovey, Mary (1985). *The Proper Lady and the Woman Writer. Ideology as Style in the Works of Mary Wollstonecraft, Mary Shelley, and Jane Austen*. Chicago and London: The University of Chicago Press, xi.

[20] Jones, Vivien (2002). "Mary Wollstonecraft and the Literature of Advice and Instruction." Ed. Claudia L. Johnson. *The Cambridge Companion to Mary Wollstonecraft*. Cambridge: Cambridge University Press, 119-140, 121.

[21] *Ibid.*, 119.

[22] *Ibid.*, 124.

[23] Gunther-Canada (1997), 20-21.

[24] Jones (2002), 133.

25 Gordon, Lyndall (2005). *Mary Wollstonecraft. A New Genus.* London: Little, Brown, 2.

26 Wollstonecraft's inspirational life has produced several biographies and works on the author, most prominently by Lyndall Gordon (2005), Barbara Taylor (2002), Janet Todd (2000), Claire Tomalin (1975), Charlotte Gordon in *Romantic Outlaws* (2016), and Sylvana Tomaselli (2021). I base my short sketch on Todd's biography.

27 Bahar (2002), 67.

28 Richardson, Alan (2002). "Wollstonecraft on Education." Ed. Claudia L. Johnson. *The Cambridge Companion to Mary Wollstonecraft.* Cambridge: Cambridge University Press, 24-41, 31.

29 Todd, Janet (2000). *Mary Wollstonecraft. A Revolutionary Life.* London: Weidenfeld & Nicolson, 28.

30 Jones (2002), 119.

31 Mackay's graphic novel is aimed at primary school children but works as a simple and creative way to introduce the author to older students as well. More material can be accessed via the Newington Green Meeting House website.

32 Burke, Lauren, Hannah K. Chapman and Kayley Bayles (2021). *Why She Wrote.* San Francisco: Chronicle Books, 99.

33 Mackay, Martha (2021). *Mary Wollstonecraft: A Life In Pictures*, produced by New Unity. Newington Green Meeting House in cooperation with People's History Museum, and the Wollstonecraft Society, 9. Reprinted cover with permission by the Wollstonecraft Society and New Unity.

34 See Mark Brown's article for *The Guardian* (2020) in which he calls the statue "one of 2020's most polarising artworks". *The Guardian.* Web. 30 August 2021. https://www.theguardian.com/artanddesign/2020/dec/25/london-mary-wollstonecraft-statue-one-of-2020s-most-polarising-artworks.

35 Wollstonecraft, Mary (2009 [1792]). *A Vindication of the Rights of Woman.* Ed. Deidre Shauna Lynch. W.W. Norton, 67. (henceforth *V*)

36 From an interview with Stuart Jeffries for *the Guardian* (2020). "'There are plenty of schlongs in art' – Maggi Hambling Defends Her Nude Sculpture of Mary Wollstonecraft." *The Guardian.* Web. 30 August 2021. https://www.theguardian.com/artanddesign/2020/dec/16/plenty-schlongs-art-maggi-hambling-defends-nude-sculpture-of-mary-wollstonecraft.

37 Wollstonecraft largely addresses the rising middle class and here predominantly includes white women. Despite her proto-feminist writings, she fails to consider more thoroughly working-class women, women of colour, queer, and transgender women, foreshadowing first and second wave feminism's blind spots towards these women. BIPOC women, particularly Black women, were not included in Wollstonecraft's agenda in the *Vindication* despite her support of an abolition of the slave trade (cf. Tomaselli, 2021, 69-71).

[38] O'Brien, Karen (2009). *Women and Enlightenment in Eighteenth-Century Britain.* Cambridge: Cambridge University Press, 1.

[39] *Ibid.*

[40] *Ibid.*, 2.

[41] Sapiro, Virginia (1992). *A Vindication of Political Virtue. The Political Theory of Mary Wollstonecraft.* Chicago & London: The University of Chicago Press, xiv.

[42] *V*, 5.

[43] *Ibid.*

[44] *Ibid.*

[45] *Ibid.*

[46] Richardson (2002), 25-26.

[47] Hanley (2013), 62.

[48] *V*, 5.

[49] *Ibid.*

[50] Gubar, Susan (1994). "Feminist Misogyny: Mary Wollstonecraft and the Paradox of 'It Takes One to Know One'." *Feminist Studies* 20.3, 452-472.

[51] "wokeness." *Urban Dictionary.* Web, 20 December 2021. https://www.urban dictionary.com/define.php?term=wokeness.

[52] I suggest Stella Moss's explanation of *coverture.* See Royal Holloway's YouTube channel for (3 Sept 2021) "'No Status of Their Own' | Women and the Law in the Nineteenth Century." *YouTube.* Web. 6 November 2022. https://www.youtube.com/watch?v=MtORA2TOLQk.

[53] *V*, 5.

[54] Blackstone, William (1756). *Commentaries on the Laws of England. Vol. 1.* Oxford: Clarendon, 430.

[55] *V*, 25.

[56] *Ibid.*, 28-29.

[57] *Ibid.*, 6.

[58] *Ibid.*

[59] Sutherland (2000), 42.

[60] *V*, 7.

[61] *Ibid.*, 8.

[62] *Ibid.*, 149.

[63] *Ibid.*, 24.

[64] Johnson (2002), "Mary Wollstonecraft's Novels." Ed. Claudia L. Johnson. *The Cambridge Companion to Mary Wollstonecraft.* Cambridge: Cambridge University Press, 189-208, 190.

[65] Wollstonecraft, Mary (2009 [1788/1798]). *Mary* and *The Wrongs of Woman.* Ed. Gary Kelly. Oxford: Oxford University Press, 14. Further references to this edition will be included in the text.

[66] Hanley (2013), 97.

67 Johnson (2002), 191.
68 Armstrong (1987), 60.
69 Hanley (2013), 105.
70 Jemima's biography requires a trigger warning (physical and sexual abuse, self-harm).
71 Sutherland (2000), 26.
72 Rostek, Joanna (2021). *Women's Economic Thought in the Romantic Age. Towards a Transdisciplinary Herstory of Economic Thought.* Abingdon: Routledge, 135.
73 Wolfram, Sybil (1985). "Divorce in England 1700-1857." *Oxford Journal of Legal Studies* 5.2, 1985, 155-186, 155, 157.
74 Hanley (2013), 106.
75 Hanley (2013), 109.

Bibliography

Anonymous (2020). "Mary Wollstonecraft Statue: 'Mother of Feminism' Sculpture Provokes Backlash." *The Guardian.* Web. 30 August 2021. https://www.bbc.com/news/uk-england-london-54886813.

Armstrong, Nancy (1987). *Desire and Domestic Fiction. A Political History of the Novel.* New York and Oxford: Oxford University Press.

Bahar, Saba (2002). *Mary Wollstonecraft's Social and Aesthetic Philosophy: 'An Eve to Please Me'.* Houndmills: Basingstoke.

Blackstone, William (1756). *Commentaries on the Laws of England. Vol. 1.* Oxford: Clarendon.

Brown, Mark (2020). "Mary Wollstonecraft Statue Becomes One of 2020's Most Polarising Artworks." *The Guardian.* Web. 30 August 2021. https://www.theguardian.com/artanddesign/2020/dec/25/lon don-mary-wollstonecraft-statue-one-of-2020s-most-polarising-art works.

Burke, Lauren; Hannah K. Chapman and Kayley Bayles (2021). *Why She Wrote: A Graphic History of the Lives, Inspiration, and Influence Behind the Pens of Classic Women Writers.* San Francisco: Chronicle Books.

Cladis, Mark (2014). "Radical Romanticism: Democracy, Religion, and the Environmental Imagination." *Soundings: An Interdisciplinary Journal* 97.1, 21-49.

Gordon, Charlotte (2016). *Romantic Outlaws. The Extraordinary Lives of*

Mary Wollstonecraft and Mary Shelley. London: Windmill Books.

Gordon, Lyndall (2005). *Mary Wollstonecraft. A New Genus*. London: Little, Brown.

Gubar, Susan (1994). "Feminist Misogyny: Mary Wollstonecraft and the Paradox of 'It Takes One To Know One'." *Feminist Studies* 20.3, 452-472.

Gunther-Canada, Wendy (1997). "Teaching Mary Wollstonecraft: Women and the Canonical Conversation of Political Thought." *Feminist Teacher* 11.1, 20-29.

Hanley, Kirstin Collins (2013). *Mary Wollstonecraft, Pedagogy, and the Practice of Feminism*. Abingdon: Routledge.

Jeffries, Stuart (2020). "'There are plenty of schlongs in art' – Maggi Hambling Defends her Nude Sculpture of Mary Wollstonecraft." *The Guardian*. Web. 30 August 2021. https://www.theguardian.com/artanddesign/2020/dec/16/plenty-schlongs-art-maggi-hambling-defends-nude-sculpture-of-mary-wollstonecraft.

Johnson, Claudia (2002). "Mary Wollstonecraft's novels." Ed. Claudia L. Johnson. *The Cambridge Companion to Mary Wollstonecraft*. Cambridge: Cambridge University Press, 189-208.

Jones, Vivien (1990). *Women in the Eighteenth Century. Constructions of Femininity*. London and New York: Routledge.

--- (2002). "Mary Wollstonecraft and the Literature of Advice and Instruction." Ed. Claudia L. Johnson. *The Cambridge Companion to Mary Wollstonecraft*. Cambridge: Cambridge University Press, 119-140.

Landesinstitut für Lehrerbildung und Schulentwicklung (2009). *Bildungsplan gymnasiale Oberstufe. Neuere Fremdsprachen*. Freie und Hansestadt Hamburg. Behörde für Schule und Berufsbildung.

Mackay, Martha (2021). *Mary Wollstonecraft: A Life in Pictures*. Produced by New Unity. Newington Green Meeting House in cooperation with People's History Museum, and the Wollstonecraft Society. Web. 30 August 2021. Available to download via the Newington Green Meeting House Website. https://www.ngmh.org.uk/schools/primary-schools/maryforschools.

Myers, Mitzi (1989). "Pedagogy as Self-Expression in Mary Wollstonecraft. Exorcising the Past, Finding a Voice." *Jump* 2, 76-91.

O'Brien, Karen (2009). *Women and Enlightenment in Eighteenth-Century Britain*. Cambridge: Cambridge University Press.

Peckham, Morse (1951). "Toward a Theory of Romanticism." *PMLA* 66.2, 5-23.

Poovey, Mary (1985). *The Proper Lady and the Woman Writer. Ideology as Style in the Works of Mary Wollstonecraft, Mary Shelley, and Jane Austen*. Chicago and London: The University of Chicago Press.

Richardson, Alan (2002). "Mary Wollstonecraft on Education." *The Cambridge Companion to Mary Wollstonecraft*. Ed. Claudia L. Johnson. Cambridge: Cambridge University Press, 24-41.

Rostek, Joanna (2021). *Women's Economic Thought in the Romantic Age. Towards a Transdisciplinary Herstory of Economic Thought*. Abingdon: Routledge.

Royal Holloway (2021). "'No Status of Their Own' | Women and the Law in the Nineteenth Century" *YouTube*. Web. 6 November 2022. https://www.youtube.com/watch?v=MtORA2TOLQk.

Sapiro, Virginia (1992). *A Vindication of Political Virtue. The Political Theory of Mary Wollstonecraft*. Chicago & London: The University of Chicago Press.

Sutherland, Kathryn (2000). "Writings on Education and Conduct: Arguments for Female Improvement." Ed. Vivien Jones. *Women and Literature in Britain. 1700-1800*. Cambridge: Cambridge University Press, 25-45.

Taylor, Barbara (2003). *Mary Wollstonecraft and the Feminist Imagination*. Cambridge: Cambridge University Press.

Todd, Janet (2000). *Mary Wollstonecraft. A Revolutionary Life*. London: Weidenfeld & Nicolson.

Tomalin, Claire (1975). *The Life and Death of Mary Wollstonecraft*. London: Weidenfeld and Nicholson.

Tomaselli, Sylvana (2021). *Wollstonecraft. Philosophy, Passion and Politics*. Princeton University Press.

Wolfram, Sybil (1985). "Divorce in England 1700-1857." *Oxford Journal of Legal Studies* 5.2, 155-186.

Wollstonecraft, Mary (2009 [1792]). *A Vindication of the Rights of Woman*. Ed. Deidre Shauna Lynch. New York: W.W. Norton.

--- (2009 [1788/1789]). *Mary* and *The Wrongs of Woman*. Ed. Gary Kelly. Oxford: Oxford University Press.

"woke." *Oxford English Dictionary*. Oxford University Press. Web 29 August 2021. www.oed.com/view/Entry/58068747.

"wokeness." *Cambridge Dictionary*. Web 20 December 2021. https://

dictionary.cambridge.org/us/dictionary/english/wokeness.
"wokeness." *Urban Dictionary*. Web 20 December 2021. https://www.urbandictionary.com/define.php?term=wokeness.

Md. Monirul Islam

Teaching Romanticism in the Indian Classroom: Culture of Conformity and Pedagogies of Dissent

"Thinking is difficult, speaking the word, forbidden."

Paulo Freire. *The Adult Literacy Process as Cultural Action for Freedom.*

1. Introduction: Culture of Conformity

In *The Argumentative Indian* (2005) Amartya Sen wrote about the long-standing Indian tradition of argumentation and dissent. India, he argued, "is an immensely diverse country with many distinct pursuits, vastly disparate convictions, widely divergent customs and a veritable feast of viewpoints".[1] However, within fifteen years of publication of the book, the tradition of heterodoxy and dialogue is under unprecedented threat. The stellar rise of the exclusionary ideology of Hindutva[2] or Hindu fundamentalism[3] and the seizure of the state machinery by its advocates have led to a culture of conformity in which everyone is expected to follow a particular narrative. A nationalist rhetoric that obscures the boundaries between religious and national identities, the government, and the nation (people), has been adopted by the political parties currently running the central government.[4] Any disagreement with what is advocated by the government and dictated by the far-right organisations[5] is branded 'anti-national'. Constant effort is directed towards suppressing dissident voices. The government agencies do this systematically by frequently invoking the draconian sedition law[6] and the Unlawful Activities Prevention Act (UAPA)[7] in the most unlikely circumstances.

In addition, there is a menacing display of violence manifested in (virtual-)verbal as well as in physical form by the ideologically indoctrinated Hindutva-mob.[8] A culture of "cancellation of difference through violence"[9] has taken hold of the nation's psyche, often leading to the denial of constitutional rights for religious minorities, Dalits, and women.[10] The conformist culture has hugely impacted the academic space as free-thinking intellectuals, academics, and students have been the other prime victims of conformist oppression. The demand for conformity in higher education is most visible in institutional control that the union government exercises on educational institutions through its policy decisions. It is reflected in the curricula for a Choice-Based Credit System (CBCS) that has been recently introduced by the regulatory authority for higher education in India, the University Grants Commission (UGC) for universities and colleges across the country. Although CBCS is touted as a student-centred approach that would open up space for creativity and critical thinking as it apparently offers more choices to students, questions have been raised regarding its professed aim.

At the heart of the CBCS lies an imposed uniformity through a homogenisation of the curricula as all universities and colleges are to follow the syllabi prescribed by the UGC. The institutions are allowed to make only minor changes to what has been prescribed. Thus, it impairs the autonomy of the educational institutes, and with its top-down model of imposing a policy completely undermines the role of the "teachers in policy making and curriculum design".[11] The intended uniformity, as noted by Sikha Kapur, dents "creativity, critical thought and is against the socio-cultural diversity and realities of society".[12] Thus, the spirit of the CBCS is in line with the general demand for conformity that is seen in academia and beyond. Secondly, there has been a growing tendency to interfere with the content of teaching and research in the last few years, and phrases like 'national priorities' and 'strengthening of cultural values' have been recurrently used to justify such moves. In 2016, the Gujrat government provided a list of PhD topics to the universities,[13] and the Central University of Kerala issued the following dictate: "When fellows are being admitted for PhDs, the topics for the thesis should be in accordance with the national priorities".[14] Thirdly, as noted by renowned historian Benjamin Zachariah in his article "Academic Freedom Under Threat in India", the selection of Hindutva ideologues in different administrative posts has posed a huge challenge to academic autonomy. These officials work in collusion with the education ministry, and they impose on academic freedom, be it through the selection of faculty members or PhD dissertation topics.[15] Finally, in the name of 'Hindu sentiment' as dictated by the Rashtriya Swayamsevak Sangh (RSS), various Hindutva organisations are engaged in creating fear and anxiety among students and academics, who are forced to self-censor in order to avoid confrontation.[16] *The Free Think Report* (2020), prepared by the international group Scholars at Risk, has highlighted the issue of "clampdown on scholar and student dissent in India under the country's nationalist ruling party" as a major concern.[17] In the face of all this, teachers, scholars and students are compelled to rethink their strategies of teaching and research. The present article on teaching Romantic dissent emerges in this context, and it probes the question whether introducing Romantic dissent in the Indian classroom can help sustain a critical dissent amidst the prevailing culture of conformity.

2. Why Romanticism: Some Considerations

Three primary considerations have directed my enquiry into this question. Firstly, the eerie similarity between the Romantic period in England and twenty-first century India: Just as the culture of conformity dictates terms of living in contemporary India, a similar form of orthodoxy dominated late eighteenth- and early nineteenth-century England. There was a rising demand for political and civil rights from different dissenting religious groups[18] in the eighteenth century, and Dissenters and radical leaders tried to turn the tide in their favour with the revolutionary fervour growing in England in the 1790s. However, there was a quick reaction to this on the part of the British government, and radical activities were supressed by every possible means. A number of acts were instituted to persecute radical thinkers and leaders, especially after the outbreak of the Anglo-French war in 1793. The Seditious Meetings Act and the Treasonable Practices Act of 1795 had gagging effects on any form of dissent, including writing and speech. *Habeas Corpus* was suspended in fear of radical uprising and an extensive network of spies was developed by the Pitt government for surveillance on people. Additionally, with the Anglo-French war, there was an upsurge in nationalist sentiments, and several pro-government groups overzealously watched over radical activities.

Secondly, the intimate connection between Romanticism and dissent: Romanticism emerged as a counter-cultural movement against literary and political orthodoxies. Romantic writers were targeted by the government and the orthodox lobbies, both for their radical poetics and politics. Persecuted by the government and its supporters, Romantic writers adopted the method of setting their poems in some distant place and time, where they could explore their revolutionary consciousness, evading government censure and public scrutiny, yet still challenging the conventional socio-political order. Whether this Romantic policy of distancing can be adopted in the Indian context to avoid hounding by authorities (and mobs) will form an important dimension of this article.

Thirdly, English Studies is one of the most important disciplines in post-colonial India, and Romanticism forms an integral part of almost every college and university curriculum, both for Bachelor of Arts (BA) and Master of Arts (MA) in English studies. When it comes to the BA course in English studies, canonical Romantic poems such as "Tintern Abbey", "Immortality Ode", "Ode to a Nightingale", "To Autumn", selections from *Songs of Innocence and Experience*, "Ozymandias", "To a Skylark", or "Ode to the West Wind" form the core group of texts, along with some classic essays by Charles Lamb, William Hazlitt or Thomas De Quincey, and a novel or two by Mary Shelley, Jane Austen or Walter Scott.

For the MA courses, along with the shorter lyrical texts, classics like *The Prelude*, *Rime of the Ancient Mariner*, or *Prometheus Unbound* often find a place along with critical texts such as the Preface to *Lyrical Ballads*, *A Defence of Poetry*, and selections from *Biographia Literaria*. In terms of genre, poetry dominates the curriculum and considering this, Romantic dissent will be examined here with reference to two poets, William Blake and Percy Bysshe Shelley, as both had unflinching commitments to non-conformist positions. Although many of Blake and Shelley's poems can be read in terms of dissent and raising consciousness about society and the self, this article will mainly concentrate on Blake's "The Chimney Sweeper" poems and "London" from his *Songs of Innocence and of Experience* and on *Prometheus Unbound* by Shelley. The primary factor that determined this choice is the unwavering presence of these texts in the English literature curriculum across many Indian universities and colleges. Some notions from pedagogies of dissent, especially, Paulo Freire's conceptualisation of critical pedagogy, or what he calls 'pedagogy of the oppressed', will be employed to reach a theoretical vantage point. Key concepts in Freire's critical pedagogy such as conscientization, dialogue, critical dissent, and emancipation will be employed to make sense of the Romantic aesthetic as a form of dissent and reconsider Romantic ethics and 'wokeness' in order to examine whether a re-reading of Romantics texts can possibly facilitate a shift towards a more inclusive worldview welcoming of differing opinions.[19]

3. Questions of Pedagogy: Paulo Freire and the Idea of Critical Education

The word 'dissent' derives from the Latin *dissentire*, which literally means to disagree, to feel apart, to have different sentiment or feeling. As conceived by several theorists, dissent is not merely a reactionary negative gesture; rather it is a non-conformist move against the tide. It involves the will and ability to subvert the normative (and dominant) order of socio-political institutions.[20] A pedagogy of dissent, therefore, prioritises freedom of thought and speech in the learning process and centralises the question of disputation and dialogue. It takes into account the fact that the process of sharing knowledge in the classroom is intimately linked to larger cultural and historical processes and that critical thinking developed in the classroom enables learners to engage in critical praxis with society at large. However, the culture of disputation and debate in academia faces several obstacles, because the learning process is not "solely sustained by the teachers and the students", but larger players like the bureaucratic systems that govern the institution, state, and society are major determining factors.[21] Another structural problem with the method of sharing knowledge lies in what Paulo Freire terms the 'banking' system of education, "in which the students are depositories and the teacher is the depositor. Instead of communicating, the teacher issues communiques and 'makes deposits' which the students patiently receive, memorize and repeat".[22] In this system the learner is not considered to be "a conscious being (*corpo consciente*)" but "an empty 'mind' passively open to the reception of deposits of reality from the world outside".[23]

Moreover, as Freire argues, "[i]mplicit in the banking concept is the assumption of a dichotomy between human beings and the world: a person is merely in the world, not with the world or with others; the individual is spectator, not re-creator".[24] The mainstream practice of education in India mostly follows this 'banking system' in which the didactic process fails to connect to the "variety of social, political and moral orientations [...] brought into play" by the actors involved.[25] Thus,

97

the 'banking system' of education becomes a means for maintaining the *status quo* and perpetuating the existing hegemony because in 'banking' education, the learner fails to realise her or his agency. Freire argues that this system of education should be replaced by critical education involving a critical pedagogy. The critical education would do away with the disconnect between the academia and the larger socio-cultural processes that characterise the 'banking system' of education. What Freire means by critical education can also be gauged from the definition of literacy he provides in the foreword to *Literacy: Reading the Word and the World*. He defines literacy not merely as "the treatment of letters and words as a purely mechanical domain" but as "the relationship of learners to the world, mediated by the transforming practice of this world taking place in the very general milieu in which learners travel".[26] He argues that the critical curiosity of the learners should move beyond the classroom to connect it to the larger cultural historical processes, so that learners "become the actors of their own histories".[27] Thus, the critical pedagogy proposed by Freire has an emancipatory dimension to it, in terms of emancipating both the self and society.[28] Central to this project of emancipation is what he terms conscientization.[29]

In a footnote to the essay "Cultural Action and Conscientization", Freire defines conscientization as "the process in which men, not as recipients, but as knowing subjects, achieve a deepening awareness both of the socio-cultural reality which shapes their lives and of their capacity to transform that reality" (452).[30] He observes that conscientization "is a joint project in that it takes place in a man [*sic*!] among other men, men united by their action and by their reflection upon that action and upon the world".[31] Fundamental to Freire's critical pedagogy and the process of conscientization is dialogue. Genuine dialogue, Freire argues, is a "form of humanizing praxis" as it involves belief "in the ability of the others 'to name the world'".[32] In other words, dialogue is an inclusive act premised upon mutual respect, or, as Freire puts it, 'love': "Dialogue cannot exist [...] in the absence of love for the world and the people. [...] Love is [...] the foundation of dialogue [...] and cannot exist in a relation of domination".[33]

4. Romanticism and Dissent: Subversive Promises

If an emphasis on voicing dissent, nurturing a critical consciousness, and working towards an inclusive society are central tenets of critical pedagogy, the British Romantics come very close to practising such a pedagogy of dissent as far as their aesthetics and politics are concerned. Romantic writers asserted their free spirit against the aesthetic and moral conservatism of late eighteenth- and early nineteenth-century England. They decolonised[34] poetry and poetics from the dominance of neoclassicism, subverted existing forms, experimented with new forms and techniques, and dealt with themes and issues formerly considered unfit for poetic treatment. William Wordsworth declared in the Preface to *Lyrical Ballads* that "incidents and situations from common life" form his poetic subject, and the poems are written "as far as was possible in a selection of language really used by men".[35] It was a revolutionary move towards democratisation of poetics and had deep political implications for late-eighteenth-century England that saw a great surge in republican spirit in the aftermath of the French Revolution. Similarly, the egalitarian move of William Blake with his treatment of all forms of life in his *Songs of Innocence and of Experience*, using a language that is simple and direct, liberated poetry from the sanctimonious language of neoclassicism and opened up the poetical and 'ideological' space for (the) "previously marginalised 'Others', social, racial, cultural, and aesthetic".[36] The introduction of figures like the aged Cumberland Beggar, Michael, Simon Lee, Lucy, the chimney sweeper, the clerk, the harlots of London, the peasants, the industrial labourers, the racial Others in Romantic poetry marked a new culture of inclusiveness that the Romantics embraced.[37]

The tendency to break free from the shackles, political or poetical, also characterised second-generation Romantics like Shelley, Keats and Byron, who defied political, moral and aesthetic Augustanism. There was a strong convergence of aesthetics and politics in the Romantic period, and the creation of a political frontline between the radicals and supporters of the government also "entailed aesthetic frontline formation"[38] in post-1789 Britain. The conservative critics condemned Romantic writers' disregard for "Neoclassicist norms as undermining what they believed to be the universally valid feudal constitution of society instituted by the will of God".[39] In other words, there was an increasing demand for literary conformity, especially after the start of the

99

Anglo-French war and, as noted by C.C. Barfoot, by the end of the eighteenth century, the aesthetic principles of Augustanism were easing out, but political and moral Augustanism created pressure on the writers.[40] Thus, the Romantics were dubbed "heretical 'schools': the Satanic School, the Lake School, the Cockney School, the Jacobinical School etc., designating a multiplicity of heresies opposed to the one true school of Augustan neoclassical tradition of rule and reason".[41] Although some of the Romantics buckled under pressure and could not sustain their radical politics throughout their lives,[42] they nonetheless espoused an egalitarian principle aiming at a fundamental transformation of society through their poetry and politics. In a nutshell, Romanticism was characterised by a persistent spirit of non-conformity. Introducing this spirit of dissidence in the classroom, the article contends, has the potential to subvert and transform the prevalent exclusionary ideologies of our time.

5. Blake: Conscientization and Unlearning the Language of Abuse

At the heart of Romantic dissent there was a 'wokeness', both in the sense of alertness to racial or social discrimination and injustice[43] and in the sense of nurturing a critical consciousness aimed at challenging existing hegemonies. The process of raising critical consciousness can be explained with reference to Blake's "London" and "The Chimney Sweeper" poems. In "The Chimney Sweeper" from *Songs of Innocence*, we find a group of young sweepers oblivious to their abuse as they have been tutored to believe that suffering is a part of their life on earth and redemption will come only after death. The dream of Tom Dacre is used by Blake to illustrate how the chimney sweepers have internalised the language of abuse. The young sweepers endure their present state of suffering, believing that their future redemption will come if they "do their duty".[44] The implication is that the children are gullible because they are ignorant of their exploitation by society. The state of innocence is problematised as abetting the exploitation of the chimney sweepers.

In contrast, the speaker of "The Chimney Sweeper" in *Songs of Experience* is deeply aware of his[45] subjection by society: his plight, the "clothes of death" and the forces behind it, "God & his Priest & King".[46] In the state of experience, the child has achieved literacy in the Freirean sense and is intensely conscious of his place in the chain of exploitation.

The journey from innocence to experience becomes a journey from ignorance to 'wokeness', and it is illustrative of the child's *Bildung*.[47] This education is about un-learning the language of abuse. Blake suggests that the chimney sweepers can free themselves from the "mind-forged-manacles"[48] only by undoing the teachings of the oppressive institutions; it is a precondition for the oppressed to end their plight. Thus, once the young chimney sweeper is able to unravel the language of oppression, he can no longer accept his misery as normal, and the tone of the second chimney sweeper poem becomes very bitter. The bitterness not only reflects the sweeper's dissatisfaction with his state of affairs, but embedded in his discontent is his desire to change it. However, Blake seems to suggest that unlearning the language of oppression on the part of the oppressed is not enough. The oppressor and all those with complicity in the process of exploitation should go through a similar process of education and must develop 'wokeness' (and learn) to imagine themselves in the place of the abject chimney sweepers. It suggests possibility of resistance through an identification with the victim. The image of the lone chimney sweeper on the plate of the second chimney sweeper poem enlightens us to this. He is portrayed with his eyes raised towards the onlookers. The raised eyes seem to accuse the onlookers of their complicity and demand an alertness on the part of the readers to the chimney sweepers' plight. Interestingly, through this gesture the boy appears to be reclaiming his right to speak for himself, the "primordial right to speak their word" to borrow a phrase from Freire,[49] and not allow others to 'name' the world for him as it happens in the case of the chimney sweepers in the poem from *Songs of Innocence*.

To read it in a slightly different way, the chimney sweeper's gesture of looking up can also be construed as the act of questioning society (by the subaltern) – raising questions and demanding to be heard. Blake's "London" centres on this need to attend to the unheard voices as prerequisite to developing 'wokeness'. Blake's speaker wanders through the industrial districts of London and 'marks' the pain ingrained in every face s/he meets and 'hears' the cries of people in distress. Through a recurrent use of the words 'mark' and 'hear', readers are "constantly reminded of the need to listen".[50] A look at the earlier draft of the poem reveals that Blake changed 'see' to 'mark'. It indicates that Blake wanted to accentuate the need to remain alert to the plights of others as a part of the process of conscientization. The argument gains strength once we consider that Blake's "London" was written as a kind of rejoinder to Isaac Watts's song "Praise for Mercies Spiritual and Temporal".[51] In Watts's song the self-righteous speaker witnesses people in misery, but remains completely indifferent to their suffering. The speaker feels blessed that God has given him all he needed compared to those who suffer in the street. He reasons that they suffer because they "Swear / And Cry, and Lye and Steal",[52] while he has been rewarded for his faithful prayers to God. Fearing God and praying is the solution that Watts provides. Blake reverses this blinding logic of Watts's song, in which the speaker's eyes are wide open, but the mind remains shut, and suggests that "[b]y opening our ears and our eyes […] we may also open our minds".[53] For Blake, the "key to redemption lies"[54] in this awakening through our investment in the world, not in increasing the hours of prayer. The image of the little boy leading Urizen[55] out of the shadows of darkness towards a bright gate on the plate of "London" is clearly suggestive of this. Thus, characterised by a similar sense of bitterness as "The Chimney Sweeper" in *Songs of Experience*, but more encompassing in its scope, Blake's "London" seems to illustrate a process by which we can develop an alertness towards the plights of others as a step towards transformation of the world governed by Urizenic forces. Reading Blake, therefore, can be very rewarding in terms of an evolving critical awareness based on Romantic ethics and this in turn can play a vital role in forming the readers' perspectives on injustices and inequalities afflicting our contemporary world.

6. Shelley: Towards a Pedagogy of Love

If Blake's poems are concerned with raising consciousness or conscientization as reflection, Shelley's *Prometheus Unbound* goes a step further and dramatises the possible transformation of the order of oppression through a praxis of love. Dialogue is the crucial component of Freire's notion of conscientization. Illustrating his idea of dialogue, Freire maintains that it is founded upon "love, humility, and faith".[56] Shelley's *Prometheus Unbound* seems to develop the full implication of the Freirean notion of dialogue as love, as humility. Following the Greek myth, the poem begins with Prometheus chained in the (Indian) Caucasus. In the opening sequence, we are provided with some glimpses of Prometheus's suffering under Jupiter's tyranny and Prometheus's hatred for the despot. However, Prometheus soon realises that it is his blind hatred that binds him to Jupiter. To free himself of the cycle of hatred, Prometheus recalls and revokes his curse on Jupiter: "It doth repent me; words are quick and vain; / Grief for a while is blind, and so was mine. / I wish no living thing to suffer pain".[57] Following this moment of epiphany, hatred is replaced by sympathy and love. This moment of *anagnorisis*[58] forms the climax of the poem and can be interpreted as the most significant point in Prometheus's *Bildung*. Prometheus's act of forgiving underlines the importance of humility and sets love (Asia)[59] in motion, initiating the transformation of the world that follows. In the very next scene (Act II, Scene 2) we find Panthea and Asia led by a voice towards Demogorgon's cave where a long dialogue between Asia and Demogorgon ensues. It is presented in the form of a catechism in which the pupil seems to be questioning the all-knowing teacher on equal terms.

Once the conversation is over, two chariots set out from there: Won over by the principle of love (Asia), Demogorgon starts on his mission to end the reign of hatred by bringing down Jupiter, while Asia goes to meet her beloved Prometheus, who is unbound by Hercules. The 'self-realisation' of Prometheus initiates the long chain of events that effects a radical transformation of the socio-political order. A new world order is born in which everyone is their own sovereign: where "thrones were kingless"[60] and "altars, judgment-seats, and prisons"[61] were "ghosts of a no-more-remembered fame".[62] It is the end of Jupiter's tyranny and the hegemonic structure that sustained it, but not only that, because the change is not the result of any violent social and political revolution but ensues from a deep transformation of the self and society through a praxis of love. In this transformed world governed by love, "[n]one fawned, none trampled; hate, disdain, or fear, / Self-love or self-contempt, on human brows / No more inscribed, as o'er the gate of hell".[63] The binary of the self and the other crumbled the moment Prometheus revoked the curse on Jupiter. It was the moment when love was liberated from the bondage of hatred, effecting a complete transformation of the human situation as hate and revenge are no longer the guiding principles. Instead, love and forgiveness take over. Demogorgon's final speech on freedom suggests the forces which sustain the new world order: "Gentleness, Virtue, Wisdom, and Endurance / These are the seals of that most firm assurance".[64]

The transformation in *Prometheus Unbound* has a profound philosophical dimension: Jupiter's empire was built on a dualism of the self and the other, and hatred, as conceived by Shelley, ensued from this dualistic mode of thinking. The change effected by Prometheus's self-transformation suggests a non-dualist, non-violent ethics to counter Jupiter-like forces.

The emancipatory promise of non-dualism to free oneself from the bonds of hatred through a process of recognising the connection between the self and the other realised in *Prometheus Unbound* bears a deep significance in the Indian context. The problem plaguing contemporary Indian society can primarily be defined as an expression of violence rooted in dualism. Based on a dualistic logic, there is constant generation and regeneration of the 'enemy-within' in the form of religious minorities, Dalits, women, the working class or any other marginalised group, depending on the context. The ethics of non-violence and the message of love embodied in *Prometheus Unbound* can act as an antidote to this politics of hatred and can generate hope for a state of harmony in a society fractured at multiple levels. Moreover, Shelley's non-dualism, as has been noted by critics, was inspired by the Indian *advaita* philosophy.[65] Also, it is pertinent to remember in this context that *Prometheus Unbound* is set in the Indian Caucasus and Asia sets out on her journey from a valley in Kashmir in her conquest of love, effecting the birth of a new ethical sensibility that encompasses the whole planet. So, the narrative structure also suggests the Indian roots of the revolutionary transformation witnessed in the poem. Thus, reading the poem in terms of its non-dualist, non-violent ethics can strike a chord with Indian readers and re-kindle dormant traces of *advaita darshan*[66] in the Indian mind. Interestingly, Mahatma Gandhi, the greatest advocate of non-violence in the modern world, found inspiration in Shelley's non-violent ethics.[67] Conversely, *Prometheus Unbound* has been defined as the "most Gandhian" of Shelley's long poems.[68] Just like Shelley, Gandhi was also deeply influenced by the *advaita* tradition.[69]

7. Adopting the Romantic Strategy of Distancing: Problems and Possibilities

Finally, let us turn to the question of adopting the Romantics' policy of distancing to bypass oppressive authorities at home. It must be noted at the very outset that this method of distancing has its own problems. The primary problem with such distancing is that it can be construed as escapism, a means to evade responsibility to stand against the immediate forces of oppression. Seen from this perspective, the Romantic 'wokeness' can be questioned as pretended alertness to injustice and oppression without appropriate commitment to the cause. Interestingly, it draws our attention to the double-edgedness of the term 'woke', and here 'wokeness' becomes more of a fashionable gesture than a pledge to social transformation.[70] It also provokes one to question the positions of privilege from which the Romantic writers waged their poetic (read political) battle.[71] However, it can also be contended that a form of de-centred (de-)contextualised critique of the repressive forces at home can sustain counter-cultural notions in times of extreme repression. The policy of distancing becomes very relevant to present-day India, where there is enormous pressure to conform and free speech is under severe threat. The pressure is exerted not merely through the state apparatuses, but also through mob violence. In this intimidating atmosphere, distanced criticism might prove a more sustainable and subversive method because direct voices can easily be identified and silenced. Apart from adopting the method of distanced criticism from the Romantics, another rewarding practice can be teaching Romantic texts that were set in India to dodge authorities in Britain.

These texts are critical of despotism on multiple levels, and introducing them to the learners might help them draw easy parallels with contemporary events. A remarkable poem in this context is Robert Southey's 'Indian epic' *The Curse of Kehama*. The poem centres on a conflict between an oppressive king (and priest), Kehama, and a lower caste (lower class) duo, Kailyal and Ladurlad. In this battle of unequal forces, the oppressed father-daughter duo refuses to be subdued by the despotic Kehama and ultimately emerges victorious. The dictatorial Kehama can form an obvious parallel to modern-day despotism in India or elsewhere, and the rebelling father-daughter pair can be a model for fierce resistance to systematic oppression. On another level, the poem can be effectively read to sensitise the student community against oppression of the Dalits in the Indian sub-continent as the caste identity of Kailyal and Ladurlad is central to their tale of suffering. Thus, the tactic of setting their poems in some distant time and space adopted by the Romantics to criticise oppressive political culture at home can provide us with important directions in regard to the practice of pedagogies of dissent in the Indian classroom today.

8. Conclusion

Teaching Romanticism in the Indian classroom to conscientize and foster dissenting sensibilities, therefore, has several dimensions to it. Considering Romantic avant-garde poetics, Romantic aesthetics can be defined as a pedagogy of dissent and thus an introduction to the Romantic movement can itself be a praxis of dissent. Romantic poetics can be adopted as a critical pedagogy to nurture a counter-culture because, as Isaiah Berlin puts it, Romanticism was characterised by a "great revolution in consciousness".[72] It was rooted in an awareness that "[t]here was no structure of things because that would hem us in, that would suffocate us".[73] It rejected the long-standing proposition that "there is a nature of things, there is a *rerum natura*, there is a structure of things".[74] Thus, by its very philosophy, Romanticism is counter-hegemonic and its dissemination can potentially help generate a critical consciousness and initiate a process of conscientization for the readers, which in turn may create a potential space for an emancipatory discourse in society at large. Further, close reading of Romantic texts can aid the process of conscientization, and the Romantic tactic of distanced criticism can be employed to evade conformist pressure. Despite its double-edgedness, 'wokeness' as embodied in Romantic literature can assist in developing sympathy and love and motivate students to challenge the exclusionary ideologies plaguing the Indian society. However, it must be admitted that there are several pedagogical obstacles in realising these radical possibilities. The choice of texts and pedagogical approaches for instance, can make a huge difference. Teachers need to explore the radical dimensions of Romanticism and their contemporary relevance, rather than merely repeat the conventional readings of the texts that emphasise Romantic lyricism, theories of imagination and exploration of human

106

passions. Adopting the Freirean critical pedagogy that allows dialogue to nurture critical consciousness and puts emphasis on the lived experience of the learners can help us overcome some of the pedagogical problems.

Notes

[1] Sen, Amartya (2005). *The Argumentative Indian: Writings on Indian History, Culture and Identity*. London: Penguin Books, ix.

[2] Banerjee, Sumanta (1991). "'Hindutva': Ideology and Social Psychology." *Economic and Political Weekly* 26.3, 97-101. See also Sharma, Aravinda (2002). "On Hindu, Hindustan, Hinduism and Hindutva." *Numen* 49.1, 1-36.

[3] Ram-Prasad, C. (1993). "Hindutva Ideology: Extracting the Fundamentals." *Contemporary South Asia*, 2.3, 285-309.

[4] The Nationalist Democratic Alliance (NDA) led by the (right-wing) Bharatiya Janata Party (BJP) has been in power since 2014.

[5] See note 15 below.

[6] The sedition law was originally enacted by the British in India in 1860 to suppress dissent against the British Raj. After India's independence the law was removed from the Constitution as it was considered inappropriate for a democracy. However, the law was re-imposed in 1951 through an amendment. Although it was supposed to be applied in rarest instances, it has been frequently invoked in recent times to frame the dissenters. See Manga, Meher (2021). "Sedition law: A Threat to Indian Democracy." *Observer Research Foundation* 26 July 2021. Web. 20 April 2022. https://www.orfonline.org/expert-speak/sedition-law-threat-indian-democracy/.

[7] The 1967 act was amended in 2019 to give government agencies more power over the people. See Bhandari, Deepali and Deeksha Pokhriyal (2020). "The Continuing Threat of India's Unlawful Activities Prevention Act to Free Speech." *Jurist* 2 June 2020. Web. 19 March 2022. https://www.jurist.org/commentary/2020/06/bhandari-pokhriyal-uapa-free-speech/.

[8] Ramachandran, Sudha (2020). "Hindutva Violence in India: Trends and Implications." *Counter-Terrorist Trends and Analyses* 12.4, 15-20. Ramachandran argues that although the primary target of the Hindutva groups are Muslims, the Hindutva radicals jeopardise the security of all Indians.

[9] McLaren, Peter (2002). *Critical Pedagogy and Predatory Culture: Oppositional Politics in a Postmodern Era*. London: Taylor & Francis, 146.

[10] To give an instance, despite huge public protests, the Citizenship Amendment Bill (CAB) 2019, which is discriminatory against Muslim minorities, was enacted, and protesters were persecuted by the government agencies (Anon. 2021, "'Invocation of Sedition Laws, UAPA Against CAA Protesters Illegal,'

Say Activists." *The Wire,* 24 April 2021. Web. 12 March 2022. https://thewire.in/rights/anti-caa-protesters-uapa-caa.). The hounding of the Dalit activists since the Bhima Karegaoon violence in 2018 forms another instance of state oppression against voices of dissent. See Katakam, Anupama (2020). "Elgar Parishad Case: Victims of Vendetta", *The Frontline* 28 August 2020. Web. 12 June 2022. https://frontline.thehindu.com/the-nation/victims-of-vendetta/article32298401.ece.

[11] Kapur, Sikha (2017). "Choice Based Credit System (CBCS) and Higher Education in India." *Jamia Journal of Education* 3, 100-112, 106. It should also be mentioned here that the government of India has introduced a new education policy in 2020. The implications of the new National Education Policy for society at large have been a matter of public debate since its draft was released in 2019. See Chakrabarty, Nidra (2020) "Implications of the National Education Policy 2020 on higher education in India." *Times of India.* Aug 14. Web. 3 November 2022. https://timesofindia.indiatimes.com/readersblog/slowlyandsteadilymovingforward/implications-of-the-national-education-policy-2020-on-higher-education-in-india-24554/.

[12] *Ibid.*

[13] Bharat, Yagnik and Ashish Chauhan (2016). "Gujarat govt gives universities list of topics for PhD thesis." *Times of India*, 26 April 2016. Web. 12 January 2022. https://timesofindia.indiatimes.com/india/gujarat-govt-gives-universities-list-of-topics-for-phd-theses/articleshow/51986510.cms.

[14] Menon, Gautam I. (2019). "Research Has to Be Nudged into 'National Interest' Areas – Not Sledgehammered."*The Wire*, 18 March 2019. Web. 12 March 2022. https://thewire.in/the-sciences/research-has-to-be-nudged-into-national-interest-areas-not-sledgehammered.

[15] Zachariah, Benjamin (2021). "Academic Freedom under Threat in India." *Geschichte der Gegenwart*, 23 February 2021. Web. 12 July 2022. https://geschichtedergegenwart.ch/academic-freedom-under-threat-in-india/.

[16] The mother organisation for the Hindutva groups is the RSS. It is a right-wing paramilitary organisation, and ideologically, the RSS and its affiliates believe in Hindu supremacy, and its professed aim is to turn India to a Hindu nation. See Andersen, Walter K. (1987). *The Brotherhood in Saffron: The Rashtriya Swayamsevak Sangh and Hindu Revivalism*. Boulder: Westview Press.

[17] *The Free Think Report* (November 2020) has reflected on the gradual loss of academic freedom in India: in 2014 India had an AFi score of 0.68, but in 2019, "India's AFi score dropped to 0.35, lower than that of neighbouring Nepal (0.73), Pakistan (0.55), and Sri Lanka (0.51)." See Sundar, Nadini and Gowhar Fazli (2020). "Academic Freedom in India: A Status Report 2020." *The India Forum*, 27 August 2020. Web. 19 January 2022. https://www.theindiaforum.in/article/academic-freedom-india.)

18 Because the Corporations Act (1661) and Test Acts (1673 and 1678) were in force, notwithstanding the Toleration Act of 1689 Dissenters were denied certain vital rights.

19 See the "Introduction" to this volume by Marie Hologa and Sophia Lange.

20 Pandey, Rakesh (2016). "The Problem." *Pedagogy of Dissent*. Web. 12 March 2022.https://www.india-seminar.com/2016/686/686_the_problem.htm.

21 *Ibid.*

22 Freire, Paulo (2000). *Pedagogy of the Oppressed*. New York: Continuum, 72.

23 *Ibid.*, 73.

24 *Ibid.*

25 Pandey, Rakesh (2016), n.pag.

26 Freire, Paulo and D. Macedo (1987). *Literacy: Reading the Word and the World*. South Hadley, MA: Bergin and Garvey, viii.

27 Jahanbegloo, Ramin (2021). *Pedagogy of Dissent*. Hyderabad: Orient BlackSwan, 40.

28 *Ibid.*, 33.

29 The term is derived from the Portuguese *conscientização* and is translated as 'consciousness raising' or 'critical consciousness'. As noted by Keqi Liu (2014), "the concept is basically about education for critical consciousness" ("The Key Elements of Conscientization." *Conscientization and the Cultivation of Conscience*. New York: Peter Lang, 31-51, 31).

30 Freire, Paulo (1970). "Cultural Action as Conscientization." Trans. Loretta Slover. *Harvard Educational Review* 40.3, 452.

31 *Ibid.*, 471

32 Roberts, Peter. (1998) "Knowledge Dialogue and Humanization: The Moral Philosophy of Paulo Freire." *The Journal of Educational Thought (JET)/Revue de La Pensée Éducative* 32. 2, 95-117, 106-107.

33 Freire (2000), 89-90.

34 The term 'decolonised' is used here to refer to the process of liberation of British poetry from the over-determining role (and rules) of neoclassicism in the hands of the Romantics, who looked elsewhere for poetic inspiration and formulated an alternative aesthetic principle that gave a new direction to British poetry.

35 Wordsworth, William (1962 [1802]). "Preface to Lyrical Ballads." *English Critical Texts: Sixteenth Century to Twentieth Century*. Eds. D.J. Enright and Ernst De Chickera, Oxford: Oxford University Press, 162-189, 164.

36 Athanassoglou-Kallmyer, Nina (1993). "Romanticism: Breaking the Canon." *Art Journal* 52.2, 18-21, 19.

37 This indicates the general spirit of Romanticism, but it is also to be noted that the Romantics were not free of cultural, racial, class or gender prejudices and their attitude towards the 'Other(s)' altered with time. Coleridge, for instance,

was an anti-slavery advocate and wrote and lectured against slavery in the 1790s, but, as noted by J.H. Haeger, by 1830 Coleridge's early writing on slavery became an anomaly. See Haeger, J.H. (1974). "Coleridge's Speculations on Race." *Studies in Romanticism* 13.4, 333-357. The similar transformation of Southey is noted by Carol Bolton (2007). *Writing the Empire: Robert Southey and Romantic Colonialism.* London: Pickering and Chatto. Secondly, most Romantic writers in fact wrote from a position of privilege in terms of class, ethnicity, gender mostly – while appropriating the voice of the marginalised, e.g. the enslaved, or Wordsworth using the 'ordinary language of man', while not effectively being hit by discrimination. Thus, the Romantics have been accused of pretended 'wokeness'.

[38] Lessenich, Rolf (2017). "The European Context." *Handbook of British Romanticism*, 164-182, 167.

[39] *Ibid.*

[40] Barfoot, C.C. (1988). "English Romantic Poets and the 'Free Floating Orient'." *Oriental Prospects: Western Literature and the Lure of the East*. Eds. Barfoot, C. C., and Theo D'haen. Amsterdam: Rodopi, 71.

[41] Lessenich (2017), 167.

[42] For instance, William Wordsworth embraced revolutionary ideals in youthful days, but moved away from his earlier position later in his life under growing nationalist fervour. Douglas, W.W. (1948). "The Problem of Wordsworth's Conservatism." *Science & Society* 12.4, 387-399. Coleridge, who was a radical Jacobin and a Unitarian in the 1790s, later became a supporter of the Anglican Church. See Elizabeth Schneider's (1953) *Coleridge Opium and Kubla Khan.* Chicago: Chicago University Press.

[43] "woke adjective *earlier than 2008.*" *OED* 25 June 2017. Web. 20 January 2022. https:// public.oed.com/appeals/woke/.

[44] Blake, William (2004). *Blake's Poetry and Designs*. Eds. Lynn Johnson and John E. Grant. New York: W. W. Norton, 26. Further references to this edition will be included in the text.

[45] The author is fully aware of the fact that both young boys and girls were employed as chimney sweeps during the eighteenth and nineteenth centuries. However, the pronouns 'he' and 'his' are used following the common practice, see e.g. Linda Freedman (2014). "Looking at the manuscript of William Blake's "London"." n.pag. Web. 20 December 2021. https://www.bl.uk/ romantics-and-victorians/articles/looking-at-the-manuscript-of-william-blakes-london. Also, reading the two chimney sweeper poems as a pair leads the reader to identify the speaker as male.

[46] Blake (2004), 46.

[47] The German term *Bildung* carries loads of meaning, but it is used here to make sense of the development of the child's ethical (and political) consciousness.

The author has in mind the association of the term with education and learning as we see in the nineteenth-century *Bildungsroman*.

48   Blake (2004), "London", line 8.

49   Freire, Paulo (2000), 88.

50   Freedman, Linda (2014), n.pag.

51   This is the fourth song of Isaac Watts's *Divine Songs*.

52   Watts, Isaac (2004 [1761]). *Divine Songs Attempted in Easy Language for the Use of Children*. 25th edition, London: J. Buckland. Project Gutenberg. EBook, 7. Web 12 January 2022. https://www.gutenberg.org/ebooks/13439.

53   Freedman (2014), n.pag.

54   *Ibid.*

55   In Blake's mythology Urizen stands for reason as opposed to Orc, who represents energy. He is "limiter of Energy, the lawmaker, and the avenging conscience", as S. Foster Damon puts it in *A Blake Dictionary* (1988). It is the repressive Urizenic institutions (e.g. the Church, the State) that, for Blake, are responsible for the plights of children and ordinary people. Thus, Urizen led out of his dark claustrophobic chamber is a sign of hope and change. Blake envisioned a regenerated world freed from the clutches of Urizenic forces.

56   Freire (2000), 91.

57   *Prometheus Unbound*, Act I, 2. 303-305. All quotes from the poem are from the 1820 edition, *Prometheus Unbound: A Lyrical Drama in Four Act with Other Poems*. A digital copy of the text is accessible at http://knarf. english.upenn.edu/PShelley/promtp.html.

58   The term *anagnorisis*, which literally means 'recognition', is usually employed in theatre criticism to refer to the moment of realization of some important truth on the part of the tragic protagonist.

59   In *Prometheus Unbound* Asia is Prometheus's beloved. In the scheme of the poem, she is the principle of love and plays a key role in the transformation of the world-order. Panthea and Ione are two sisters of Asia.

60   *Prometheus Unbound,* Act III, scene 4, line 131.

61   *Ibid.,* line 164.

62   *Ibid.,* line 161.

63   *Ibid.,* lines 131-133.

64   *Ibid.* Act IV, scene 1, lines 56-63.

65   Leask, Nigel (2004 [1992]). *British Romantic Writers and the East: Anxieties of Empire*. Cambridge: Cambridge University Press. In the second chapter titled "'Sharp Philanthropy': Percy Bysshe Shelley and Romantic India", Leask traces the influence of Indian (*advaita*) philosophy on Shelley and *Prometheus Unbound*. 68-154. The most relevant pages are 134-146.

66   *darshan* means philosophy, but in the Indian context it can also be the philosophy one lives by.

[67] That Gandhi was influenced by Shelley is proven by the fact that Gandhi quoted several stanzas from *The Mask of Anarchy* in support of his notion of non-violence when he was interviewed by some Christian missionaries in 1938. See Gandhi, M.K. "Discussions with Christian Missionaries." *The Collected Works of Mahatma Gandhi* 74, 307-313.

[68] Ashe, Geoffrey (1968). *Gandhi*. New York: Stein and Day, 249-250.

[69] Richards, Glyn. (1986) "Gandhi's Concept of Truth and the Advaita Tradition." *Religious Studies* 22.1, 1-14.

[70] "wokeness." *Urban Dictionary*, top definition by Fata Morgana. 2019. Web. 25 June 2021.

[71] See the "Introduction" to this volume by Marie Hologa and Sophia Lange.

[72] Berlin, Isaiah (1999). *The Roots of Romanticism*. Princeton: Princeton University Press, 24.

[73] *Ibid.*, 133

[74] *Ibid.*

Bibliography

Andersen, Walter K. (1987). *The Brotherhood in Saffron: The Rashtriya Swayamsevak Sangh and Hindu Revivalism*. Boulder: Westview Press.

Anon. (2020). "Invocation of Sedition Laws, UAPA Against CAA Protesters Illegal,' Say Activists." *The Wire*, 24 April 2020. Web. 12 July 2022. https://thewire.in/rights/anti-caa-protesters-uapa-caa.

Ashe, Geoffrey (1968). *Gandhi*. New York: Stein and Day.

Athanassoglou-Kallmyer, Nina (1993). "Romanticism: Breaking the Canon." *Art Journal* 52.2, 18-21.

Barfoot, C.C. (1988) "English Romantic Poets and the 'Free Floating Orient'." *Oriental Prospects: Western Literature and the Lure of the East*. Eds. C.C. Barfoot and Theo D'haen. Amsterdam: Rodopi, 65-96.

Berlin, Isaiah (2013). *The Roots of Romanticism*. Princeton: Princeton University Press.

Bhandari, Deepali and Deeksha Pokhriyal (2020). "The Continuing Threat of India's Unlawful Activities Prevention Act to Free Speech." *Jurist* 2 June 2020. Web. 19 March 2022. https://www.jurist.org/commentary/2020/06/bhandari-pokhriyal-uapa-free-speech/.

Bharat, Yagnik and Ashish Chauhan (2016). "Gujarat govt gives universities list of topics for PhD thesis." Times of India, 26 April 2016. Web. 12 January 2022. https://timesofindia.indiatimes.com/india/gujarat-govt-gives-universities-list-of-topics-for-phd-theses/articleshow/51986510.cms.

Blake, William (2004). *Blake's Poetry and Designs*. Eds. Lynn Johnson and John E Grant. New York: W.W. Norton.

Bolton, Carol (2007). *Writing the Empire: Robert Southey and Romantic Colonialism*. London: Pickering and Chatto.

Chakrabarty, Nidra (2020) "Implications of the National Education Policy 2020 on higher education in India." *Times of India*. Web. 3 November 2022. https://timesofindia.indiatimes.com/readersblog/slowlyand steadilymovingforward/implications-of-the-national-education-policy-2020-on-higher-education-in-india-24554/.

Damon, S. Foster (2010 [1924]). *William Blake: His Philosophy and Symbols*. Whitefish, Mont.: Kessinger Publishing, LLC.

Douglas, W.W. (1948). "The Problem of Wordsworth's Conservatism." *Science & Society* 12.4, 387-399.

Freedman, Linda (2014). "Looking at the manuscript of William Blake's "London." n.pag. Web. 20 December 2021. https://www.bl.uk/romantics-and-victorians/articles/looking-at-the-manuscript-of-william-blakes-london.

Freire, Paulo (1970). "Cultural Action as Conscientization." Trans. Loretta Slover. *Harvard Educational Review* 40.3, 452-477.

---. "The Adult Literacy Process as Cultural Action for Freedom." *Harvard Educational Review* 40.2, 205-225.

--- (2000). *Pedagogy of the Oppressed*. New York: Continuum.

--- and D. Macedo (1987). *Literacy: Reading the Word and the World. South Hadley* MA: Bergin and Garvey.

Gandhi, M.K. (1999). "Discussions with Christian Missionaries." *The Collected Works of Mahatma Gandhi*. 98 Volumes. New Delhi: Publications Division Government of India 74, 307-313.

Haeger, J.H. (1974). "Coleridge's Speculations on Race." *Studies in Romanticism* 13.4, 333-357.

Jahanbegloo, Ramin (2021). *Pedagogy of Dissent*. Hyderabad: Orient BlackSwan.

Kapur, Sikha (2017). "Choice Based Credit System (CBCS) and Higher Education in India." *Jamia Journal of Education* 3.2, 100-112.

Katakam, Anupama (2020). "Elgar Parishad Case: Victims of Vendetta." *The Frontline*. 28 August. https://frontline.thehindu.com/the-nation/victims-of-vendetta/article32298401.ece.

Leask, Nigel (2004 [1992]). *British Romantic Writers and the East: Anxieties of Empire*. Cambridge: Cambridge University Press.

Lessenich, Rolf (2017). "The European Context." *Handbook of British Romanticism*. Ed. Ralf Haekel. Berlin: de Gruyter, 164-182.

Liu, Keqi (2014.). "The Key Elements of Conscientization." *Conscientization and the Cultivation of Conscience*. New York: Peter Lang, 31-51.

McLaren, Peter. (2002 [1995]). *Critical Pedagogy and Predatory Culture: Oppositional Politics in a Postmodern Era*. London: Taylor & Francis.

Manga, Meher (2021). "Sedition law: A Threat to Indian Democracy." *Observer Research Foundation*. 26 July 2021. Web. 20 April 2022. https://www.orfonline.org/expert-speak/sedition-law-threat-indian-democracy/.

Menon, Gautam I. (2019). "Research Has to Be Nudged Into 'National Interest' Areas – Not Sledgehammered." *The Wire* 18 March 2019. Web. 12 March 2022. https://thewire.in/the-sciences/research-has-to-be-nudged-into-national-interest-areas-not-sledgehammered.

Pandey, Rakesh (2016). "The Problem." *Pedagogy of Dissent*. Seminar.com. Web. 12 March 2022. https://www.india-seminar.com/2016/686/686_the_problem.htm.

Ramachandran, Sudha (2020). "Hindutva Violence in India: Trends and Implications." *Counter-Terrorist Trends and Analyses* 12.4, 15-20.

Ram-Prasad, C (1993). "Hindutva ideology: Extracting the fundamentals." *Contemporary South Asia* 2.3, 285-309.

Richards, Glyn (1986). "Gandhi's Concept of Truth and the Advaita Tradition." *Religious Studies* 22.1, 1-14.

Roberts, Peter (1998). "Knowledge, Dialogue, and Humanization: The Moral Philosophy of Paulo Freire." *The Journal of Educational Thought (JET)/Revue de La Pensée Éducative* 32.2, 95-117.

Sathyamala, C. (2019). "Meat-eating in India: Whose food, whose politics, and whose rights?" *Policy Futures in Education* 17.7, 878-891.

Schneider, Elizabeth (1953). *Coleridge, Opium and Kubla Khan*. Chicago: University of Chicago Press.

Sen, Amartya (2005). *The Argumentative Indian: Writings on Indian History, Culture and Identity*. London: Penguin Books.

Sharma, Arvind (2002). "On Hindu, Hindustān, Hinduism and Hindutva." *Numen* 49.1, 1-36.

Shelley, Percy Bysshe (1820). *Prometheus Unbound: A Lyrical Drama in Four Acts with Other Poems*. London: C. and J. Ollier.

Sundar, Nandini and Gowhar Fazli (2020). "Academic Freedom in India: A Status Report 2020." *The India Forum*, 27 August 2020. Web 19 January 2022. https://www.theindiaforum.in/article/academic-freedom-india.

Watts, Isaac (2004 [1761]). *Divine Songs*. Project Gutenberg. EBook. Web. 12 January 2022. https://www.gutenberg.org/ebooks/13439.

"woke adjective earlier than 2008." *Oxford English Dictionary*. 25 June 2017. Web. 20 January 2022. https:// public.oed.com/appeals/woke/.

Wordsworth, William (1962 [1802]). "Preface to Lyrical Ballads." *English Critical Texts: Sixteenth Century to Twentieth Century*. Eds. D.J. Enright and Ernst De Chickera. Oxford: Oxford University Press, 162-189.

Yagnik, Bharat and Ashish Chauhan (2016). "Gujarat govt gives universities list of topics for PhD thesis." *Times of India*, 26 April 2016. Web 12 January 2022. https://timesofindia.indiatimes.com/india/gujarat-govt-gives-universities-list-of-topics-for-phd-theses/articleshow/51986510.cms.

Zachariah, Benjamin (2021). "Academic Freedom under Threat in India." *Geschichte der Gegenwart* 23 Feb. 2021. Web. 12 July 2022. https:// geschichtedergegenwart.ch/academic-freedom-under-threat-in-india/.

Sérgio Das Neves

Novalis and the Alchemical Expansion of Consciousness

1. Introduction

Alchemy is an ancient natural philosophy that catalysed the emergence of early modern sciences. It gained major popularity in the Middle Ages and later inspired Renaissance humanists to perceive the human as alchemical vessel that must achieve balance with nature and the universe to improve the world. Alchemy can be understood as an ancient and syncretic theoretical-practical system that attempts to turn common metals into silver and gold and to create the Philosopher's Stone that will concede immortal life, health, and the wisdom and moral perfection to transform the world. The process involves the conjunction of opposites, such as stable and volatile substances (e.g., sulphur and mercury respectively), and through the repetitive transmutations of the metals, the state of perfection is achieved. The process has two parts – dissolution and coagulation – and four stages: death, rebirth, purification, and perfection. The stage of perfection is never perennial, and the process therefore requires to be redone repeatedly. On the one hand, the alchemical system can be a metaphor for the reconstruction of the self in interaction with and response to our experiences in society. On the other hand, alchemists believed every creational process to be structured according to the four stages of alchemical transmutation. The state of perfection in alchemy, symbolised through the Philosopher's Stone, is equated to the perfection of the human mind, a state of elevation, a spiritual wokeness. Alchemy was not just employed to describe chemical and metallurgical processes, but was also used in a mystical sense, teaching the spiritual improvements that must occur in the self. In the latter, alchemy works towards the expansion of consciousness.

These ideas were taken up and developed further in German Idealism and Romanticism, especially by Novalis, for whom this expansion results from the return to a primordial unity with the world. His writings reveal the link between knowledge and love, showing us that a conscious individual is intimately concerned about the world. This article intends to demonstrate how the alchemical process was thought to lead to the expansion of consciousness and how Novalis reworked this idea in his literary productions. Moreover, I shall link Novalis's thought to the question of how a (re-)confrontation with Romantic poetry and its reconceptualisations of alchemy may catalyse its readers' own (spiritual) awakening and the development of a more conscious and thus perhaps 'woke' outlook on the world.

2. Novalis, an Alchemical Poet

In addition to his literary activity, Novalis cultivated a mystical approach to life, combined with philosophical studies, chemistry, geology, and mathematics. Ralf Liedtke observes how alchemy was integrated into Novalis's life, showing the fusion between the philosophy of Nature and the modern path of chemistry that Novalis sought to exercise, the so-called "dritte Weg",[1] the third path. In *Heinrich von Ofterdingen* (1801), a celebrated work by Novalis, the main character is a young poet, Heinrich, who travels and then meets his poetical mentor Klingsohr and the love of his life, Mathilde. Heinrich finds his true self on his journeys as he realises his destiny as poet and prophet of a new world in which man and nature are (re-)united. During the entire novel the same symbol is pursued: the blue flower. The blue flower is a key symbol of German Romanticism representing a never-ending longing inside the poet's soul for a unity with nature and the world. In *Ofterdingen*, the blue flower is pursued as a symbol of individualism and humanism, which can thus be connected to basic alchemical ideas. It is an archetypal form that combines spirit and matter, restoring the primordial androgynous form.

Novalis soon became attached to Romanticism. The appeal to him of a movement that incites a wild imagination and a torrent of frantic inspiration is however disputed by Littlejohns, commenting that Schlegel and Novalis argued that the "inspiration has to be contained and even negated by the contrary impulse of rationality, by self-awareness and self-regulation".[2] Novalis was an early Romantic writer, whose ideas go against an unrestrained enthusiasm favoured by later Romantics or the earlier *Sturm und Drang* writers. In 1798, Novalis published in the

Athenaeum for the first time with *Glauben und Liebe*, a set of fragments that metaphorically construct his utopia of humanity, relating it to a monarchic ideal. The king and queen symbolize a state of perfection through education: "das Erziehungsmittel [...] ist ein König".[3] The royal pair has a major importance for alchemy, since the king and the queen, sulphur and mercury respectively, constitute the conjunction of the opposites, *coincidentia oppositorum*: male-female or sun-moon pairs.[4] Through this conjunction, the hermetical child (the philosopher's son), i.e. the Philosopher's Stone, is born. When Novalis uses the royal pair metaphor, he is not defending the monarchy as a political, but as a moral system. Becoming a king means reaching an absolute identity with divinity, a total expansion of consciousness or, as Jung concludes: "Gott wird Mensch",[5] God becomes human. An ethical wokeness emerges within the human who achieves the freedom and power to rebuild the world and to reconstruct her/his perception of reality. For Novalis, this leads to the acknowledgment of the self and to a state of empathy, tolerance, and benevolence towards the world.

Indeed, we can perceive that in Novalis's poem "Kenne dich selbst!"

> [n]ur der vernünftige Mensch der echte Adept [ist] – er verwandelt / Alles in Leben und Gold – braucht Elixiere nicht mehr. / In ihm dampfet der heilige Kolben – der König ist in ihm – / Delphos auch, und er fasst endlich das: Kenne dich selbst![6]

The adept, the alchemist, or the initiated must find the king inside themselves, which also means the gold, the Philosopher's Stone, God/Christ, or even the full consciousness of the being. Finding the king inside ourselves is representative of knowing our deepest self, guided by moral implications, as a profound work in the world that improves our human nature. After the Philosopher's Stone is found inside the alchemist himself, he must proceed with the so-called alchemical *amplification*, *multiplication*, and *proiectio*: multiplication of the gold transmutation, and projection of the virtues of the Stone to the world. This is another metaphor revealing the moral operation that should occur: an awakened individual consciousness (microcosm) can change the world (macrocosm).

One of the most striking examples of the presence of the royal figure appears in *Heinrich von Ofterdingen*. The first time Novalis evokes the figure of the king is by way of allegory in a dream of Heinrich's father.

There, everything becomes dark, and Heinrich's future mother appears with a baby in her arms, who emanates a sort of mystical light. This baby then grows wings and lifts up his parents to the sky. This is a preview of future Heinrich, a metaphor for the alchemical pair, king and queen, giving birth to the Philosopher's Stone. Heinrich's parents are about to create an elevated being capable of elevating others: a poet. The philosopher and alchemist Thomas Vaughan's treatise *Lumen de Lumine* presents the man who wanders in darkness until he finds the light of nature (symbolised by the mother) containing the pure and luminous child, who will discover "the green dragon",[7] the Philosopher's Stone. Novalis equated the power of the poet with the power of the Philosopher's Stone, functioning as a guide for the world to moral and spiritual perfection, and achieving a symbolical immortality. The poet is thus enabled to change the perception of reality with words and images since he has discovered his true self and can therefore become a mentor for the initiation of the discovery of the true self in each human being. The poet becomes the Philosopher's Stone working on himself through his poetry. Since he becomes the Philosopher's Stone, he has achieved a level of consciousness that will allow him to transmute the entire world. In *Ofterdingen*, to speak about poets is to speak about the Philosopher's Stone and thus about entities powerful enough to change the world.

The figure of the king appears again in *Ofterdingen*, this time in a story narrated by merchants travelling to Augsburg, which is the hometown of Heinrich's mother. Here, it is said that a king is not merely a king because of his crown, but because of "jenes volle, überfließende Gefühl der Glückseligkeit".[8] For Jung, the idea of plenitude is alchemical perfection. The crown, in alchemy, is a symbol of plenitude, of royal (and real) totality, and not of power or wealth. This totality also has to do with the conjunction of opposites, the multiple that is one, as the paracelsic mystic Jakob Böhme, well-known to Novalis, conceives through the image of God. Following this path, he who reaches perfection, i.e. plenitude or even God, by unifying all oppositions will be king. This shows that everyone can try to reach his/her own plenitude, understood as moral perfection, by expanding one's consciousness. Becoming an alchemical king means working on the psyche in the same way that the alchemists work on metal. Then, evoking the figure of the king is to speak about poets too, and therefore, once again, the Philosopher's Stone.

Nevertheless, the Philosopher's Stone remains a utopia, and it is here that the real meaning of alchemy metaphorised by Novalis in his writings is revealed. It does not matter if we never achieve this perfection of mind because what matters is the process itself. The simple fact that we try to reach perfection will change our attitude towards the world, even if we know that the Philosopher's Stone is impossible to produce, and moral perfection is impossible to obtain. Alchemists recognised that impossibility, but they continued to search for their Philosopher's Stone nonetheless. Novalis, as an artist, did more: he attempted to reach perfection through art, in which seemingly utopian ideas can be played out, which may then positively impact the lives of those who receive these works. That is why he enabled Heinrich to transform the world through poetry, seen as an eternal experiment of language, as a work in process of the matter of life. The text's main thesis is therefore that humanity needs art to improve consciousness and positively shape the world.

Novalis coined a striking symbol of this unity of the mind and the world: the blue flower, whose maximum expression is ensured by the metaphorical union of Heinrich and Mathilde in *Ofterdingen*. The symbol of the blue flower, as a "model of fantastic expectations destined to be realized",[9] becomes the most important legacy left to subsequent generations of Romantic writers. The search for the blue flower is the search for the intellectual formation of the being, a clear anticipation of the *Bildungsroman*. Helmut Gebelein observes that Novalis communicates "die hermetische Weisheit",[10] hermetic wisdom, through the blue flower as alchemical symbol of psychological experience in Romanticism. Alchemically, the blue flower is a flower that is born from the hermetic egg, the beginning of life. From the same egg the ouroboros snake will also be born, which devours its own tail and symbolises the primal matter, as shown in the anonymous treatise *Pandora*, edited by Hieronymus Reussner, which was a source of inspiration for *Ofterdingen*.[11] The primal matter is the formless base matter which exists in everything or every being of the world. It is that matter that the alchemists try to transform, which is, in metaphorical terms, the matter reworked by art itself. The pursuit of the blue flower by Heinrich, as a pursuit of his own vocation as a poet, evokes the quest of the alchemist for the Philosopher's Stone.

The blue flower born from ouroboros teaches the individual to return to a primal state, which is, for Novalis, the "primitive and perhaps future union of the universal family of the stone, the plant, the animal and the human" (translation by the author).[12] Thus, exploring the symbol of the blue flower represents hermetic wisdom, realised through love, which also becomes a symbol of the expansion of consciousness. Therefore, Novalis finds the essential paths to improve the human being and to expand his consciousness in poetry and love. Carl Seelig, editor of Novalis's work, comments: "auf dem Weg der pantheistischen Mystik ist er [...] zum magischen Idealismus gelangt, durch den er die unfassbare Macht Gottes, die in jeder Menschenbrust wirkt, in die romantische Naturphilosophie einbezogen hat".[13] The unity of the self with nature constitutes God and is inscribed in "the living image of an Ouroboros Snake, a uroproctological hen to pan [...] symbol".[14] *Hen to pan* means 'all is one'; it is symbolised by ouroboros, but also by the Philosopher's Stone: microcosm and macrocosm, human and God, good and bad: all is one. This expression with its Egyptian and Greek routes is similar to the German philosophical term 'Alleinheit', both inspired by Neoplatonism. In this sense, nature and God are one.

It is difficult to distinguish the alchemical from the mystical, religious, and philosophical influences on Novalis, since he aimed at a very complete synthesis, combining different lines that invoke the same sensual and spiritual power of love. It is for this reason that Burkhard Dohm, when thinking about Novalis's poetic construction, considers it an "Aufnahme und Verarbeitung mystisch-alchemistischer Transformationsmodelle".[15] In Novalis, philosophy, chemistry and religion permeate the alchemical discourse. Dohm puts it as follows: "die irdische Liebe [erlangt] bei Novalis die Schlüsselfunktion zur Erlösung des Menschen wie des Kosmos".[16] The poet finds this redemption working on the primal matter of language, doing poetry, as a metallurgical work to obtain the Philosopher's Stone.

3. Alchemy and the Romantics

Romantics and alchemists defend the self-improvement of the being through the poetics of conscience. This does not mean that their only concern is moral perfectibility, but it sheds a light on the intersections between the art of transmutation and the art of imagination, both representing arts of creation allied to social-cultural questions. This reveals a relevant connection to Romantic ethics and wokeness, since the artistic work has a direct influence on individual conscience, and vice-versa. The artistic matter is, after all, the matter of life and the human itself. In the early phase of German Idealism, Kant showed that rationality is limited by our subjective perception, so Fichte concludes that "if all perceptions of reality are conditioned by our consciousness, [...] then in a sense we determine that reality".[17] Thus, exploring the imagination does not exclude or annul the primacy of reason because, if reality belongs to consciousness, imagination can transmute it and create "new worlds through poetic experiment".[18] *Ofterdingen* is a paradigm of this postulate. Throughout the entire novel, the reader witnesses a radically different world in which imagination, knowledge, love, and poetry are the transmuters of reality.

It is Idealism, moreover, that contributes to this alteration in the *poesis* of Romanticism, especially with Fichte. The philosopher understood that the human self and the self of nature are identical, desiring to be united and/or reconnected. This thought is essential for Novalis, present in several of his writings and used as a guiding theme for *Heinrich von Ofterdingen*. In fact, the author writes in his *Fichte-Studien* (1796): "das oberste Prinzip muß schlechterdings nichts Gegebenes, sondern ein frey Gemachtes, ein Erdichtetes, Erdachtes seyn, um ein allgemeines metaphysisches System zu begründen, das von Freyheit anfängt und zu Freyheit geht".[19] *Erdichten* was only possible by freeing the imagination.

In this sense, Gaston Bachelard agrees with Novalis in understanding imagination as action and becoming and rejecting imagination as a mimicry produced by reality or even as dependent on any of the five senses, especially vision. The imagination becomes independent and emerges as a sixth sense. Novalis's philosophy fits in with Bachelard's idea that "[t]he philosopher runs to the absolute. He is wary of pictures; he does not need pictures. Ideas are enough for him" (translation by the author).[20] Distrusting images and becoming attached to ideas, Novalis rejects the rationalist tendency and privileges the act of creating or making (*poiein*). And if the idea itself is enough for him, then the attempt to reach the absolute becomes essential. As Eustaquio Barjau summarises in the preface to the Castilian edition of *Hymnen an die Nacht*, Novalis as poet-philosopher searches for "the ascension of the universe to God; the anti-enlightened reaction of his time, the night-light confrontation, reason-feeling: through the night and feeling man can access everything, the hereafter, the absolute" (translation by the author).[21] The absolute also configures the synthesis of opposites so dear to alchemy as a mark of complete perfection. Although Novalis considers the complete relationship between polarities impossible, he recognises that the attempt to turn everything into gold sharpens our consciousness to create the spatio-temporal absolute. The attempt to search for the absolute, the Philosopher's Stone, is a necessary process for self-knowledge. This process brings together the opposites and develops through transmutation, which Novalis and Schlegel call the *menstruum universale*, the universal solvent of the alchemists, which fuses the real and the imaginary. In this sense, the horizon of the absolute gains consistency in the union of reason and imagination. At least in potency, "thought contains the potential for development, for self-transcendence, even self-contradiction, or at least contains a built-in awareness of its own incompleteness, in other words that it is capable of self-ironizing".[22] The spirit of Romanticism thus reconciles a religious background and an intellectual education.

Personal experience, a freedom of imagination, a focus on awareness and the empowerment of self-expression encapsulated in Romanticism reflect the political and social instabilities of its time. The French Revolution and its overthrow of the monarchy, Robespierre's dictatorship, and the consequent rise to power of Bonaparte disturbed what was then the Holy Roman Empire, already in crisis, culminating in its dissolution in 1806. This pan-European fracturing questioned the idea of national identities and called for an interpretation of the phenomenal reality dependent on the individual consciousness proposed by Idealism: the subject's experience becomes the protagonist in the experience of the world. Here, Romanticism still echoes into today's ethical and political discourses, in a time of empowerment of the identity, in which each singular conscience is unique and needs a space for its own self-expression, just like the free action of the Romantic talent in art and the world. At the same time, the more unique consciences are awakened and valorised, the more the world can change into a free, ethic and empathic environment. For Romantic authors, humans are the matter that is awakened in imagination and poetic experiment through the awareness of the fragmentation of the self.

Dutch Enlightenment philosopher Frans Hemsterhuis's thinking was crucial for Novalis, especially the idea that love constitutes a world through metaphysical power. He combines Neoplatonic thought with

124

modern science and "die Liebe wird als Grundverlangen der menschlichen Seele und aller Wesen begriffen, wieder in den Zusammenhang des Universums zurückzukehren, die ursprüngliche Einheit des Alls wiederherzustellen".[23] The difference lies in the power of poetry. For Hemsterhuis there is a passive aesthetic, which makes him yearn for life after death, since on earth the soul is never fully satisfied in the desired unity. For Novalis, however, poetry is the transmuting power that will bring that lost unity to the soul. This salvation and the poet as a guide are the central keys to Romantic wokeness, whose process leads to a conscience sensitive towards contemporary issues.

Gabriele Rommel states that "with regard to the history of the sciences and the pre-scientific stages of scientific development such as alchemy, mysticism, and magic, Novalis argued for a symbolic treatment of physics as a poetic treatment of nature" (translation by the author),[24] a way of poetising chemistry or, going further, modern science and rational thinking. This poetic treatment of nature helps to establish the bridge between the alchemist and the poet in Novalis's conception: by transmuting metals and words, the world is a place that can be improved, and this is the great mission: an 'ethical' project in the sense that he seeks to better the world through poetry.

The study of alchemy allows Novalis to have a holistic view of the world, i.e., an integral one, bringing together all phenomena and knowledge, whose main symbol is again the ouroboros. Alchemy would then be for Novalis "eine Weisheitslehre",[25] a teaching of wisdom. The same thought is corroborated by Mähl when he states that the early Romantic idea of a universal science in Novalis is understood "als Selbstoffenbarung Gottes im Menschen",[26] God's self-revelation in man. Alchemy is itself a language of revelation that immanentises the transcendent, and gives it matter. We can find the same idea in poetry, in literature and art in general, as a way of merging the matter of life and the matter of language and thereby offering new perspectives on the world.

The longing and desire for primordial unity, symbolised by the blue flower, "die Erweckung hermetischer Sehnsucht",[27] is represented in alchemy by the hermetic androgynous or hermaphrodite pair. This pair is the result of the reconciliation of opposites and its myth "is in the centre of the romantics theories, Böhme's followers. It is the active force that makes it possible to reintroduce eternity into time",[28] the same force found in the symbol of ouroboros. After the *Märchen*, in *Ofterdingen*, and the transmutation of all reality, the second part opens with the poem "Astralis", with which the empire of love [der Liebe Reich] is inaugurated through the conjunction: "nicht einzeln mehr nur Heinrich und Mathilde, / Vereinten beide sich zu einem Bilde".[29] It is the image of the hermaphrodite, the primordial being, prime and ultimate matter, the Philosopher's Stone, representative of the very image of God, a divine spark present in all beings, from human to stone, as the same poem still indicates: "eins in allem und alles in einem, / Gottes Bild auf Kräutern und Steinen / Gottes Geist in Menschen und Tieren" (304).[30] The dreamed and prophesied universal family comes to pass, or rather, consciousness is expanded.

In this sense, the poet is superior to ordinary individuals because he connects with nature as it is, in a relationship of contemplation rather than domination. That is precisely why the poet is thought of as the Philosopher's Stone or the gold amongst the metals, due to his moral and artistic superiority. For this reason, Heinrich's path will be the encounter with his vocation as a poet, "the purest revelation of mankind",[31] which alchemy also carries in its womb. To be a poet is, in short, to return to the archetypal human being, to the primordial hermaphrodite, created from the "verbo de amor",[32] the verb of love. Novalis writes in *Blütenstaub*: "Dichter und Priester waren im Anfang eins",[33] or even, in a fragment from the year 1798, "der Zauberer ist Poet",[34] a sorcerer is also a poet as he illuminates, reveals, and transforms nature.

Giorgio Agamben, thinking about alchemists and their alchemical work, concludes that there was "the failure of the Romantic attempt at uniting mystical practice and poetry, work on oneself and the production of a work".[35] I can only disagree with the philosopher, reading Novalis, but also other key Romantic poets such as Lord Byron, Percy Bysshe Shelley, Gérard de Nerval, or even Johann Wolfgang von Goethe. Without exploring Novalis biographically, closing in on his literary production, his work gives to humanity the poetics of transmutation, teaching the reader to build a path of wisdom and love, a path of improvement for themselves and the world by looking at this world through a poet's eyes. This worldview breaks down prejudices, cultivates tolerance and respect, and creates family ties with everything that exists.

4. Alchemical Human Perfectibility

After this brief exposition of the relationship between Romanticism and alchemy as exemplified through Novalis, I return to the initial question: how can a (re-)confrontation with Romantic poetry and its re-conceptualisations of alchemy catalyse its readers' own (spiritual) awakening and the development of a more conscious and thus perhaps 'woke' outlook on the world? The short answer is: through human perfectibility. According to alchemy, we are the alchemical work itself, we are the metal to be transmuted, we are the Philosopher's Stone to be discovered. This means that the knowledge of how to become one with the world and thus improve the world through love is already inherent in us as humans. It is through poetry, or even all art, that we learn how to arrive at perfection. Alchemically speaking, the metal must be released from its impurities and improved until becoming gold. The alchemist, as intervening creator, transmutes and dissolves the polarities to create the Philosopher's Stone. The Novalisian poet similarly frees meanings, fusing the material of language with the material of imagination, questioning the limits of the impossible. The alchemical process is a poetic process, and Novalis turns his works into alchemical acts, teaching that literature, and more specifically poetry, awakens human consciousness, giving clarity about how we should live wisely and with benevolence. For Yvette Centeno "alchemy is the art that best helps to decode the hidden path of literary creation [...]. The matter of works, alchemical or literary, is the matter of life" (translation by the author).[36] Particularly, in *Ofterdingen*, Heinrich desires to discover new words to better understand the world.[37] His search will lead him to the perceived pinnacle of poetic writing, which becomes truer the more poetic it is,[38] confirming that the poet is "um segundo deus",[39] a second god, just like the alchemist.

One of the teachings of the *Corpus Hermeticum*, mystical and philosophical texts allegedly written by Hermes Trismegistus, the father of alchemy (100-300 a. D.), is the revelation that the alchemical work and its meaning are within each person. For this reason, alchemy has been compared to artistic creation due to its internal process, which leads to the artist's rebirth. This is one of the ways of conceiving the relationship between alchemy and art. However, considering the creation of an artistic work as necessarily linked to the transformation of the artist would mean to substitute the creature for the creator. To avoid this substitution, the

127

relationship between created and creator can be understood as reciprocal: Art is as alive as its creator, and both transform the world and each other. Instead of Agamben's pessimistic view mentioned above, the philosopher highlights the dimension of alchemical transmutation in literary language. The poet as an artistic creator uses language and his poetic texts to shape the world and guide the readers, offering impossible ways to describe reality, illogical linguistic constructions and, moreover, images of a world not yet in existence. The *Märchen* told by Klingsohr is an example of that new reality, showing to Heinrich and his readers the potentials of literature as a matter capable of changing lives. As he teaches Heinrich, "the more man masters language, the more he will want to be able to master the world, and express himself freely" (translation by the author).[40] The same principle is prevalent in alchemical thought: the more the alchemist masters the metals and substances, the more he will master a thorough understanding of the world through the Philosopher's Stone.

The alchemist-artist is also the alchemical retort itself and must perform the alchemical procedure as many times as needed. The Stone is produced, i.e. the artistic, literary, or moral work is created, after finding the raw and primordial material and purifying it: in this sense, the primal matter can be understood as the true nature of all things. The literary work purifies it, giving form to matter through language. Believing that perfection is never reached, the work never ends because the experience amplifies, multiplies, and projects itself onto nature to improve it. It is not just the artist who operates in this transmutation. In line with reader-response theory, the reading of the artist's work will produce a certain effect in the metaphorical alchemical work of the reader, which means that they will be inspired to better themselves through the confrontation with poetical works. This is part of the alchemical process known as *amplificatio*, *multiplication*, and *projection*: the amplification, multiplication, and projection of the power of the Philosopher's Stone, in this case, the artist's work. We can notice this in the end of the *Märchen*, because it corresponds to the end of the reality as we perceive it, too: "empirical reality is totally supplanted and Heinrich moves only in a supernatural world where the restrictions of time and space have disappeared".[41] To this temporal and spatial suppression, Liedtke ascribed a jump to a mythological time, made by the alchemical process.[42] The poetic language has created life and, in fact, a new world: poetry, *poesis*, becomes *poiein*, the action of creation. As stressed in *Ofterdingen*, the

128

ordinary becomes wonderful,[43] *i.e.*, perfected. Moreover, after the union of Heinrich with Mathilde, she apparently dies, but in fact they merge into each other,[44] returning to their primordial hermaphrodite origin. In the second part of *Ofterdingen*, the reader is transported into this mythological time, in which the tree speaks with Mathilde's voice, and Heinrich meets another girl with Mathilde's memories and soul, reinforcing the ouroboric circle of life: the unification of opposites is successfully accomplished. The transformation and the return to a primordial nature are caused by the *Märchen* as such and by Heinrich's poetry in the *Märchen*. Alchemically, this is the return to the "first mercurial matter",[45] i.e., to the hermetic egg, the beginning. Once discovered, we can finally make the Philosopher's Stone, *i.e.*, we can finally expand our consciousness.

Novalis's character Heinrich also undergoes what can be called alchemical processes and is therefore representative of the reader. These alchemical transmutation processes allow thinking of an alchemical poetics of the transmutation of consciousness. A sense of contemplation and a sense of (self-)reflection: contemplating art, reading, and exploring the work of Romantics like Novalis will inspire us to reflect on ourselves, improving the understanding of ourselves and others. In *Ofterdingen*, this self-reflection is notorious. Heinrich teaches that the success of the alchemical conjunction results in a work that fuses imagination and reality, making a point that the process of imagination is so powerful that it can affect the world. Novalis and other Romantic poets would therefore potentially advise us as 21st-century readers to use our imagination to build bridges to improve our understanding of others and ourselves.

Ofterdingen is therefore a quintessential novel of apprenticeship because it shows how a young poet can develop his skills and discover himself through experiences in and interaction with society: the stories told by the merchants during their travels; the shared dreams of others; the social life in Augsburg; the teachings of Klingsohr and, finally, the discovery of love. The construction of the novel is influenced by the alchemical system. First, there is an evolution of the self and the transformation of moral/spiritual matter. In a second step, the same stages of the alchemical process are played out: The departure from his homeland (death); the travels and the arrival in a new land (rebirth); increased understanding and intellectual and moral achievements (purification); and finally, the union with Mathilde and the fusion of the real world with the poetical (perfection). Analysing the text through the alchemical lens helps to understand wokeness as a discovery of our true self, putting us at the service of society. This can be conceptualised as helping others to better know themselves, adding value to the Humanities and the Arts, respecting our own vocation and, above all, creating a collective consciousness. As Sylvester, another mystical character in *Ofterdingen*, shows to Heinrich, consciousness is the essence of the human in constant transmutation; it is the celestial image of the human.[46] Through reading Novalis and learning about alchemical processes, we understand that love and poetry work together in the construction of a better world.

5. Conclusion

Reading Novalis, I feel that there still is a blue flower to be searched and found. In other words, Novalis writes of the possibility of believing in the power of literature, or art in general, as something that can change the world, starting with the reader. Alchemical matter and literary matter are self-reflective. And that matters to this essay because the imagination of a harmonious unity, so longed for by the Romantics, expands our consciousness simply through imagining its existence. Of course, knowing its impossibility is also very important to avoid the pressure of pursuing a utopian idea. Romantic ethics enable us to be more conscious, to be in-the-present, thinking, criticising, destroying and reconstructing moral, ethical or social barriers, trying to improve our being and existence in relationship with others and the natural world. Romantic literature, in this case Novalis's *Ofterdingen*, is constantly questioning moral issues, reflecting on desires and passions, analysing our emotions, offering rich images of individual perceptions of reality, which, in summary, helps readers to better understand humanity.

Alchemical treatises are alchemy's greatest contribution to how humans think about culture and art. Its formulas, philosophy and the compilation of teachings resulting from different cultures, times and religions constitute a source of discourses that question our sense of self and language. By dissolving language, merging symbols, and improving imagination, human identity is questioned and reconstructed. These reconstructions are worked on by Romantic poets but are perceived as emerging in the study of literature itself. Arts, literature, and poetry are crucial when we want to interpret what is happening in the world, when we want to observe and theorise actions and reactions. Literature and literary studies promote an urgent reflection on the world, since they try to "understand across barriers of time and culture, the actions and creations of other human beings".[47]

By way of conclusion, the words of Romantic poets create reality, they alter us through reading them, and our consciousness expands. Novalis and other Romantics noticed that and found, for example, in alchemy a source of learning, with a powerful symbolic and metaphorical language that could be used to awaken the consciousness, since the simple quest of interpreting a text can increase our understanding of other people's actions. There is an urgency of investing in the humanities and appealing to the need to create reading habits to foster our self-improvement. To ignore the usefulness of artistic creation, in this case literary texts, is to silently agree with those who discard what is not, at first sight, useful, or rather, quantitatively useful. If the physical and mental health of human beings are valuable assets, so is the well-being of a society. This health is also achieved through reading and questioning political attitudes and socio-political criticism, inspiring a continuous working on the expansion of one's own consciousness as symbolised in Novalis's alchemy.

Notes

[1] Liedtke, Ralf (2003). *Das romantische Paradigma der Chemie Friedrich von Hardenbergs Naturphilosophie zwischen Empirie und alchemistischer Spekulation*. Paderborn: Mentis, 312.

[2] Littlejohns, Richard (2004). "Early Romanticism." *The Camden House History of German Literature*. Vol. 8. *The Literature of German Romanticism*. Ed. Dennis Mahoney. Rochester: Camden House, 61-77, 61.

[3] Novalis (1945b). *Gesammelte Werke*. Vol. 2. Zurich: Bühl, 55, "The means of education to this distant goal is a king" (translation by the author).

[4] Sulphur is the stable, active substance that attracts the volatile and passive mercury. Mercury dissolves sulphur and after that it is responsible for its rebirth and purification. The renewed sulphur will coagulate with mercury, forming a new, improved substance. Certainly, there is an implied sexual metaphor.

[5] Jung, Carl Gustav (1963). *Gesammelte Werke*. Vol. 11. *Zur Psychologie westlicher und östlicher Religion*. Zurich: Rascher, 431.

[6] Novalis (1945b), 103, "Only the reasonable person is the real adept – he transmutes / everything into life and gold – no longer needs elixirs. / The holy retort steams in him – the king is in him – / Delphos too, and he finally understands this: Know yourself!" (translation by the author).

[7] Vaughan, Thomas [Eugenius Philalethes] (1919). *The Works of Thomas Vaughan. Eugenius Philalethes*. London: Thesophical Publishing House, 268.

[8] Novalis (1945). *Gesammelte Werke*. Vol. I. Zurich: Bühl, 169, "that full, overflowing feeling of bliss" (translation by the author).

[9] Mahoney, Dennis (2004). "Introduction." *The Camden House History of German Literature*. Vol. 8. *The Literature of German Romanticism*. Ed. Dennis Mahoney. Rochester: Camden House, 1-24, 16.

[10] Gebelein, Helmut (2000). *Alchemie*. Munich: Diederichs, 238.

[11] Rommel, Gabriele (1998). *Geheimnisvolle Zeichen: Alchemie, Magie, Mystik und Natur bei Novalis*. Leipzig: Edition Leipzig, 148.

[12] Marques, Manuela de Sousa (1947). "O romantismo em Novalis." *Revista da Faculdade de Letras* 8.2, 44-52, 47, "união primitiva e talvez futura da família universal da pedra, da planta, do animal e do homem".

[13] Novalis (1946b). *Gesammelte Werke*. Vol. V. Zurich: Bühl, 374, "On the path of pantheistic mysticism, he [...] came at magical idealism, through which he incorporated the inconceivable power of God, which works in every human breast, into romantic natural philosophy" (translation by the author).

[14] Ceronetti, Guido (1993). *The Silence of the Body. Materials for the Study of Medicine*. New York: Harper Collins, 36.

[15] Dohm, Burkhard (2000). *Poetische Alchemie. Öffnung zur Sinnlichkeit in der Hohelied- und Bibeldichtung von der protestantischen Barockmystik bis zum Pietismus*. Tübingen: Niemeyer, 365, "Recording and processing of mystical-alchemical transformation models" (translation by the author).

[16] Dohm (2000), 365, "In Novalis, earthly love attains the key function for the redemption of man and the cosmos" (translation by the author).

[17] Littlejohns (2004), 65.

[18] Mahoney (2004), 8.

[19] Novalis (1945b), 177, "The supreme principle must absolutely be nothing given, but something freely made, something fabricated/poetised, invented, in order to establish a general metaphysical system that begins with freedom and goes on to freedom" (translation by the author).

[20] Bachelard, Gaston (1968). *Fragments d'une Poétique du Feu*. Paris: Presses Universitaires de France, 11, "le philosophe court à l'absolu. Il se méfie des images, il n'a pas besoin des images. Les idées lui suffisent".

[21] Novalis (1982). *Himnos a la Noche y Enrique de Ofterdingen*. Barcelona: Ediciones Orbis S.A., 1, "La ascensión del Universo a Dios; la reacción

antiilustrada de su tiempo, el enfrentamiento Noche-Luz, razón-sentimiento: a través de la noche y del sentimiento el hombre puede acceder a todo, al Más Allá, al Absoluto".

[22] Littlejohns (2004), 67.

[23] Mähl, Hans-Joachim (1994). *Die Idee des goldenen Zeitalters im Werk des Novalis.* Tübingen: Niemeyer, 267, "Love is understood as the basic desire of the human soul and all beings will return to the context of the universe and restore the original unity of the universe" (translation by the author).

[24] Rommel, Gabriele (2004). "Romanticism and Natural Science." *The Camden House History of German Literature.* Vol. 8. *The Literature of German Romanticism*, Ed. Dennis Mahoney. Rochester: Camden House, 209-228, 218.

[25] Rommel (1998), 136.

[26] Mähl (1994), 240.

[27] Liedtke, Ralf (1996). *Die Hermetik: traditionelle Philosophie der Differenz.* Paderborn: Ferdinand Schöningh Verlag, 27, "the awakening of the hermetic Sehnsucht" (translation by the author).

[28] Centeno, Yvette (1987). *Literatura e Alquimia. Ensaios.* Lisbon: Editorial Presença, 80, "está no centro das especulações dos românticos, seguidores de Böhme. É a força actuante que permite reintroduzir a eternidade no tempo" (translation by the author).

[29] Novalis (1945), 303, "No longer just Heinrich and Mathilde, / both united to form one picture" (translation by the author).

[30] Novalis (1945), 304, "One in all and all in one, / God's image on herbs and stones / God's spirit in people and animals" (translation by the author).

[31] Marques (1947), 47, "a mais pura revelação da humanidade" (translation by the author).

[32] Marques (1947), 47.

[33] Novalis (1945), 25, "Poet and priest were one at the beginning" (translation by the author).

[34] Novalis (1946). *Gesammelte Werke.* Vol. III. Ed. Carl Seelig. Zurich: Bühl, 97.

[35] Agamben, Giorgio (2017). *The Fire and the Tale.* California: Stanford University Press, 116.

[36] Centeno (1987), 7, "a alquimia é a arte que melhor ajuda a descodificar o caminho oculto da criação literária [...]. A matéria das obras, alquímica ou literária, é a matéria da vida" (translation by the author).

[37] Novalis (1945), 128.

[38] Novalis (1946), 141.

[39] Marques (1947), 51.

[40] Novalis (1945), 259.

[41] Littlejohns (2004), 69.

[42] Liedtke (1996), 135.
[43] Novalis (1945), 303.
[44] Novalis (1945), 263.
[45] Gray, Ronald Douglas (2010). *Goethe, the Alchemist. A Study of Alchemical Symbolism in Goethe's Literary and Scientific Works.* New York: Cambridge University Press, 16.
[46] Novalis (1945), 322.
[47] Collini, Stefan (2012). *What Are Universities for?* London: Penguin Books, 63.

Bibliography

Agamben, Giorgio (2017). *The Fire and the Tale.* Trans. Lorenzo Chiesa. California: Stanford University Press.

Bachelard, Gaston (1988). *Fragments d'une Poétique du Feu.* Paris: Presses Universitaires de France.

Balcarová, Markéta (2016). *Die Schlange als Reflexionsmittel in den Künstlertexten der deutschen Romantik.* Prague: University of Karlova, 2016. Web. 28 July 2021. https://is.cuni.cz/webapps/zzp/detail/104964/.

Borges, Jorge Luis (1998). *El Hacedor.* Madrid: Alianza Editorial.

Centeno, Yvette (1987). *Literatura e Alquimia. Ensaios.* Lisbon: Editorial Presença.

Ceronetti, Guido (1993). *The Silence of the Body. Materials for the Study of Medicine.* Trans. Michael Moore. New York: Harper Collins.

Collini, Stefan (2012). *What Are Universities for?* London: Penguin Books.

Dohm, Burkhard (2000). *Poetische Alchemie. Öffnung zur Sinnlichkeit in der Hohelied- und Bibeldichtung von der protestantischen Barockmystik bis zum Pietismus.* Tübingen: Niemeyer.

Gebelein, Helmut (2000). *Alchemie.* Munich: Diederichs.

Gray, Ronald Douglas (2010). *Goethe, the Alchemist. A Study of Alchemical Symbolism in Goethe's Literary and Scientific Works.* New York: Cambridge University Press

Jung, Carl Gustav (1963). *Gesammelte Werke.* Vol. 11. *Zur Psychologie westlicher und östlicher Religion.* Zurich: Rascher.

--- (1972). *Gesammelte Werke.* Vol. 12. *Psychologie und Alchemie.* Zurich: Rascher.

Liedtke, Ralf (1996). *Die Hermetik: traditionelle Philosophie der Differenz*. Paderborn: Ferdinand Schöningh Verlag.

--- (2003). *Das romantische Paradigma der Chemie Friedrich von Hardenbergs Naturphilosophie zwischen Empirie und alchemistischer Spekulation*. Paderborn: Mentis.

Littlejohns, Richard (2004). "Early Romanticism." *The Camden House History of German Literature*. Vol. 8. *The Literature of German Romanticism*. Ed. Dennis Mahoney. Rochester: Camden House, 61-77.

Mähl, Hans-Joachim (1994). *Die Idee des goldenen Zeitalters im Werk des Novalis*. Tübingen: Max Niemeyer.

Mahoney, Dennis (2004). "Introduction." *The Camden House History of German Literature*. Vol. 8. *The Literature of German Romanticism*. Ed. Dennis Mahoney. Rochester: Camden House, 1-24.

Marques, Manuela de Sousa (1947). "O romantismo em Novalis." *Revista da Faculdade de Letras* 8.2, 44-52.

Martins, Frias Manuel (1995). *Matéria Negra. Uma Teoria da Literatura e da Crítica Literária*. Lisbon: Edições Cosmos.

Novalis (1945). *Gesammelte Werke*. Vol. 2. Ed. Carl Seelig. Zurich: Bühl.

--- (1945b). *Gesammelte Werke*. Vol. 2. Ed. Carl Seelig. Zurich: Bühl.

--- (1946). *Gesammelte Werke*. Vol. 3. Ed. Carl Seelig. Zurich: Bühl.

--- (1946b). *Gesammelte Werke*. Vol. 5. Ed. Carl Seelig. Zurich: Bühl.

--- (1982). *Himnos a la Noche y Enrique de Ofterdingen*. Trans. Eustaquio Barjau. Barcelona: Ediciones Orbis S.A.

Rommel, Gabriele (1998). *Geheimnisvolle Zeichen: Alchemie, Magie, Mystik und Natur bei Novalis*. Leipzig: Edition Leipzig.

--- (2004). "Romanticism and Natural Science." *The Camden House History of German Literature*. Vol. 8. *The Literature of German Romanticism*. Ed. Dennis Mahoney. Rochester: Camden House, 209-228.

Vaughan, Thomas [Eugenius Philalethes] (1919). *The Works of Thomas Vaughan. Eugenius Philalethes*. Trans. and ed. Arthur Edward Waite. London: Thesophical Publishing House.

Lorenz A. Hindrichsen

Erasing Intersectionality: Silencing Female Black Voices in English Romantic Texts

1. Introduction

Despite frequently advocating for abolition and the rights of women, workers, children, and the poor, English Romantics collectively tend to erase women of colour through a systemic marginalisation that has gone largely unnoticed in literary criticism. That coloured women should be more extensively marginalised than other demographics is consistent with Critical Race Theory, according to which intersectional groups are particularly prone to systemic discrimination.[1] The complicity of Romantic writers and artists in this process questions their alleged woke credentials and calls for a closer examination of the ways in which intersectional silencing is disseminated throughout the Romantic period.

Representations of black women attain particular significance given that the Romantic period constitutes a key chapter in abolitionist history, commencing with the Somerset case (1772), which outlaws slavery on English soil,[2] and culminating in the Slavery Abolition Act of 1833, which forbids the purchase and ownership of slaves in the British empire.[3] The same dates mark cornerstones in intersectional publishing: Phillis Wheatley's *Poems on Various Subjects, Religious and Moral* (1772), the first literary work in print by a black female author, and *The History of Mary Prince* (1831), the first female slave narrative in the English language. Reading Romantic intersectional representations against these abolitionist trajectories not only furthers our understanding of how black female intersectionality is shaped by social and legal contexts in conjunction with artistic representation; it also highlights notable contradictions and blind spots within woke Romantic discourse.

The need to reassess Romantic representations of black women is underscored by the highly mediated nature of intersectional writing during that period, which limits the reconstruction of authentic subaltern voices. Phillis Wheatley's distinctly Eurocentric poetry, replete with neoclassical tropes, offers limited insight into her identity as an intersectional writer.[4] Similarly, the *History of Mary Prince*, on account of its heavy editing by Thomas Pringle, appears highly constructed in places, raising doubts about the authenticity of the narrative voice.[5] Such editorial censuring and self-censoring uncannily echoes the silencing of black women in many canonical Romantic texts, and points towards a larger pattern of suppression that informs later intersectional archetypes such as the 'mad woman in the attic' in *Jane Eyre* (1847).[6]

Close-reading the erasure of black women in Romantic texts, then, promises to bridge significant gaps in our understanding of Western epistemology and artistic representations. That such erasure is not author-dependent but constitutes a larger trend shall be demonstrated by sampling intersectional representations from signature pieces by five canonical Romantics: Mary Wollstonecraft, Samuel Taylor Coleridge, Charlotte Smith, Mary Shelley, and William Blake. The texts chosen cover a range of literary and non-literary genres (political writing, serialised novels, lyrical poetry, and book illustrations) to emphasise that intersectional bias cuts across many verbal and visual textualities.

The following readings reveal significant discrepancies between Romantic notions of 'wokeness' on the one hand – often expressed through metaphors of awakening ("England! awake! awake! awake!")[7] – and 21st-century notions of inclusivity on the other. Mimicking the (self)censoring of black female voices from Phillis Wheatley to Mary Prince, Romantic writers deploy a range of strategies (such as Oriental tropes) to erase women of colour narratively, figuratively, and iconographically. Such silencing is sometimes sustained by authors, editors, illustrators, and readers working in concert, a pattern which may account for the pervasiveness of intersectional bias throughout the Romantic period.

2. Mary Wollstonecraft: Endorsing Intersectional Tropes

Mary Wollstonecraft, a staunch abolitionist and arguably the most influential advocate for women's rights in the period, assumes a surprisingly ambivalent position towards black women. While black men feature prominently in the *Vindication of the Rights of Man* (1791) and the *Vindication of the Rights of Woman* (1792) as victims of slavery and as metaphorical placeholders for the 'enslavement' of Western women,[8]

138

women of colour are conspicuously absent from both texts. Probably the only instance where Wollstonecraft specifically mentions black women appears in a lesser-known passage from the *Vindication of the Rights of Woman*, where she challenges the "physically degrad[ing]" nature of polygamy by quoting the *Account of the Isles of the South Seas* (1778) by Johann Reinhold Forster, an ethnographer on James Cook's second expedition:

> [I]t is evident that the men [in Africa], accustomed to polygamy, are enervated by the use of so many women, and therefore less vigorous; the women, on the contrary, are of a hotter constitution, not only on account of their more irritable nerves, more sensitive organization, and more lively fancy; but likewise because they are deprived in their matrimony of that share of physical love which, in a monogamous condition, would all be theirs; and thus for the above reasons, the generality of children are born females.[9]

Wollstonecraft's uncritical endorsement of Forster's theories – she calls them "pertinent observations" (90) and does not qualify them in any way – seems deeply problematic given the intersectional tropes rehearsed here: myths of a "hotter" constitution, which echo racist and misogynist narratives from the medieval to the modern period; notions of "irritable nerves", which foreshadow nineteenth-century writings on hysteria; and suggestions of a "more lively fancy", a reference to early modern theories on maternal impression, according to which ethnicity is imprinted onto unmarked white foetuses by way of an impressionable female psyche.[10]

Wollstonecraft's tacit acceptance of such theories clashes with her scepticism towards racial anthropology in other instances, as when she mocks Johann Lavater's teachings on physiognomy in her private letters,[11] and undercuts her iconic status as a "proto-intersectional philosopher" spearheading a universal "quest for egalitarian social justice".[12] Endorsing a text that reduces African women to impressionable dependents whose lack of matrimonial love generates mostly female offspring also runs against the foundational principles of *A Vindication of the Rights of Woman*, which asserts equality of the sexes on the basis of equality in intellect, a parity Forster visibly denies.

Embracing a racial anthropology that defines African women in terms of absence – as male dependents whose humoral[13] imbalance triggers a cyclical reproduction of their intersectional deficiencies – Wollstonecraft undermines the egalitarian vision of the *Vindication of the Rights of Woman*, and reveals a striking double standard when it comes to women of colour, whose intersectional bodies are "almost the same, but not quite".[14] Although she merely quotes Forster without further elaborating on his discriminatory views, her endorsement aligns with a conspicuous absence of non-white women throughout the rest of the *Vindication*. Wollstonecraft's ready acceptance of Forster also reveals a lack of critical distance towards a racial anthropology that informs Enlightenment thinking from Kant to Burke and summarily dismisses non-Western cultures as barbaric, uncultivated, and deficient in reason.[15]

Wollstonecraft's advocacy for social justice, then, is compromised by exclusionary positions on intersectionality which cloud her status as a feminist and abolitionist icon. Acknowledging such blind spots in Wollstonecraft's thinking is vital for a critical appreciation of her voice, and for recognising the limitations of her woke discourse, which powerfully exposes sexual discrimination and racial oppression, yet sustains and normalises prejudice against women of colour.

3. Charlotte Smith: Dramatising Colonial Fears

Wollstonecraft's marginalising of intersectionality is echoed in Charlotte Smith's *Story of Henrietta* (1800), which narrates the escape of a white planter's daughter from the dual threats of a tyrannical father and a savage maroon tribe in revolt-stricken Jamaica. Informed by Smith's experience as the daughter of a London-based West Indian planter and the wife of an abusive husband with investments in Jamaica, the novel blends Gothic tropes with colonial contexts, casting the protagonist as a damsel in distress who is preyed upon by authoritarian patriarchs and sexual predators. While the main physical, economic and sexual threats are unmistakably male, black women play a key role as enablers of oppressive polygamists and as degenerates that fill the protagonist with fear and disgust.

The narrative includes three groups of intersectional women: the servants accompanying Henrietta to the father's estate in Jamaica, the protagonist's biological stepsisters at her father's estate, and the tribal women guarding Henrietta when she is held prisoner by maroons. While the coloured servants are mostly eclipsed from the narrative arc, assertive intersectional figures in the shape of Henrietta's stepsisters and tribal women trigger intense emotive responses in the protagonist, casting somatic difference and cultural alterity as threats to white status and privilege.

Attitudes to intersectionality are first distinctly articulated when Henrietta, upon arriving at a Jamaican port, is informed by Mr. Grabb, a servant of her father's, that she must board his coach unaccompanied, an order meant to separate Henrietta from her governess Mrs. Apthorp. Henrietta complies, yet curiously enters Grabb's coach together with the coloured slave Juana, who "attend[s]" to her[16] and accompanies her to her father's estate. Grabb neither comments on, nor takes issue with Juana's presence despite having just declared that he would "not [...] suffer any person whatsoever to go with [Henrietta]",[17] indicating that he obviously does not consider Juana a 'person' – an opinion tacitly shared by her mistress, who collaborates in the casual negating of Juana's personhood.

The offhand silencing of Juana, a subordinate, contrasts with a more vehement rejection of intersectional figures Henrietta views as a threat to her status and fortune. Upon meeting her coloured half-sisters at her father's estate, she states: "I saw strange female faces of many shades around me",[18] using obfuscating language to reduce unwanted kin to a depersonalised, spectral presence. Henrietta's voice becomes increasingly tense as she tries to downplay the effect her sisters' presence has on her:

> I have had nothing to add to my narrative for some days, at least nothing that I like to write on, or that you [Denbigh, her fiancé] would like to read; and for the persons who surround me, I would I could escape ever naming them! [...] [T]here are three young women here, living in the house, of colour, as they are called, who are, I understand, my sisters by the half blood![19]

Oscillating between outright denial and violent rejection, Henrietta struggles to find a language that can capture her emotional distress. Her sisters' physical proximity, family ties and mixed ethnicity disturb Henrietta, as does their unfamiliar idiolect. "They speak an odd sort of dialect, more resembling that of the negroes than the English spoken in England"[20] she notes, questioning their sisterhood by foregrounding cultural differences.

Henrietta continues to list her stepsisters' "odd manners, their love of finery, and curiosity about my clothes and ornaments" along with "their

141

total insensibility to their own situation",[21] visibly distressed by their closeness and family ties, as well as by a physical resemblance to the youngest of her half-sisters. She is "nearly as fair as I am",[22] Henrietta confirms, voicing her fears of 'going native', or of being perceived as coloured herself: "As I am a native of this island, perhaps I have the same cast of countenance without being conscious of it",[23] she reasons. Henrietta fears an eroding of boundaries between herself and her half-sisters, between her white privilege and the liminal status of her father's mixed offspring. To assert her perceived supremacy over her step sisters, she deploys a wide arsenal of racial, linguistic and cultural stereotypes to resurrect the social and familial boundaries that have been erased. In her attempt to escape the "slave[ry]"[24] of a hateful arranged marriage – a metaphor inspired by Wollstonecraft's analogy of female oppression as enslavement – she resurrects a colonial racial code to assert herself as the sole heir to her family's estate.

Another facet of Henrietta's silencing of intersectional bodies occurs in the dramatic finale when she finds herself taken prisoner by a maroon chief keen to add her "to the number of his wives".[25] Guarded by "three wild-looking female dark faces"[26] resembling the Obeah women introduced earlier in the narrative,[27] Henrietta is stripped of her jewellery and finest clothing by an old "sorceress" and two younger women, who "appropriat[e]" her possessions "without ceremony".[28] Just when Henrietta seems irredeemably lost, cornered in a cave in the Jamaican jungle, her three female guardians change track and decide to release her, perceiving her as a rival threatening their status as the leader's favourite wives. Henrietta is convinced that she owes her liberty to the wives' self-interest rather than pity, claiming that they would have surely "murder[ed]"[29] her should she have chosen to marry the maroon leader.

Smith's *deus-ex-machina* resolution thus effectively dramatises the biased reasoning of Forster's quote in the *Vindication of the Rights of Woman*, according to which polygamist native women "are of a hotter constitution" than their husbands, being denied the "physical love which in a monogamous condition would all be theirs". Consumed by jealousy, Smith's maroon women seem driven by "the desire to appropriate this hero of the hills [the maroon leader] to themselves",[30] authenticating the teachings on intersectionality promoted in Wollstonecraft's text. The *Story of Henrietta*, then, relays three archetypal narratives that actively 'other' intersectionality in distinct socio-cultural settings: as a marker of slavery (personified in Juana), intersectionality renders black women invisible, eroding their personhood; as an indicator of mixed origins (embodied in Henrietta's half-sisters), intersectionality threatens the colour bar upon which white privilege is based; and as a marker of savagery (personified in the maroon women), intersectionality amplifies a culturally encoded otherness that threatens white purity by sustaining a polygamist regime.

While it is difficult to attribute Smith's outlook on intersectionality to a single source, the narrative seems informed by multiple biographical, historical and economic contexts. The protagonist's intense rejection of the step-sisters' appearance and vernacular draws from Smith's own estrangement from her West Indian step-mother, whom she criticised for her skin colour and "monotonous drawl and pronunciation peculiar to the natives of the West Indies".[31] The stereotyping of maroon women as Obeah witches relies heavily on the writings of apologists like Edward Long and Jonathan Edwards, whose accounts she perused while writing the novel.[32] The foregrounding of maroon violence in the final section of the novel reflects anxieties about slave insurrections and the Haitian Revolution (starting in 1791), which threatened to upend colonial rule in the Caribbean.[33] Smith's own economic interests seem equally relevant: the writing of *The Story of Henrietta* overlaps with the author's attempt to reclaim her father-in-law's Barbados estate on behalf of her children in a lawsuit, which prompts her to write a personal letter that specifies the monetary value of each of the slaves on her father's plantation.[34] Significantly, the novel culminates in a similar foregrounding of financial interests by having Henrietta's husband and legal ward Denbigh "divest himself [...] of all his [formerly her] property on the other side [of] the Atlantic",[35] a resolution which conveniently monetises colonial property while shielding the protagonist and her fiancé from the colonial context through which such wealth was generated.

A similarly intense rejection of intersectionality is echoed in other Romantic novels such as John Thelwall's *The Daughter of Adoption: A Tale of Modern Times* (1801), which dramatises the victimisation of white femininity by black male sexual predators while "attribut[ing] [white] sexual predatory behaviour and desires to characteristics arising from within the objects of those desires": hypersexualised intersectional temptresses who lure planters into compromising relationships.[36] Charlotte Smith's novel, then, articulates – and perhaps even sets – a pronounced trend in turn-of-the-century Romantic novels, which stage colonial violence for the purpose of promoting an ameliorationist or apologist agenda, effectively deploying stereotypes of intersectional depravity for that purpose.

4. Samuel Taylor Coleridge: Rehearsing Racial Stereotypes

Racial anthropology also informs the writings of Samuel Taylor Coleridge, whose literary works and lectures frequently echo problematic stereotypes. Despite vociferously campaigning for abolishing the slave trade, Coleridge – echoing other abolitionists of his day – expresses distinctly racist views, notably in his notorious comments on Othello's ethnicity,[37] but also in lesser-known unpublished manuscripts, such as a shorter fragment entitled *Degeneration and Race*.[38] Coleridge's views on race also shape his representation of intersectional figures in poetry and prose, which features two distinct types: the orientalised, acculturated damsel versus the degenerate, demonic witch. By strategically deploying these stereotypes, Coleridge constructs a gendered and racialised hierarchy reminiscent of contemporary racial anthropologies in which women of colour are commodified and stratified as discrete subgroups representing various disenfranchised communities.

The duality of exotic damsel versus intersectional witch is memorably dramatised in *Kubla Khan*, where an orientalised princess – the "Abyssinian maid [...] [s]inging of Mount Abora" (37-39)[39] – contrasts with an eroticised "savage place" (14) resounding with the cries of "[a] woman wailing for her demon lover" (16). Blending in with sexualised landmarks ("deep romantic chasm", 12) whose natural phenomena mimic erotically charged human behaviour ("with ceaseless turmoil seething", "in fast thick pants [...] breathing", 17-18), the 'wailing' woman resembles the desperate, lovelorn tribal women described in Wollstonecraft and Smith who suffer from male neglect. The woman's "wailing" also marks her as unmistakably intersectional, being distinctly gendered, culturally othered, and pathologised as mentally unstable.

Merging with a savage colonial landscape to be 'discovered',[40] the wailing woman and her surrounding scenery form a single entity whose consummation is figuratively expressed through phallic imagery ("A mighty fountain momently was forced / Amid whose swift half-

intermitted burst / Huge fragments vaulted like rebounding hail", 19-21),
followed by an anticlimactic serenity that consolidates her conquest:
"Five miles meandering with a mazy motion / Through wood and dale the
sacred river ran / Then reached the cavern measureless to man / And sank
in tumult to a lifeless ocean", 25-28). In a distinctly Oedipal twist, the
conquest of the woman associated with this "savage place" triggers
violent male rivalry ("And 'mid this tumult Kubla heard from far /
Ancestral voices prophesying war", 29-30), suggesting circular patterns
of conquest and sexual consummation, warfare and pain (hence the
"wailing") that animates this timeless universe.

By way of contrast, the cultured "Abyssinian maid" inhabits a psychic
landscape of cultured refinement, mysterious seclusion and artistic
expression:

> A damsel with a dulcimer
> In a vision once I saw:
> It was an Abyssinian maid
> And on her dulcimer she played,
> Singing of Mount Abora. (37-41)

Celebrated through the language of courtly love, the "damsel" – a term
suggesting noble birth – expresses her longing through a "dulcimer", an
instrument whose etymology encodes sweetness. The romantic charge of
her refined response is expressed through her singing of "Mount Abora"
("Mount Amhara" in the original manuscript),[41] the famed royal prison
where Ethiopian heirs were kept to avoid armed conflicts with their ruling
fathers, a place where, according to Purchas,"[n]o woman may ascend".[42]
The romantic conflict established here – of lovers separated perhaps
indefinitely to honour royal custom – contrasts with the impulsive and
seemingly unrestrained "wailing for [a] demon lover".

The paganism and sinfulness of the savage woman's "chasm" are
likewise contrasted with paradisiacal, innocent bliss of life on top of
Mount "Amhara". Purchas describes at great length how Mount Amhara
represents the cradle of Ethiopian Christianity; the Ethiopian empress
Candace's eunuch from the *Acts of the Apostles* (Acts 8:27-36) was –
according to local legend – baptised there.[43] Mount Amhara/Abora in
Coleridge's poem thus encapsulates a place whose sacredness eclipses the
alleged 'holiness' ("holy and enchanted", 14) of the savage chasm; it
functions as a safeguard that ensures a peaceful transfer of power, thereby

eliminating the 'prophecies of war' (or wars of succession) associated with the savage chasm.

The poem's two contrasting visions – of sinfulness versus enforced chastity, instant gratification versus tragic longing, and savagery versus Christianity – evoke two distinct exotic universes that function as complementary spheres in colonial discourse. "Ethiopia" or "Abyssinia" (both reference the Ethiopian kingdom in the Horn of Africa)[44] represents a Christian enclave in a continent otherwise constructed as 'savage'. As the realm of "Prester John" – the mythical Christian ruler European explorers attempt to locate throughout the early modern period – Ethiopia/Abyssinia becomes an object of desire associated with the riches of the Orient. As the cradle of the Blue Nile (allegedly discovered by the Scottish explorer James Bruce in the 1790s) and the home of a scriptural legacy that preserved texts like the *Book of Enoch* in old Ethiopic script (Ge'ez), Ethiopia/Abyssinia becomes a Christianised version of the Moorish or Arab traditions Coleridge celebrates in his lectures on *Othello*.

The "Abyssinian maid" is, accordingly, pictured as a courtly damsel associated with royal Mount Amhara. The ambiguous term 'maid' conveniently blurs the boundaries between freedom ('maiden') and servitude ('maidservant'), inviting readings that construct her as royal (hence desirable) and unfree (hence available). The damsel's physical displacement – she sings of Mount Amhara rather than observing it – accentuates her distress, and evokes colonial fantasies: has she been displaced to the pleasure dome at Xanadu? Else, how might she relate to the central "Vision" articulated in this "Fragment"? As a counterpoint to the Abyssinian, the "wailing" woman evokes uncultivated savagery Coleridge associates with tribes inhabiting the African continent and with the "Mongolian Asiatics" he calls "degenerate" in his unpublished manuscript *Degeneration and Race*.[45] In the same document, he echoes the theory of a "low estimation of women", or a neglect of their sexual desires in non-European cultures,[46] a theme dramatised in the wailing savage, and still liminally present in the Abyssinian's expressive singing of her lover.

In *Kubla Khan*, then, Coleridge operates with a colonial frame that iconises Westernised, vaguely orientalised femininity (embodied in the Abyssinian maid) while demonising somatic difference and cultural alterity (associated with Xanadu's 'savage' place). Such a stratifying of otherness, which lies at the heart of racial anthropology, is consistent with views expressed by contemporaries like De Quincey, who in his *Confessions of an Opium-Eater* condemns the "barbarity" of Africa while praising the "mere antiquity of Asiatic things".[47] Coleridge's vociferous protesting against the slave trade, and his genuine commitment to liberating and enfranchising slaves and common labourers,[48] contrasts with his literary representation of intersectional women, who – in the texts above – are reduced to animalistic constructs (the 'wailing' woman) or highly mediated, eroticised oriental tropes (the Abyssinian maid) whose Christian attributes compromise their cultural alterity, and turn them into legitimate objects of desire. Acknowledging these blind spots compromising Coleridge's vision of wokeness seems crucial for a nuanced understanding of his writing, and for an informed interpretation of his literary oeuvre.

5. Mary Wollstonecraft Shelley: Questioning Intersectional Tropes

Mary Shelley's *Frankenstein* operates with a similar dichotomy like *Kubla Khan*, pitching a Christianised damsel (Safie, Felix de Lacey's fiancé) against a demonised witch (the Creature's[49] inanimate companion) whose power renders her problematic and feared. Even though the novel does not explicitly associate the Creature with a colonial context, contemporary readers commonly read it in such terms, which lends the Creature's companion distinct intersectional overtones. By demonising the uncontrollable female Creature while celebrating Safie's successful acculturation, the novel portrays intersectionality through culturally defined power dynamics as well as by gender politics, reflected in Victor Frankenstein's misogyny, which fundamentally shapes the novel.

That *Frankenstein* was commonly associated with imperial rule emerges from a parliamentary debate on the "Amelioration of the Condition of the Slave Population of the West Indies" in 1824, in which the Leader of the House of Commons George Canning drew a direct link between Victor's rebellious Creature and enslaved labourers:

> In dealing with the negro, Sir, we must remember that we are dealing with a being possessing the form and strength of a man, but the intellect only of a child. To turn him loose in the manhood of his physical strength, in the maturity of his passions, but in the infancy of his uninstructed reason, would be to raise up a creature resembling the splendid fiction of a recent

romance; the hero of which constructs a human form, with all the corporeal capabilities of man, and with the thews and sinews of a giant; but being unable to impart to the work of his hands a perception of right and wrong, he finds too late that he has only created a more than mortal power of doing mischief, and himself recoils from the monster which he has made.[50]

Canning's reading of the Creature as a rebellious slave using his "mortal power" to "d[o] mischief" was apparently appreciated by Mary Shelley, who stated in a letter to a friend (Edward John Trelawny) that Canning "paid a complement to *Frankenstein* in a manner sufficiently pleasing to me".[51] The ironic touch of her statement leaves no doubt that she favoured the narrative being read as an imperial allegory; in fact, her manuscript draft contains passages where the original wording described the Creature in language evoking non-Western alterity. The scene when Victor destroys the female companion, for example, is introduced by a description of the onlooking Creature as displaying "the utmost extent of malice & barbarity", a phrase that is altered to "the utmost extent of malice & treachery",[52] thus erasing the non-Western encoded in 'barbarity', a key term in oriental and colonial discourse.

The central plot point on which the novel's tragic second half hinges is exactly that moment when Victor breaks his promise of creating a female companion, thereby unleashing the Creature's killing spree sealing the fate of Clerval, Elizabeth, Alphonse, Victor and the Creature himself. Victor rationalises his impulsive destruction of the female companion in a passage often discussed in feminist readings,[53] using language that gradually shifts from contemplative and analytical to speculative and agitated:

> I was now about to form another being, of whose dispositions I was alike ignorant; she might become ten thousand times more malignant than her mate, and delight, for its own sake, in murder and wretchedness. He had sworn to quit the neighbourhood of man, and hide himself in deserts; but she had not; and she, who in all probability was to become a thinking and reasoning animal, might refuse to comply with a compact made before her creation. They might even hate each other; the creature who already lived loathed his own deformity, and might he not conceive a greater abhorrence for it when it came before his eyes in the female form? She also might turn with disgust from him to the superior beauty of man; she

might quit him, and he be again alone, exasperated by the fresh provocation of being deserted by one of his own species.

Even if they were to leave Europe, and inhabit the deserts of the new world, yet one of the first results of those sympathies for which the daemon thirsted could be children, and a race of devils would be propagated upon the earth, who might make the very existence of the species of man a condition precarious and full of terror. Had I a right, for my own benefit, to inflict this curse upon everlasting generations?[54]

In quick succession, Victor piles hypotheticals upon hypotheticals, culminating in two scenarios that, in Victor's eyes, seem equally horrendous: the female Creature reproducing uncontrollably, or her engaging in sexual relations with humans. Victor's frantic prose here leverages sensationalist tropes commonly found in colonial discourse. The spectre of miscegenation is dramatised through emotive language that masks highly subjective opinion as objective truth, emulating a connoisseur physiognomist's passing of informed judgment.[55] The insistence that the Creature's companion might propagate and "inflict this curse upon everlasting generations" echoes colonialist fears of being outnumbered by native demographics, with the term "curse" referencing the propagandist myth of Noah's curse on Ham, according to which (non-white skin-)colour arose as a punishment for Ham's irreverence towards his father.[56]

The various nightmare scenarios also have a distinctly misogynist bent. The premise that "she might become ten thousand times more malignant than her mate" assumes an inherent flaw rooted in the female gender, while the speculation that she might "refuse to comply with a compact made before her creation" casts her as an inconstant Eve using her "thinking and reasoning" to selfish ends. This notion of inconstancy is continued in the speculation that she "might quit him", while labelling her as an "animal" (not a Creature) dehumanises her – a process feeding into the destruction of her body through "an image that suggests violent rape": "[T]rembling with passion, [I] tore to pieces the thing on which I was engaged."[57] Using language that objectifies her, Victor negates the significance of the violence inflicted while painting the male Creature's disturbed response ("howl of devilish despair and revenge")[58] in animalistic terms reminiscent of the uncontrollable "wailing" of the demon's lover in *Kubla Khan*. By dismissing the Creature's mental anguish as barbaric and malignant, Victor further degrades the female

Creature, and reduces her body to a legitimate site for his proxy war against the male Creature.

Destroying the female Creature – an act Shelley implicitly questions by systematically undercutting Victor's narrative through the preceding narrative by the Creature – contrasts with the celebration of Turkish Safie, whose name (*sapientia*) bespeaks her wisdom. Having absconded from an ungrateful, tyrannical father, who failed to honour his promises toward Felix and hoped to "immur[e] [her] within the walls of a harem",[59] Safie actively seeks out the de Laceys in their exile, demonstrating her agency in the process. Her conversion to Christianity represents both an act of acculturation and emancipation: as the daughter of a "Christian Arab, seized and made a slave by the Turks",[60] she aspires to "marrying a Christian *and* remaining in a country where women [a]re allowed to take a rank in society".[61] The linking of status and Christianity (offering "an independence of spirit [...] [forbidden] to followers of Mahomet")[62] echoes statements by Mary Shelley's mother, Mary Wollstonecraft, who frequently conjures up stock images of oppressed women in Islamic communities to vindicate the rights of (Western) women.[63]

Safie's conversion and acculturation, her independence and thirst for learning, and her loyalty and purity mark her as an idealised Westernised oriental princess whose ready availability turns her into a rewarding colonial conquest. Unlike the faceless, nameless Abyssinian maid singing of Mount Amhara, Safie's distinct identity and self-empowerment elevate her above a mere colonial trope. By centring her narrative in the heart of the novel – framed by the Creature's, Victor's and Walton's narratives – the author validates and celebrates her figure, casting her as a cultural rebel who dismantles familiar stereotypes through her own agency. *Frankenstein*, then, offers a set of contrasting intersectional figures who broadly correspond to the savages and oriental figures in the previous texts. Unlike the hapless Abyssinian maid, Turkish Safie has agency and voice, and even assumes protagonism within her own tale. The Creature's companion represents a tragic figure who is merely represented as, rather than embodies, the savage type replicated in Wollstonecraft, Smith and Coleridge.

Shelley's skilful balancing of conflicting voices (Victor's and the Creature's) constantly raises doubts about the legitimacy of Victor's demonising of the female companion. A straightforward assessment of Mary Shelley's wokeness in *Frankenstein* is complicated by the rhetorical contest between Victor and the Creature, whose dialectic undercuts the validity of the colonial trope Victor promotes. While endorsing problematic racial and orientalist stereotypes, some of which feature in her mother's writing, Mary Shelley asserts the importance of questioning demeaning rhetoric by giving the subaltern a voice, thus demonstrating sensibility towards the plight of silenced voices.

6. William Blake and Cristoforo Dall'Acqua: Erasing Black Femininity

Intersectional figures are not purely marginalised as a result of authorial choices; discriminatory codes are likewise sustained through networks of textual production and consumption that popularise such othering. Compelling evidence that demonstrates how intersectional bias was endorsed by publishers, illustrators and readers can be found in book illustrations where generations of readers touched or poked at visual representations of racialised figures, thereby literally marking or erasing such characters from a given page.

Good examples of such haptic erasure can be found among the etchings William Blake created for John Gabriel Stedman's *Narrative, of a Five Years' Expedition, against the Revolted Negroes of Surinam* (1798), a text well-known to other Romantics like Coleridge,[64] which visualise the brutalising of rebellious slaves by white planters and their black henchmen. The illustrations, based on Stedman's own drawings, feature a number of coloured female figures, including Joanna, who plays a prominent role as his love interest in his overly romanticised *Narrative*.[65]

Blake's etching (Fig. 1) shows her dressed as a colonial consort, wearing eye-catching jewellery (necklace, earrings, bracelets at wrists and ankles), a loose dress revealing her right breast and shoulder (iconographically matching the figure of Temptation from George Richardson's *Iconology*, 1797),[66] and holding a colonial hat in her right hand. The mismatch between material wealth and regal pose on the one hand and sexual availability on the other casts her as an erotic object bridging the divide between a white plantocracy (represented through a conservatively dressed lady with child in the background) and the black and mulatto slaves in other images. That readers viewed Joanna as a consumable body emerges from the marks anonymous readers left on the manuscript surface. The distinct yellow brown blotch enveloping her head was generated by readers repeatedly touching her head and upper body, literally marking her in the process.

Figure 1. *Joanna* by William Blake (1798).[67]

Figure 2. *Giovanna* by Cristoforo Dall'Acqua (1796).[68]

Similar haptic traces are visible on a hand-coloured version by the Italian engraver Cristoforo Dall'Acqua (1796) (Fig. 2), which modifies a mirrored, slightly enlarged template of Blake's version by removing the white mother and child and showing Joanna (spelled "Giovanna") wearing an elaborate headdress with a rose. The Dall'Acqua version shows traces of readers repeatedly touching Giovanna's hair and rose along with her shoulder and bared breast, blurring some of the colouring in the process. While the haptic traces are less distinct than in the Blake version, the colouring amplifies colonial connotations by accentuating her coral necklace along with a golden collar, a stylised version of slave collars in Western art.[69]

In both versions, the commodification of Joanna/Giovanna is sustained by multiple stakeholders: Stedman the planter (owning and naming Joanna), Stedman the author (iconising her), the engravers

Dall'Acqua and Blake (replicating her image through sets of simulacra), the anonymous colourist (enhancing Dall'Acqua's engraving), and anonymous readers purchasing those reproductions, and 'owning' Joanna/Giovanna by consummating her physical reproduction on the page. Significantly, this process of commodification is pan-European and multilingual, with Stedman the Scottish planter, Dall'Acqua the Italian engraver and international readers purchasing editions in English, Dutch, Swedish, German, French and Italian contributing towards a wider dissemination and commodification of Joanna/Giovanna's image. The images also reveal a symbiosis between illustrators creating erotically charged images that allow for an intimate owning of figures like Joanna/Giovanna, and audiences engaging in a performative reading that rehearses such 'owning' through physical contact with the page.

A similar process can be observed with images staging a violating of intersectional bodies. A coloured version of William Blake's *Flagellation of a Female Samboe Slave* (1796), also from Stedman's *Narrative* (Fig. 3), shows traces of readers smudging the victim's head and hair. While such contact may arguably reflect a pitying of the victim and a desire to share her pain, such pointing also disturbingly mimics the pointing fingers of colonial figures in the background, whose theatrical gesturing is directed at the central space occupied by the flagellated female slave. Readers seemingly followed the deictic directions by white overseers and marked the female slave haptically, while the figures in the background – the originators of such violence – remain unmarked. The overseers, in other words, act as conduits orchestrating the stigmatising of the intersectional body, whose suffering is vicariously shared by unidentifiable readers complicit in the marking of a suffering intersectional body.

A corresponding Italian version by Dall'Acqua (Fig. 4) shows haptic readers creating a halo around the victim's tied hands, as if to accentuate her inability to escape. Such markings arguably reveal a wish to release the victim instead of silencing her. The removal of white overseers in the background changes the narrative encoded in the image, as the threat to the Sambo slave arises from two unaccompanied black figures carrying massive whips, connoting native savagery rather than colonial violence. Readers touching the rope tying the Sambo slave arguably intended to free her from black violence, in contrast to readers of Blake (Fig. 3), who endorse the silencing of the tortured slave.

One particularly disturbing aspect of Blake's and Dall'Acqua's visions of flagellation (Figs. 3-4) is that they rely on the illustrations of Joanna/Giovanna (Figs. 1-2), using them as a template. The peculiar positioning of the victims' heads – seemingly attaching them to the shoulder – suggests a crude modification of a generic torso, which appears almost identical in shape and tilt in all four illustrations (Figs. 1-4). The flagellated Sambo slave, then, resembles a violated Joanna/Giovanna, whose suffering is silenced (Fig. 3) or witnessed (Fig. 4) by haptic readers – a conflating of figures Stedman himself mimics in his prose when describing the tortured girl as "a truly beautiful Samboe Girl of about 18",[70] using language more suitable for his erotic muse Joanna/Giovanna. Haptic readers seem to have followed Stedman's footsteps by visiting their "pornographic" desire[71] onto the page by desiring and silencing a suffering intersectional body in colonial visions (Fig. 3) while graciously liberating a similar victim from native savagery (Fig. 4).

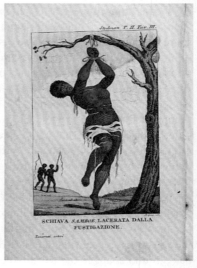

Figure 3. *Flagellation of a Female Samboe Slave* by William Blake (1796).[72]

Figure 4. *Schiava Samboe Lacerata Dalla Fustigazione* by Cristoforo Dall'Acqua (1798).[73]

Such haptic markings likewise echo the apologist position Stedman verbalises in his narrative, according to which enslaved intersectional natives are happiest when ruled by white planters. Stedman memorably expresses this position through an illustration showing a nuclear colonial 'family' (consisting of father, mother, child and infant) who personify a "State of Tranquil Happiness" facilitated by a "mild Government" that frees natives from "every Anxiety". Thriving under their beloved "Masters", these subjects enjoy a healthy diet (fish and fruit), entrepreneurial spirit (spinning, hunting, fishing, making baskets), sensory pleasure (the smoking of a pipe), and physical wellbeing (performing labour that is "no [...] more than a Healthy Exercise"). Colonial governance allegedly also facilitates monogamy, as the habitual "[e]xchanging [a partner] for another the Moment He, or She is Tired [of them]" becomes rarer than in "European [forms] of matrimony", Stedman claims.[74]

The physical mark of such a utopian state is visually imprinted onto the chest of the muscular male servant in the form of a tattoo, showing "the letters J.G.S. being the enitials [*sic*] of my name, And Supposed to be the Cypher by which each master knows his Property".[75] By physically imprinting his name, Stedman turns the naked colonial body into a "Cypher" he owns, governs, commodifies, consummates. In a similar vein, the haptic marks readers leave on intersectional bodies signal ownership (over bodies and text), unlimited access (to sexualised bodies), freedom to censure (through stigmatisation), the right to liberate eroticised bodies at will. As an expression of power, haptic reading offers ultimate control over mediated intersectional bodies, complementing narrative forms of erasure that reverberate through the Romantic canon.

7. Conclusion

Surveying representations of intersectionality across a range of canonical texts reveals a disturbing pattern of erasure in a variety of genres – poetry and prose, text and image – whereby black, coloured and non-Christian women are silenced in a number of ways. Common strategies include typecasting intersectional women as irrational savages, promoting Westernised and Christianised ideals of normative alterity (as in

Coleridge's Abyssinian maid or Mary Shelley's Safie), and reducing women of colour to *femmes fatales* and pornographic objects.

The impulses giving rise to such intersectional bias are often difficult to trace. In some cases, intersectional bias can be attributed to an identifiable source, as with Mary Wollstonecraft, whose quoting of a racial anthropologist significantly compromises her woke credentials. In other instances, as with Charlotte Smith or Coleridge, determining how and why these writers espouse a certain position can be difficult. Significantly, an echoing of intersectional tropes does not necessarily equate with a promoting of such views: as Mary Shelley demonstrates in *Frankenstein*, intersectional prejudice articulated from a position of privilege (Victor Frankenstein's) may be parroted to expose the fallacies of such rhetoric.

A key finding rarely discussed in literature on intersectionality is the interplay between various stakeholders involved in textual production and consumption. Writers, translators, illustrators, engravers, illuminators, and readers often collaborated in a collective marketing and silencing of intersectional bodies in the shape of book illustrations, feeding a market reducing intersectional women to fungible objects. As the haptic marks on many illustrations reveal, readers seem to have gratuitously engaged with the suffering of intersectional figures, rehearsing colonial fantasies on the page. Physical traces on non-English editions of Stedman's narrative act as a useful reminder that intersectional bias is not limited to a particular linguistic or cultural tradition but pan-European in origin. Assessing intersectional bias in the Romantic period, in other words, calls for research that looks beyond the narrow confines of a single national tradition.

Given the limited sampling of material covered above, how reliable is this preliminary assessment of Romantic wokeness? One can undoubtedly find texts that run counter to the trends sketched out above. Robert Southey's ballad "The Sailor Who Had Served in the Slave-Trade", for example, rewrites Coleridge's *Rime of the Ancient Mariner* from an intersectional perspective, replacing the unspecified guilt crippling Coleridge's narrator with a sailor's trauma from witnessing the torturing of an intersectional heroine defying enslavement. Long buried in a canon largely oblivious to intersectionality, Southey's poem will in all likelihood become a modern classic along with other long-forgotten texts as scholarship embraces a turn towards Critical Race Theory. Looking at the

156

Romantic canon at large, though, Southey's poem represents in all likelihood an exception that proves the rule that Romantic inclusivity is less inclusive than one might assume, and particularly hostile towards intersectionally marked women.

Acknowledging the limitations of Romantic notions of wokeness – their internal contradictions, cultural biases and close ties to anthropological racism – seems key to a critical engagement with Romantic writing in the 21st century. Recognising the privileged stance of Romantic writers and their tendency to replicate vestiges of privilege in their writing is arguably a must for any critic approaching Romantic writing within a socio-cultural, political, economic, philosophical, or indeed imperial context. At the same time, though, readers are well advised to examine their own position of privilege in order to lend their examination of Romantic privilege substance and credibility. As movements like BLM or #MeToo have demonstrated, global communities are still widely discriminatory and structurally unjust. Addressing such inequities alongside and through criticism can contribute to a more just and equitable world.

Notes

[1] Hopkins, Peter (2017). "Social Geography I: Intersectionality." *Progress in Human Geography* 43.5, 937-947.

[2] Cottrol, Robert J. (2013). *The Long, Lingering Shadow: Slavery, Race, and Law in the American Hemisphere*. Athens and London: The University of Georgia Press, 83.

[3] Hall, Catherine (2011). "Troubling memories: Nineteenth-Century Histories of the Slave Trade and Slavery." *Transactions of the Royal Historical Society* 21, 148.

[4] For a vocal critique of Wheatley's supposed lack of race consciousness, see R.L. Matson (1972). "Phillis Wheatley – Soul Sister?" *Phylon* 33.3, 222-230. A reevaluation of Wheatley as a celebrity artist who negotiated conflicting concepts of freedom offers Pinto, Samantha (2020). "Fantasies of Freedom: Phillis Wheatley and the 'Deathless Fame' of Black Feminist Thought." *Infamous Bodies: Early Black Women's Celebrity and the Afterlives of Rights*. Durham, North Carolina: Duke UP. 31-64.

[5] Banner, Rachel (2013). "Surface and Stasis: Re-reading Slave Narrative via *The History of Mary Prince*." *Callaloo* 36.2, 298-311. 11 July 2021. Helena Woodard calls Mary Prince's narrative "ghostwritten" ("The Two Marys

(Prince and Shelley) on the Textual Meeting Ground of Race, Gender, and Genre. Witnesses and Practitioners." 17).

[6] Gilbert, Sandra M. and Susan Gubar (1979). *The Madwoman In The Attic: The Woman Writer and the Nineteenth-Century Literary Imagination*. New Haven and London: Yale University Press.

[7] Blake, William (1904 [1808]). *The Prophetic Books: Jerusalem*. Ed. R.D. Maclagan and A.G.B. Russell. London: Chiswick Press, 3.77.

[8] "Throughout the *Vindication*, Wollstonecraft uses the term slavery in both a literal and a metaphorical sense. She believes that the institution of marriage in England in 1792 is legal slavery, no different in kind from that imposed on Africans in the American colonies", Mellor, Anne K. (1995)."Sex, Violence, and Slavery: Blake and Wollstonecraft." *Huntington Library Quarterly* 58.3/4, 364).

[9] Wollstonecraft, Mary (2004 [1792]). *A Vindication of the Rights of Woman*. Ed. Miriam Brody, rev. ed. London: Penguin Books, 90-91.

[10] For early modern sources echoing the theory of material impression, see Loomba, Ania and Jonathan Burton. (2007). *Race in Early Modern England: A Documentary Companion*. Basingstoke: Springer, 100, 114, 165, 236.

[11] Juengel, Scott (2001). "Countenancing History: Mary Wollstonecraft, Samuel Stanhope Smith, and Enlightenment Racial Science." *ELH* 68.4, 913-914.

[12] Botting, Eileen Hunt (2019). "Wollstonecraft's Contributions to Modern Political Philosophy." 355-356.

[13] Racial anthropology frequently echoes Galenic humoral theory, according to which human traits are defined through humoral fluids. See for example François Bernier, who in *A New Division of the Earth* (1684) describes natives of the Cape of Good Hope as "small, thin, *dry*, ugly, quick in running, passionately fond of carrion [...] and speaking a language altogether strange" (Loomba and Burton (2006). *Race in Early Modern England*, 274, emphasis added).

[14] Bhabha, Homi (1984). "Of Mimicry and Man: The Ambivalence of Colonial Discourse." *October* 28, *Discipleship: A Special Issue on Psychoanalysis*, 125-133. 127.

[15] Armstrong, Meg (1996). "'The Effects of Blackness': Gender, Race, and the Sublime in Aesthetic Theories of Burke and Kant." *The Journal of Aesthetics and Art Criticism* 54.3, 213-236.

[16] Smith, Charlotte (2012 [1800]). *The Story of Henrietta*. Ed. Janina Nordius. Kansas City: Valancourt Books, 27.

[17] *Ibid.*, 26-27.

[18] *Ibid.*, 28.

[19] *Ibid.*

[20] *Ibid.*, 29.

[21] *Ibid.*

22 *Ibid.*

23 *Ibid.*

24 Significantly, the analogy of arranged marriage as slavery is emphasised by naming Henrietta's prospective husband "Sawkins" (31), an unusual name that references John Hawkins, the notorious Elizabethan slave trader, see Kelsey, Harry (2003). *Sir John Hawkins: Queen Elizabeth's Slave Trader*. New Haven: Yale University Press.

25 Smith, 143.

26 *Ibid.*

27 *Ibid.*, 47.

28 *Ibid.*, 145.

29 *Ibid.*, 147.

30 *Ibid.*

31 Nordius, Janina (2012). "Introduction." Smith, Charlotte [1800]. *The Story of Henrietta*. Kansas City: Valancourt Books, vii-l. x.

32 *Ibid.*, xxi.

33 *Ibid.*, xxiii

34 *Ibid.*, xiv.

35 Smith, Charlotte (2012 [1800]), 148.

36 Kitson, Peter (2010). "John Thelwall in Saint Domingue: Race, Slavery, and Revolution in *The Daughter of Adoption: A Tale of Modern Times* (1801)." *Romanticism* 16.2, 120-138. 127.

37 Coleridge, Samuel T. (1890). *Lectures and Notes on Shakespeare and Other English Poets*. Ed. Thomas Ashe. London: George Bell and Sons, 385-386.

38 Haeger, J.H. (1974). "Coleridge's Speculations on Race." *Studies in Romanticism* 13.4, 333-357.

39 All quotes are taken from Samuel Taylor Coleridge (1993). "Kubla Khan." *The Norton Anthology of English literature*. 6th ed. Vol. 2. Ed. M.H. Abrams. New York: W.W. Norton & Company, 346-349.

40 On the theme of colonial discovery, see Hulme, Peter (1986). *Colonial Encounters: Europe and the Native Caribbean, 1492-1797*. London and New York: Methuen, 1-2.

41 Coleridge, Samuel T. "Manuscript of Samuel Taylor Coleridge's 'Kubla Khan'." *The British Library*. Web. 30 August 2021. https://www.bl.uk/collection-items/manuscript-of-s-t-coleridges-kubla-khan.

42 Purchas, Samuel (1614). *Purchas his Pilgrimage*. London: William Stansby. 7.5. 680. Archive.org. Web. 31 August 2021. https://archive.org/details/case_g_12_71_v_5.

43 *Ibid.*, 7.5. 673.

44 Auf der Maur, Lorenz (2006). "Ethiopia and Abyssinia in English Writing up to 1790." *Proceedings of the XVth International Conference of Ethiopian*

Studies. Eds. Siegbert Uhlig, et al. Wiesbaden: Otto Harrassowitz Verlag. 523-531.

[45] Haeger, J.H. (1974). "Coleridge's Speculations on Race." *Studies in Romanticism* 13.4, 333-357. 340.

[46] *Ibid.*, 341.

[47] Kitson, Peter (2000). "'Bales of Living Anguish': Representations of Race and the Slave in Romantic Writing." *ELH* 67.2, 515-537. 516.

[48] See the brilliant flourish with which he ends the lecture on the slave trade: "It has been asserted by more than one Writer on the subject, that the planation slaves are at least as well off as the peasantry in England. Now I appeal to common sense, whether to affirm that the slaves are as well off as our peasantry, be not the same as to assert that our peasantry are as bad off as negro-slaves? And whether if our peasantry believed it, they would not be inclined to rebel?" (Coleridge, 1796, 140)

[49] Editors' note: In our collection, the two contributors writing on Shelley's *Frankenstein* have made the conscious choice to use 'Creature' or 'Being' respectively depending on their individual preference (see Jean in this volume).

[50] Hansard, column 1103 of 16 March 1824. Wollstonecraft Shelley, Mary (1996). *The Frankenstein Notebooks: A Facsimile Edition of Mary Shelley's Manuscript Novel, 1816-17* (with Alterations in the Hand of Percy Bysshe Shelley). Ed. Charles E. Robinson. New York and London: Garland, ci.

[51] *Ibid.*

[52] Shelley, Mary W. "Frankenstein Volume II Draft in Chapter Sequence." *Shelley-Godwin Archive*. Web. 30 August 2021, 109. http://shelleygodwinarchive.org/contents/frankenstein/.

[53] See for example Anne K. Mellor (1996). "Possessing Nature: The Female in Frankenstein." *Mary Shelley. Frankenstein*. Ed. Paul J. Hunter. New York: Norton, 274-286. 278.

[54] Shelley, Mary W. (2003 [1818]). *Frankenstein*. Ed. Maurice Hindle. rev. ed. London: Penguin Books. 170-171.

[55] Percival, Melissa (2008). "Johann Caspar Lavater: Physiognomy and Connoisseurship." *Journal for Eighteenth-Century Studies* 26.1, 77-90.

[56] Haynes, Stephen R. (2002). *Noah's Curse: The Biblical Justification of American Slavery*. New York: Oxford University Press.

[57] Mellor, Anne K. "Possessing Nature: The Female in Frankenstein." 279.

[58] Mary W. Shelley (2003 [1818]). *Frankenstein*. Ed. Maurice Hindle. rev. ed. London: Penguin Books. 171.

[59] *Ibid.*, 127.

[60] *Ibid.*, 126.

[61] *Ibid.*, 127.

[62] *Ibid.*

[63] See for example Mary Wollstonecraft's reading of Milton's Eve, where she equates misogynist tropes with Islamic culture: "Thus Milton describes our first frail mother; though when he tells us that women are formed for softness and sweet attractive grace, I cannot comprehend his meaning, *unless, in the true Mahometan strain*, he meant to deprive us of souls, and insinuate that we were beings only designed by sweet attractive grace, and docile blind obedience, to gratify the senses of man when he can no longer soar on the wing of contemplation" (*A Vindication* 28, emphasis added).

[64] Johnson, Mary L. (1982). "Coleridge's Prose and a Blake Plate in Stedman's *Narrative*: Unfastening the 'Hooks & Eyes' of Memory." *The Wordsworth Circle* 13.1, 36-38.

[65] Stedman portrays Joanna very differently in his published *Narrative* and his personal journals. Mary Louise Pratt considers these changes from the outspoken journal to an embellished public narrative a "romantic transformation of a particular form of colonial sexual exploitation" (Pratt 2007, 93).

[66] Brienen, Rebecca P. (2016). "Joanna and her Sisters: Mulatto Women in Print and Image, 1602-1796." *Early Modern Women: An Interdisciplinary Journal* 10.2, 65-94. 94.

[67] Blake, William (1793). *Joanna*. Engraving produced for Stedman, John Gabriel (1796). *Narrative, of a Five Years' Expedition; against the Revolted Negroes of Surinam*, 89. Rare Books and Manuscripts, Eberly Family Special Collections Library, Penn State University Libraries. Used with permission.

[68] Dall'Acqua, Christoforo (1796). *Giovanna*. Allard Pierson Museum, University of Amsterdam, UBM: NOK 95-155, pl. 3 t.o.p. 108 (engraving). Used with permission.

[69] Boffey, Daniel. "Rijksmuseum Slavery Exhibition Confronts Cruelty of Dutch Trade." *The Guardian*. Web. 18 May 2021. https://www.theguardian.com/world/2021/may/18/rijksmuseum-slavery-exhibition-confronts-cruelty-of-dutch-trade.

[70] Stedman, John Gabriel (1796). *Narrative, of a Five Years' Expedition; against the Revolted Negroes of Surinam*, 325. Web. 31 August 2021. https://quod.lib.umich.edu/e/ecco/004897533.0001.001?rgn=main;view=fulltext.

[71] Klarer, Mario (2005). "Humanitarian Pornography: John Gabriel Stedman's *Narrative of a Five Years' Expedition Against the Revolting Negroes of Surinam* (1796)." *New Literary History* 36.4, 559-587.

[72] Blake, William (1796). *Flagellation of a Female Samboe Slave*. Collection of Robert N. Essick. Object 9 (Bentley 499.8). Copyright © 2022 William Blake Archive. Used with permission.

[73] Dall'Acqua, Christoforo (1798). *Schiava Samboe Lacerata Dalla Fustigazione*. Allard Pierson Museum, University of Amsterdam, UBM: NOK 95-156, pl. 3 t.o.p. 11 (engraving). Used with permission.

[74] The full passage is quoted in Mellor, Anne K. (1995). "Sex, Violence, and Slavery: Blake and Wollstonecraft." *Huntington Library Quarterly* 58.3/4, 356.

[75] *Ibid.*

Bibliography

Armstrong, Meg (1996). "'The Effects of Blackness': Gender, Race, and the Sublime in Aesthetic Theories of Burke and Kant." *The Journal of Aesthetics and Art Criticism* 54.3, 213-236.

Auf der Maur, Lorenz (2006). "Ethiopia and Abyssinia in English Writing up to 1790." *Proceedings of the XVth International Conference of Ethiopian Studies, Hamburg, July 20-25, 2003*. Eds. Siegbert Uhlig et al. Wiesbaden: Otto Harrassowitz Verlag, 523-531.

Banner, Rachel (2013). "Surface and Stasis: Re-reading Slave Narrative via *The History of Mary Prince*." *Callaloo* 36.2, 298-311.

Bhabha, Homi (1984). "Of Mimicry and Man: The Ambivalence of Colonial Discourse." *October* 28, *Discipleship: A Special Issue on Psychoanalysis*, 125-133.

Blake, Wiliam (1793). *Joanna*. Engraving produced for Stedman, John Gabriel (1796). *Narrative, of a Five Years' Expedition; against the Revolted Negroes of Surinam*, 89. Rare Books and Manuscripts, Eberly Family Special Collections Library, Penn State University Libraries.

--- (1796). *Flagellation of a Female Samboe Slave*. Collection of Robert N. Essick. Object 9 (Bentley 499.8). Copyright © 2022 William Blake Archive.

--- (1798). "The Execution of Breaking on the Rack." *Digital Collections: Library Company of Philadelphia Digital Collections*. Web. 31 August 2021.

--- (1904 [1808]). *The Prophetic Books: Jersusalem*. Ed. R.D. Maclagan and A.G.B. Russell. London: Chiswick Press.

Boffey, Daniel (2021). "Rijksmuseum Slavery Exhibition Confronts Cruelty of Dutch Trade." *The Guardian*. Web. 18 May 2021. https://www.theguardian.com/world/2021/may/18/rijksmuseum-slavery-exhibition-confronts-cruelty-of-dutch-trade.

Botting, Eileen Hunt (2019). "Wollstonecraft's Contributions to Modern Political Philosophy: Intersectionality and the Quest for Egalitarian Social Justice." *Feminist History of Philosophy: The Recovery and Evaluation of Women's Philosophical Thought*. Eds. Eileen O'Neill, Marcy P. Lascano. Basingstoke: Springer Nature. 355-377.

Brienen, Rebecca P. (2016). "Joanna and her Sisters: Mulatto Women in Print and Image, 1602-1796." *Early Modern Women: An Interdisciplinary Journal* 10.2, 65-94.

Coleridge, Samuel T. (1993 [1816]). "Kubla Khan." *The Norton Anthology of English Literature*. 6th ed., Vol. 2. Ed. M.H. Abrams. New York: W.W. Norton & Company, 346-349.

--- (1890). *Lectures and Notes on Shakespeare and Other English Poets*. Ed. Thomas Ashe. London: George Bell and Sons.

--- (1797). "Manuscript of Samuel Taylor Coleridge's 'Kubla Khan'." *The British Library*. Web. 31 August 2021.https://www.bl.uk/collection-items/manuscript-of-s-t-coleridges-kubla-khan/.

--- (1970 [1796]). "Lecture on the Slave-Trade." *The Collected Works of Samuel Taylor Coleridge: The Watchman*. Ed. Lewis Patton. Milton Park: Routledge, 130-140.

Cottrol, Robert J. (2013). *The Long, Lingering Shadow: Slavery, Race, and Law in the American Hemisphere*. Athens and London: The University of Georgia Press.

Dall'Acqua, Christoforo (1796). *Giovanna*. Allard Pierson Museum, University of Amsterdam, UBM: NOK 95-155, pl. 3 t.o.p. 108 (engraving).

--- (1798). *Schiava Samboe Lacerata Dalla Fustigazione*. Allard Pierson Museum, University of Amsterdam, UBM: NOK 95-156, pl. 3 t.o.p. 11 (engraving).

Gilbert, Sandra M. and Susan Gubar (1979). *The Madwoman in The Attic: The Woman Writer and the Nineteenth-Century Literary Imagination*. New Haven and London: Yale University Press.

Haeger, J.H. (1974). "Coleridge's Speculations on Race." *Studies in Romanticism* 13.4, 333-357.

Hall, Catherine (2011). "Troubling Memories: Nineteenth-Century Histories of the Slave Trade and Slavery." *Transactions of the Royal Historical Society* 21, 147-169.

Haynes, Stephen R. (2002). *Noah's Curse: The Biblical Justification of American Slavery*. New York: Oxford University Press.

Hopkins, Peter (2017). "Social Geography I: Intersectionality." *Progress in Human Geography* 43.5, 937-947.

Hulme, Peter (1986). *Colonial Encounters: Europe and the Native Caribbean, 1492-1797*. London and New York: Methuen.

Johnson, Mary L. (1982). "Coleridge's Prose and a Blake Plate in Stedman's 'Narrative': Unfastening the 'Hooks & Eyes' of Memory." *The Wordsworth Circle* 13.1, 36-38.

Juengel, Scott (2001). "Countenancing History: Mary Wollstonecraft, Samuel Stanhope Smith, and Enlightenment Racial Science." *ELH* 68.4, 897-927.

Kelsey, Harry (2003). *Sir John Hawkins: Queen Elizabeth's Slave Trader*. New Haven and London: Yale University Press.

Kitson, Peter (2000). "'Bales of Living Anguish': Representations of Race and the Slave in Romantic Writing." *ELH* 67.2, 515-537.

--- (2007). *Romantic Literature, Race, and Colonial Encounter*. New York and Basingstoke: Palgrave Macmillan.

Klarer, Mario (2005). "Humanitarian Pornography: John Gabriel Stedman's *Narrative of a Five Years' Expedition Against the Revolting Negroes of Surinam* (1796)." *New Literary History* 36.4, 559-587.

Loomba, Ania, and Jonathan Burton (2007). *Race in Early Modern England: A Documentary Companion*. Basingstoke: Springer.

Matson, R. L. (1972). "Phillis Wheatley – Soul Sister?" *Phylon* 33.3, 222-230.

Mellor, Anne K. (1995). "Sex, Violence, and Slavery: Blake and Wollstonecraft." *Huntington Library Quarterly* 58.3/4, 345-370.

--- (1996). "Possessing Nature: The Female in *Frankenstein*." *Mary Shelley. Frankenstein*. 274-286. New York: Norton.

Nordius, Jana (2012). "Introduction". Smith, Charlotte [1800]. *The Story of Henrietta*. Kansas City: Valancourt Books, vii-l.

Percival, Melissa (2008). "Johann Caspar Lavater: Physiognomy and Connoisseurship." *Journal for Eighteenth-Century Studies* 26.1, 77-90.

Pinto, Samantha (2020). "Fantasies of Freedom: Phillis Wheatley and the 'Deathless Fame' of Black Feminist Thought." *Infamous Bodies: Early Black Women's Celebrity and the Afterlives of Rights*. Durham, North Carolina: Duke University Press, 31-64.

Pratt, Mary Louise (2007). *Imperial Eyes: Travel Writing and Transculturation*. London and New York: Routledge.

Purchas, Samuel (1614). *Purchas His Pilgrimage*. London: William Stansby. Archive.org. Web. 31 August 2021. https://archive.org/details/case_g_12_71_v_5.

Shelley, Mary W. (2003 [1818]). *Frankenstein*. Ed. Maurice Hindle. rev. ed. London: Penguin Books.

--- (1996). Wollstonecraft Shelley, Mary. *The Frankenstein Notebooks: A Facsimile Edition of Mary Shelley's Manuscript Novel, 1816-17 (with Alterations in the Hand of Percy Bysshe Shelley)*. Ed. Charles E. Robinson. New York and London: Garland.

--- (1818). "Frankenstein Volume II Draft in Chapter Sequence." *Shelley-Godwin Archive*. Web. 30 August 2021. http://shelleygodwinarchive.org/contents/frankenstein/.

Simpson David (1999). "How Marxism Reads 'The Rime of the Ancient Mariner'." *Samuel Taylor Coleridge: The Rime of the Ancient Mariner*. Ed. Paul H. Fry. Boston and New York: Bedford/St. Martin's, 148-167.

Smith, Charlotte (2012 [1800]). *The Story of Henrietta*. Ed. Janina Nordius. Kansas City: Valancourt Books.

Southey, Robert (2012). "The Sailor Who Had Served in the Slave-Trade." *The Longman Anthology of British Literature*. Eds. David Damrosch and Kevin J. Dettmar. 5th ed. Boston, MA: Pearson, 270-272.

Stedman, John Gabriel (1796). *Narrative of a Five Years' Expedition; Against the Revolted Negroes of Surinam*. London: J.J. Johnson, 1796. University of Michigan Library Digital Collections. Web. 31 August 2021.https://quod.lib.umich.edu/e/ecco/004897533.0001.001?rgn=main;view=fulltext.

---, Cristoforo Dall'Acqua, and Giovanni Battista Sonzogno Lazaretti (1796). "Een Neger Slavin, Met Een Gewicht Beladen, Dat Met Een Keten Aan Haar Enkel is Vastgemaakt." *Het Geheugen*. Web. 31 August 2021. https://geheugen.delpher.nl/nl/geheugen/view/een-neger-slavin-gewicht-beladen-keten-aan-haar-enkel-is-vastgemaakt-lazaretti?facets%5BsubthemeStringNL%5D=Koloni%C3%ABn&coll=ngvn&maxperpage=4&page=539&identifier=SURI01%3ANOK95155P022PL.

--- (1796). "Eene Samboe Slavin, Wier Lichaam Door Zweepslagen is Van één Gereeten." *Het Geheugen*. Web. 31 August 2021. https://geheugen.delpher.nl/nl/geheugen/view/quot-eene-samboe-slavin-wier-lichaam-zweepslagen-is-gereeten-quot--lazaretti?coll=

ngvn&maxperpage=36&page=2&query=stedman&identifier=SURI01%3ANOK95156P111PL.

--- (1796). "Joanna." *Het Geheugen*. Web. 31 August 2021. https://geheugen.delpher.nl/nl/geheugen/view?coll=ngvn&identifier=SURI01%3ANOK95155P108PL.

Wollstonecraft, Mary (2004 [1792]). *A Vindication of the Rights of Woman*. Ed. Miriam Brody. rev. ed. London: Penguin Books.

Woodard, Helena (1996). "The Two Marys (Prince and Shelley) on the Textal Meeting Ground of Race, Gender, and Genre." *Recovered Writers/Recovered Texts*. Ed. Dolan Hubbard. Knoxville: University of Tennessee Press, 15-30.

Theadora Jean

"My Beloved Race": Mary Shelley, Racial Politics and Romanticism

1. Introduction

In the latter part of the twentieth century, numerous critics addressed the racial politics of Shelley in her most significant work, *Frankenstein*.[1] H.R. Malchow, in his book *Gothic Images of Race in the Nineteenth Century*, encapsulates the implications of the novel thus:

> the message reflects contemporary ambiguity or confusion about 'race', it entered popular culture at a time of shifting and hardening opinion and in this context, inevitably lent its weight to the construction of sensational (and more firmly pejorative) representations of race in the nineteenth century.[2]

Bohls, however, offers a comparison with postcolonial criticism's objectives, noting that "Shelley uses aesthetic concepts to probe the relationships among the scientist or explorer at the geographic and intellectual frontiers of empire" in her essay on the subject.[3]

More recently, Mulvey-Roberts outlines Shelley's thoughts on slavery and abolitionism within *Frankenstein*, in a chapter in her book *Dangerous Bodies: Historicising the Gothic Corporeal*, firmly announcing that "*Frankenstein* is a parable of the life cycle of a slave",[4] and her arguments are convincing. As well as focusing particular attention on affinities between the Being,[5] miscegenation, and fears of retaliation from enslaved peoples, Mulvey-Roberts has developed further the racialised connotations which Smith traces in *This Thing of Darkness: Racial Discourse in Mary Shelley's Frankenstein*, in which Smith concludes that the Being represents "the eighteenth-century debates over cross-racial resemblance and difference".[6] Young offers a full-length study on race and *Frankenstein* in her book on the subject *Black Frankenstein: The Making of an American Metaphor*,[7] in which her focus is on adaptation

167

and African Americans, particularly within twenty-first-century film. However, these examples focus solely on Shelley's key title, while providing supporting evidence from her autobiographical details (such as her reading habits which includes materials on the slave trade[8]). Despite these significant contributions to the study of Shelley, the pedagogy surrounding the analysis of the novel continues to marginalise these aspects of the work. *The Cambridge Companion to Frankenstein*[9] does devote a chapter to race, for example; however, this critique only serves to silence the debates, determining dismissively that the revolutionary potential of this text has far more weight. Brantlinger decides that

> [t]here is, however, no direct evidence that the struggle between Victor and the monster reflects the African slave trade, Haiti and the abolitionist movement. Mary Shelley's tale of terror more directly reflects the debates over the American and French Revolutions.[10]

In this article I will be seeking to expand the critical analysis of Shelley's wider oeuvre in relation to race and Romanticism, as well as arguing that racial politics implicit in her works should not be delegated to a position of secondary importance compared with other relevant analyses of the text. As Malchow argues effectively, a consideration of racialised paradigms within the novel offers

> at least as reasonable a reading as the claim that the Monster is a feminine-masculine composite that transcends gender, or that his alien hideousness reflects bourgeois fears of a threatening working class.[11]

Within the confines of one article, I cannot attempt to cover comprehensively all aspects of Shelley's life and works regarding race, nor can I indicate a whole-scale view of the critical works which relate to these topics. I will therefore discuss *Frankenstein* and some aspects of Shelley's autobiography, explore *The Last Man*,[12] and mention minor elements within *The Fortunes of Perkin Warbeck*.[13] Lee, in her book *Slavery in the Romantic Imagination*, argues that "[t]he African presence [...] shaped the British Romantic imagination" and further informs us that "it was inevitable that such an urgent, alarming and morally profound history would pay a major role in the Romantics' conception of the imagination".[14] This article takes a similar position, finding that racial discourses and formulations, rather than only the transatlantic eighteenth-

/nineteenth-century slave trade, have a 'presence' in Shelley's works. She is actively engaging with these discourses as a writer of the Romantic period. If we are to assess any 'woke' potential in the work, it is important to discuss that the novel contains elements which adhere to the right-wing critique of wokeness as "self-righteousness masquerading as enlightenment".[15] This is particularly the case in regard to the paternalistic arguments made against liberation of enslaved peoples, which I will discuss.

2. Mary Shelley and Racial Politics

There have been several significant biographies on Shelley, including Spark's[16] and Seymour's,[17] whose works have been republished in newer editions, and in more recent years, Gordon[18] and Sampson[19] have created fresh studies on her life and writings. Seymour notes several instances of Shelley's perceptions of racialised discourses in relation to *Frankenstein* and also suggests an alternative racial/ethnic dimension to the novel, comparing the Being to Jewish peoples: "[i]n his desolation, the Creature also seems [...] condemned to the homeless life of the wandering Jew".[20] Furthermore, Seymour establishes that Shelley had encountered black people, possibly formerly enslaved, while living in Bristol, during which time Shelley would have been working on *Frankenstein*:

> The alienated condition of black people must have preyed upon Mary's mind during her lonely weeks at Clifton, forming a significant contribution to the social intention behind the alienated Creature she brought to life in *Frankenstein* the following year.[21]

While these notations are valid, there is more complexity to Shelley's engagement with racialised discourses. Mellor, in her book *Mary Shelley: Her Life, Her Fiction, Her Monsters*, which offers a psychoanalytic approach to her life and works, writes that "we must recognise Mary Shelley's deep aversion to the lower classes and the racist chauvinism implicit in her condemnations".[22] Shelley's personal journals undeniably contain some grim, almost genocidal comments, such as that "[o]ur only wish was to annihilate such uncleansable animals. Twere easier for god to make entirely new men than attempt to purify such monsters as these [...] loathsome creepers".[23] This disturbing passage does come from her teenage years in a personal notebook; however, her writings continue in an uncomfortably similar vein as an adult. In her letters, we can find xenophobic commentary such as "[t]he Italians are so very disagreeable" and even more derogatory remarks such as "[t]he people of the country too added to one's discomfort – they are like wild savages".[24] Thus, when analysing her works, we cannot ignore the prejudicial frameworks within which Shelley perceives peoples determined as 'Other' to herself, in this instance, displaying xenophobic traits rather than racism.

3. *Frankenstein* and Racial Politics

Racist discourse and connotations of the transatlantic slave trade do feature in *Frankenstein*, however. Shelley does not write her most famous supernatural, Gothic tale of monstrosity in a socio-political vacuum. According to Gordon:

> During the final months of her pregnancy, the issue that most gripped her was slavery. Although the Abolition Act of 1807 had outlawed trafficking on English soil, slavery was still thriving in the West Indies, Brazil and Cuba as well as in North America. Deeply disturbed by the conditions of the slaves and the ill treatment they faced, Shelley read first-hand accounts of the slave trade and researched its history until her first labour pains forced her to put aside her books.[25]

Shelley even boycotts sugar as a means to defy slave-owners, seemingly aware that although slavery itself was banned in England, the trade still flourished and the produce of sugar was sold in her country: "Shelley [...] told the cook to make them the vegetarian meals he insisted on and to omit sugar from the puddings, so as not to support the slave plantations".[26] Shelley was thus clearly aware of the fates of enslaved persons while writing her novel. The similarity between the Being and enslaved persons was recognised by her peers, and even in Parliament. A Tory statesman who eventually became Prime Minister, George Canning, refers to *Frankenstein* in a speech debating emancipation:

> In dealing with the negro, Sir, we must remember that we are dealing with a being possessing the form and strength of a man, but the intellect only of a child. To turn him loose in the manhood of his physical strength, in

the maturity of his physical passions, but in the infancy of his uninstructed reason, would be to raise up a Being resembling the splendid fiction of a recent romance; the hero of which constructs a human form, with all the corporeal capabilities of man, and with the hews and sinews of a giant; but being unable to impart to the work of his hands a perception of right and wrong, he finds too late that he has only created a more than mortal power of doing mischief, and himself recoils from the monster which he has made. [...] Such would be the effect of a sudden emancipation, before the negro was prepared for the enjoyment of well-regulated liberty. I, therefore, Sir, would proceed gradually, because I would proceed safely.[27]

Shelley's thesis that the liberation of the enslaved would result in desolation and ruin directly became part of the political process arguing *against* emancipation. There are many echoes here relating to the Being; the Being is eight-foot, and physically strong, and Canning emphasises the size and strength he perceives in the black male enslaved person, and fears that emancipation of both results in a "more than mortal power of doing mischief". Seymour felt that this contradicts Shelley's intentions:

Shelley was pleased to have her book alluded to in Parliament by a politician she admired; Canning had, however, misread her intentions. She intended her Being as a warning to act against unsocial behaviour: do as you would be done by was the Godwinian message she wanted to convey. Canning's allusion was part of an argument against freedom.[28]

However, Shelley's opinions do not diverge significantly from Canning, as suggested in a letter she writes to a friend:

They are introducing some amelioration in the state of the slaves in some parts of the West Indies – during the debate on that subject Canning paid a compliment to *Frankenstein* in a manner sufficiently pleasing to me.[29]

Shelley therefore viewed her own novel as at least partially an argument for the postponing of manumission, demonstrating acceptance of paternalist amelioration instead of liberation. As Debbie Lee notes on this topic, "the interaction between Shelley's novel and the parliamentary debates demonstrates how issues of slavery were fundamental to a strain of Romantic imaginative writings" (193).[30] We can also see these elements and arguments, which she would later explore in her post-apocalyptic novel *The Last Man,* which I will discuss later in this article.

171

When Shelley expresses personal anxieties about revolution in England in her letters, she clearly values colonies as a safe harbour for the English, and certainly as rightful English possessions.

> Our colonies are just now of the mightiest import, while strange & (mighty) fearful events are in progress in Europe. Barbarism – Countless uncivilized men, long concealed under the varnish of our social system, are breaking out with the force of a volcano & threatening order – law & peace.[31]

Crucially however, for the purposes of this article, it is important to acknowledge again the racialised prejudices that Shelley is not immune from. This must inform the analysis of her works, especially if *Frankenstein* is deemed analogous to the potential of enslaved persons' uprisings.

Young makes clear in her study that the Being occupies the political category of black, being always depicted as any colour but white: "[d]escribed as yellow in the novel, painted blue in the nineteenth century, and tinted green in twentieth century [...] the monster's color nevertheless signifies symbolically [...] as black".[32] For Mulvey-Roberts, the Being is a metaphor for a mixed-race enslaved person, claiming that "Mary Shelley's monster, with his yellow skin, glossy black hair and black lips bears the inscription of mixed race".[33] Meanwhile, for Lee, the master/slave distinction is more blurred. Lee identifies the two characters (Victor and the Being) as mirroring one another and reflecting anti-abolitionist as well as anti-slavery literature and debates, defining both characters as "using the discourses of consumption, eating, vampirism, and cannibalism".[34] Lee refers to the following passage in the novel:

> His yellow skin scarcely covered the work of muscles and arteries beneath; his hair was of a lustrous black, and flowing; his teeth of pearly whiteness; but these luxuriances only formed a more horrid contrast with his watery eyes, that seemed almost of the same colour as the dun-white sockets in which they were set, his shrivelled complexion and straight black lips. (58)

The racial connotations of the yellow skin, the hair, which is a lustrous black, and the "straight black lips" denote a constructed, racialised Other, which is monstrous through the gaze of the white male European scientist, but whose features are non-specific to any one racial identity. This supports Kitson's interpretation of the Being's racialised signifiers as indicating a general, racialised, constructed difference based on physiognomy, since he states that "[t]he Creature does not appear to conclusively represent any contemporary racial type".[35] The passage is from Victor's narration, and here he is distinguishing himself from the Being, using visual cues from the Being's physiognomy, to justify his disgust. The Being is, as Halberstam has formulated, a gothic monster which offers a "multiplicity of meanings", racialised or otherwise.[36]

The projection of racial designation is reflected in the peripheral character of Safie, a mixed-race character of Turkish/Arab Christian heritage, who both mirrors and reinstates the racialised connotations of the Being. Safie's mother was "seized and made a slave by the Turks" (126) before being married to Safie's Turkish father. She – and it is difficult to refrain from drawing a comparison between Mary Wollstonecraft as feminist mother here – "instructed her daughter in the tenets of her religion and taught her to aspire to higher powers of intellect and independence of spirit forbidden to the female followers of Mahomet" (126-127) much like the white, female missionary/colonial projects of the nineteenth century. Christianity seemingly offers a liberation of women, in the formulation that Shelley offers here. Safie does act with agency, and "independence of spirit" as a result of these lessons, as she seeks to escape from Turkey and to be reunited with her white, European lover Felix: "When alone, Safie resolved in her own mind the plan of conduct that it would become her to pursue" (129). Safie as mixed-race heroine is reconfigured later in Shelley's historical novel *The Fortunes of Perkin Warbeck*,[37] which features Monina Del Fara, a woman with both Flemish and Moorish ethnic heritage, and therefore offers yet another instance in which Shelley depicts a mixed-race woman with agency.

Most significantly, when the Being encounters Safie, he immediately identifies her as a racialised Other. Safie is "a stranger" whose speech is "musical but unlike that of my friends" (119) – his 'friends' being white Europeans designated as the cottagers. Her hair is "of a shining raven black" (119) – much like the "lustrous black" (58) of the Being – and "curiously braided". Her eyes are "dark, but gentle" although her skin is not yellow but instead "wondrously fair" (119) which seems unusual in a person of Turkish/Arab ethnicity. There is a suggestion here that the white feminist education of Safie is reflected in her skin colour. Safie is constructed as exotic female Other in contrast to the hideous monstrosity of the Being, as she is described as both "beautiful" and "lovely" (119-120). In the reunion between Felix and Safie, Felix is mystically rendered as more physically attractive himself through his encounter with her: "Felix seemed ravished with delight when he saw her [...] at that moment I thought him as beautiful as the stranger" (120). This encounter between the white European male and the racially marginalised female as one which is positive for the male is echoed in Shelley's later novel *The Last Man*.

The Being's response to Safie's identity is even more significant. The Being consistently refrains from using Safie's name, and instead repeatedly designates her with her mother's ethnic heritage – she is "the Arabian" or "the lovely Arabian" or "the stranger"(120). It is effectively Felix who names her: "Felix kissed the hand of the stranger and said, 'Good night, sweet Safie'" (120) and from then on, Safie is only referred to by her name when Felix is present, and otherwise the Being returns to the racial designations. "The next morning Felix went out to his work [...] the Arabian sat at the feet of the old man" (121). The Being is nameless, and thus seems to identify with a non-European person who should also be left nameless. He also refers to Safie's father as "[t]he Turk" (126).

Safie and the Being have further kinship, via the European language of the cottagers. Upon arrival, Safie's lack of a European language is noted by the Being, "although the stranger uttered articulate sounds, and appeared to have a language of her own, she was neither understood by, nor herself understood, the cottagers" (120). Safie's language acquisition is the means by which the Being does the same: "she was endeavouring to learn their language; and the idea instantly occurred to me that I should make use of the same instructions to the same end" (120) The repetition of the word 'same' here suggests an identification between the two. Their development of their language skills is also paralleled: "she and I improved rapidly in the knowledge of the language" (121).

The constructed distinctions and hierarchies between white European languages and non-European languages are firmly emphasised. The book used by Felix for instruction is "Volney's *Ruins of Empires*"[38] (122), in which racial categorisation and labelling is made explicit. Through this book, the two learn about "the manners, governments and religion of the different nations of earth" (122). This becomes more specific, and racialised stereotypes are attributed "the slothful Asiatics", "the stupendous genius [...] of the Grecians", "the [...] wonderful virtue [...] of the early Romans" (122). As a result, the Being identifies himself directly with an enslaved person, as Mulvey-Roberts, Malchow and others have thus established in their criticism. "The words induced me to turn towards myself" (122), the Being states and recognises that those of "riches" and "high and unsullied descent" are the only beings "respected":

> without either he was considered [...] as a vagabond and a slave, doomed to waste his powers for the profit of the chosen few! And what was I? [...] I knew I possessed no money, no friends, no kind of property. I was, besides, endued with a figure hideously deformed and loathsome; I was not even of the same nature as man [...] Was I then, a monster, a blot upon the earth [...]? (123)

This moving passage, which encapsulates the sorrows of the Being, articulates the heartache and suffering caused by racialised discriminations for enslaved persons. The Being recognises himself as "a slave" whose life is sacrificed for the "profit of the chosen few" (123). He also recognises that his appearance is part of what makes him distinct from Victor and the cottagers. What is on display here is the monstrosity of enslavement, of prejudice, of the mindset which views racially determined human beings as mere tools for profit. Shelley's novel fits, in this instance, into the *Cambridge Dictionary* definition of woke as "a state of being aware, especially of social problems such as racism and inequality".[39] *Frankenstein* then, can be seen as an early example of 'wokeness' and thus shares some kinship with the concerns of the Black Lives Matter movement; however, this kinship is limited, and if Audre Lorde's maxim 'The master's tools shall never dismantle the master's house'[40] holds true, Shelley certainly has no intention of dismantling the master's house, as I will argue. However, Shelley is certainly engaged with the debates in this novel, and is simultaneously revealing prejudice and injustice, while reinscribing those same prejudices.

As I have established earlier, there are numerous instances in which the cerebral arguments made by the Being map onto contemporaneous debates and anxieties about repercussions of emancipation. When the Being vows to "revenge" his "injuries" (148), this evokes the nineteenth century fears of slave rebellions. The Being openly threatens Victor while making a direct comparison to himself as enslaved person:

175

Yet mine shall not be the submission of abject slavery. I will revenge my injuries; if I cannot inspire love, I will cause fear, and chiefly towards you my arch-enemy, because my creator, do I swear inextinguishable hatred. (148)

Crucially, what is significant about the means in which he is brought to life is that he is assembled, found, constructed. This mechanism then exemplifies racism and the construction of racialised Others, based loosely on traits and signifiers, but ultimately compiled by the racist/colonising mindset which bears little resemblance to the human beings they are meant to signify. As Malchow describes, by the time of Shelley's writing the novel, "popular racial discourse managed to conflate [...] descriptions of particular ethnic characteristics into a general image of the Negro body".[41] There is an uncomfortable contradiction at the heart of *Frankenstein* that creates racial distinctions and assignations, which are used for both the colonised subjects of the native Americans as well as the trafficked and enslaved persons of the transatlantic slave trade, while simultaneously proclaiming the injustice of such practices. Mellor establishes the contradiction in Shelley's narrative thus:

> When she voices through *Frankenstein* her belief that America should have been discovered more gradually, she implicitly casts America in the role of [...] child continent that should have been more cautiously developed [...] She does not say that America should have been left undiscovered, uncolonized, unexploited, but only that the process of imperial conquest should have occurred more slowly, less painfully.[42]

Mellor sharply identifies the contradictions at the heart of Shelley's works here – while making a vital case against the process of Othering. Nevertheless, there is a limitation to her claims. Conquest itself, either in the formation of the Being or the colonies of Britain, is acceptable, although Shelley argues for a more sophisticated process of conquest. The Being should merely have been fathered more lovingly and provided with an education.

4. *The Last Man* and Racial Politics

Aside from *Frankenstein*, Shelley scholarship has broadened to include her post-apocalyptic plague novel *The Last Man* (1826). Sterrenberg is one of the first to provide an analysis of this novel, drawing on similar themes that have been established in *Frankenstein*, namely, resonances between the text and its critique of revolution, informing us that Shelley's "disaster novel can be placed among a number of other post-Napoleonic works of literature and painting which shared analogous themes of the end of the race or the end of empire".[43] These terms (race/empire) are twinned in *The Last Man*, and Shelley's engagement with the disastrous encounter between the British imperial project/s and "alienated black people"[44] that is first found in *Frankenstein* is continued. Both terms are used with multiple meanings and intentions that intersect and blur, and Shelley focuses on the implications of these terms throughout the novel. She uses the term 'race' to signify multiple categories that are sometimes contradictory. In *The Last Man*, she at times refers to an 'English race' specifically, at others, she is more expansive and is referring to the entirety of the human race. When Verney, the narrator, finally finds himself alone, he writes in "three languages" a label of himself as "Verney, the last of the race of Englishmen" (456) in a desperate plea for the Other, as he scribbles in languages other than his own, in his note to no-one. In contrast, Shelley establishes that all of the 'races' have been destroyed by the plague "all our fellow-creatures – the inhabitants of native Europe – the luxurious Asiatic – the swarthy African and free American had been vanquished" (426). When noting her personal feelings on writing the novel in her journal, Shelley also uses the term to mean her closest friends and family, who have formed her intellectual circle, most of which have perished: "The last man! Yes I may well describe that solitary being's feelings, feeling myself as the last relic of a beloved race, my companions, extinct before me".[45] Nevertheless, amidst the confusion of a signifier which excludes and imprisons simultaneously, Shelley reinforces a white supremacist stratification of the English as successful colonisers whose greatness has been unravelled by the plague. However, while this must be noted, in other aspects of the same work, she undermines this worldview and expresses a more woke perspective via her depiction of the virus.

The plague itself is presented as a racialised Other who inflicts a reverse colonisation on European peoples, a threat hinted at later in the century in *Dracula*[46] (as argued by Arata[47]) but fully realised in *The Last Man*. Shelley, in many descriptors of the plague, employs military metaphors. Europeans are "guarding against the innumerous arrows of the plague" (223), England for a time is "still secure [...,] walls yet without a breach, between us and the plague" (231), and Verney gives a battle speech: "We will fight the enemy to the last. Plague shall not find us a ready prey; we will dispute every inch of ground [...] [and] pile invincible barriers to the progress of our foe" (246). As well as the origin of the virus being African, there are numerous instances in which Shelley depicts the plague as a racialised, feminised Other; the plague is female, the "Queen of the World" (346) which has conquered, and an "unhappy stranger" (259) – much like Safie – a plague that comes from elsewhere rather than within "preceded and caused by the contagion from the East" (223).

While Verney represents Englishmen in the novel, he first endures a process of being colonised and being a coloniser. Verney, at the start, is an uncultured shepherd, until he is educated and conquered by Adrian, heir to the throne of England.

> [H]e spoke of the old Greek sages [...]. As he spoke, I felt subject to him; and all my boasted pride and strength were subdued by the honeyed accents of this blue-eyed boy. The trim and paled demesne of civilisation, which I had before regarded from my wild jungle as inaccessible, had its wicket opened by him; I stepped within, and felt, as I entered, that I trod my native soil. (27)

In alignment with the paternalistic arguments against the liberation of enslaved peoples Shelley makes via *Frankenstein*, colonisation is glamorised by her as a process in which the uncivil become civilised, even while at the same time revealing subjection. Shelley later emphasises that in order to be considered human one must submit to social regulations.

> This was the first commencement of my friendship with Adrian, and I must commemorate this day as the most fortunate of my life. I now began to be human. I was admitted within that sacred boundary which divides the intellectual and moral nature of man from that which characterises animals (29).

Bewell summarises these moments in the novel as emblematic of the entire English people, as the products of a colonial force, England being "a colonial prototype, a region whose landscape and people have submitted to a civilising process".[48] The fear of the pending plague is described by Verney as a natural analogy to the transplantation of enslaved peoples, tearing entire societies apart to follow the triangular transatlantic enslavement routes: "It seems as if the giant waves of the ocean [...] were about to wrench the deep-rooted island from its centre; and cast it, a ruin and a wreck, upon the fields of the Atlantic" (230). In the midst of the pandemic in England, the analogy is made literal by the arrival of Americans, who first colonise Ireland and then England: "all poured with one consent into England" (297). However, this offers little terrors for the English society, including Verney, at this state of deterioration in the novel, as "[t]here was room enough indeed in our hapless country" (297). Shelley here is both preoccupied with empire and the process of colonisation, but routinely undermines any stable interpretation. Even the arrival of a conquering army on the shores of Verney's precious sceptred isle becomes a consensual encounter.

Verney romanticises European colonisers, mourning the former glories of the colonial process in the plagued world:

> [...] where was the bustle and industry characteristic of such an assemblage; the rudely constructed dwelling which was to suffice until a more commodious mansion could be build; the marking out of fields, the attempt at cultivation; the eager curiosity to discover unknown animals and herbs. (383)

Once alone, however, Verney actively seeks out racialised Others, even if that wish is one which reveals Verney as still valuing racialised difference and subjection, announcing that

> [t]he wild and cruel Caribbee, the merciless Cannibal, or worse than thee, the uncouth, the brute and remorseless veteran in the vices of civilisation, would have been to me a beloved companion, a treasure dearly prized – his nature would be kin to mine; his form cast in the same mould; human blood would flow in his veins, a human sympathy must link us for ever. (449)

Verney can only perceive racialised Others as potentially human after having become "the last of the Englishmen" (456). The novel closes with his hopeful intention to "find in some part of the wide extent a survivor" and thus to finally travel to the "tawny shore of Africa" (469). Earlier in the novel Shelley traces the origin of the plague to Africa: "This enemy to the human race had begun early in June to raise its serpent-head on the shores of the Nile" (175). Enduring the end of humanity, Verney expresses a mournful lamentation not for the varied cultures of the world but specifically for the English as supposedly superior beings, exclaiming "Thou, England, were the triumph of man [...] thou marvel of the world [...] thy tale of power and liberty at its close!" (323-324).

However, Shelley is not Verney, despite the comparisons she made between herself and the protagonist, and the racial hierarchies are unstable, akin to the complexities of *Frankenstein*. Crucially, Verney survives the plague after a Gothicised, quasi-sexual embrace between himself, an Englishman, and a black person.

> I lowered my lamp, and saw a negro half clad, writhing under the agony of disease, while he held me with a convulsive grasp. With mixed horror and impatience I strove to disengage myself, and fell on the sufferer; he wound his naked festering arms round me, his face was close to mine, and his breath, death-laden, entered my vitals. For a moment I was overcome, my head was bowed by aching nausea; till, reflection returning, I sprung up, threw the wretch from me, and darting up the staircase, entered the chamber usually inhabited by my family. (336)

While Verney expresses resistance, revulsion and disgust, the embrace of the racialised Other effectively immunises him against the virus. He experiences the symptoms of the disease, and his loved ones fear for his life, but he mysteriously survives. At the climax of the novel, before Verney embarks on his journey to Africa, he identifies himself in the same racialised stereotypes as he had hitherto depicted black people, the "wild and cruel Caribbee" (449). When finally alone, separated from all Others, he fails to recognise himself in a mirror, asking: "What wild-looking, unkempt, half-naked savage was that before me?" (455). The transformation from pastoral, uneducated peasant, to educated Englishman has now been reversed finally to a Rousseauvian 'savage',[49] and there is a certain kinship with the Being of *Frankenstein* here as his "long and tangled hair hung in elf locks" and "my dark eyes, now hollow and wild, gleamed [...] discoloured by jaundice" (455). Bewell argues that the plague merely "reverses the progress of empire";[50] in fact, the reverse colonisation process, conjured by the plague, is complete, embodied by Verney as Englishman, now turned wild.

While Sterrenberg designates *The Last Man* as "antipolitical" and "anti-intellectual" by stressing Shelley's focus on racialised paradigms, her shifting and undermining of the stratification of people of varying ethnic heritage, and at the same time reinforcing the English as "the triumph of man", it should however be clear that the novel is instead highly political.[51] However, it does not offer a didactic analogy to the complexities of empire nor "power and liberty". Finally, then, the tumult of revolution and shifting fortunes of coloniser/colonised can only be reconciled by a quest for the Other, one which may never be realised, as Verney prepares his boat to the African coast. If Romanticism is, as Hegel has expressed, a state of "absolute inwardness",[52] Verney can be construed as a Romantic figure, much like the individual in *Wanderer above the Sea of Fog*.[53] In Shelley's figuration, however, *The Last Man* is much more akin to a survivor on *The Raft of the Medusa*,[54] having endured unimaginable horrors, all around him vanquished, only to wash up on some distant shore in the hope of a return to society. For Bewell, *The Last Man* "constitutes a literary memorial to the Romantic period [...]. [Shelley] questions the confidence that underlay Romantic conceptions of nature and of human life".[55] Shelley certainly offers questions, without answers, and in that sense is less memorialising Romanticism and instead querying the concept of 'inwardness' and curiously asking her (what she assumes to be European) readers about outwardness, about encounters with racialised Others. Bewell also compares this novel to the iconic history book *The History of the Decline and Fall of the Roman Empire*, arguing that "[l]ike Gibbon's history, Shelley's is a critical elegy: both display admiration for an imperial city combined with a shrewd awareness of the limitations which have led to its collapse".[56] Shelley's novel then is highly concerned with empire, colonisation, the ways in which "the centre cannot hold",[57] and with reconfiguring racialisation, but nevertheless it is not a text in which any specific ideology can be construed from the chaos. We see here Shelley's critique of Romantic ethics as ultimately impractical and insufficient. Furthermore, however, Shelley's own wokeness is also impractical and insufficient. Her works reveal an empathy for the Other, but they betray a conservative unwillingness to deconstruct the racialised stratagems of the nineteenth century.

5. Conclusion

I am unable to comprehensively provide a complete analysis of Shelley's oeuvre within the limits of one article. She has more essays, novels, and nonfiction that would all bear analysis of the potentially xenophobic elements of her work. While there has been some discussion of slavery in relation to *Frankenstein*, the inclusion of racial discourses within this infamous text may have been consistently side-lined by the academy. There is clearly a research gap which invites further analysis of Shelley's engagement with the racialised Other, such as in in the instance of Safie and her mother. Beyond *Frankenstein*, there is also the instance of the colonial encounter in *The Last Man*, which Shelley appears to present as utopian, while reinforcing white supremacist values in other parts of the book.

The critical debates about Romantic ethics need to be expanded to discussions about race even in writers (such as Shelley) whose works may not overtly and obviously suggest racialised discourses. As Kitson has powerfully stated, "[s]tudying the race idea in the romantic period allows us to speculate about how race became so important".[58] Lee takes us further and argues that Mary Prince's writings[59] offer the most insight into Romantic values: "the most powerful representation of the ethical relationship between self and other came not from the imaginations of Romantic poets, artists and novelists, but from the voice of a former slave woman".[60] The legacies of the racial politics inherent in Shelley's works linger in 21st-century constructions of race, and as Malchow has said "[r]ace itself [...] is in its most emotive sense a construct of romanticism".[61]

I have traced the racialised dimensions of Shelley's works and to some extent her life, as an argument for further study. There must be an acknowledgement of racialised discourses being formed, as Victor's Being is formed within the context of Romantic writings, in which the self is heralded as uppermost. In the wake of the Black Lives Matter movement, as well as the Covid-19 pandemic – both of which have brought some attention to the interconnectedness of our lives, our common humanity, and the ongoing work which needs to be done to dismantle the constructions of racism – Shelley's works offer an opportunity to draw out the problematic aspects of Romanticism as well as the Enlightenment. It is crucial to accept the flaws and prejudices of our most beloved writers, especially when it comes to literary critique and academic pedagogy. The racialised aspects of *Frankenstein* should be taught in universities alongside the more established strains of critique such as feminist and Marxist analyses. The 'Black Frankenstein' that Young elucidates for us continues to proliferate: for example, Saadawi's *Frankenstein in Baghdad*[62] (which won the International Prize for Arabic Fiction for 2014) needs to become part of the canon when we discuss adaptation in relation to Shelley's text. It is also crucial that academic writing does not reinforce the racism it seeks to deconstruct, by using terms such as 'mulatto' to refer to a potentially mixed race Being in the novel. The Being's plaintive questioning of himself as "a slave, doomed to waste his powers for the profit of the chosen few" (123), even while having been written by a nineteenth-century writer endowed with white privilege and prejudices, speaks to us through the centuries.

Notes

[1]   Shelley, Mary (2003 [1831]). *Frankenstein, or The Modern Prometheus*. Ed. Maurice Hindle. New York: Penguin Books.

[2]   Malchow, H.R. (1996). *Gothic Images of Race in the Nineteenth Century*. Redwood City, CA: Stanford University Press, 38.

[3]   Bohls, Elizabeth A. (1994). "Standards of Taste, Discourses of 'Race', and the Aesthetic Education of a Monster: Critique of Empire in *Frankenstein*." *Eighteenth-Century Life* 18, 25-36.

[4]   Mulvey-Roberts, Marie (2018). *Dangerous Bodies: Historicising the Gothic Corporeal*. Manchester: Manchester University Press, 53.

[5]   In Nick Groom's introduction to the 2011 Oxford World Classics edition of *Frankenstein*, he argues that rather than 'Creature' or 'Monster', a "better term would be Being" with regard to the novel's concerns of "existence, sentience and essence". I agree with Groom's conclusions and will be referring to the nameless character as the Being (see Hindrichsen in this volume).

[6]   Smith, A.L. (2004). "'This Thing of Darkness': Racial Discourse in Mary Shelley's *Frankenstein*." *Gothic Studies* 6.2, 208-222. 220.

[7]   Young, Elizabeth (2008). *Black Frankenstein: The Making of an American Metaphor*. New York: NYU Press.

[8] For example, Malchow (1996) informs us that Shelley read works by Mungo Park and Bryan Edwards (16).

[9] Smith, Andrew (ed.) (2016). *The Cambridge Companion to Frankenstein*. Cambridge: Cambridge University Press.

[10] Brantlinger, Patrick (2016). "Race and Frankenstein." *The Cambridge Companion to Frankenstein*. Ed. Andrew Smith. Cambridge: Cambridge University Press, 128-142.

[11] Malchow (1996), 19.

[12] Shelley, Mary (2008 [1826]). *The Last Man*. Ed. Morton D. Paley. Oxford: Oxford University Press.

[13] Shelley, Mary (1996). *The Novels and Selected Works of Mary Shelley*. Vol 5. Eds. Nora Crook, Pamela Clemit and Betty T Bennett. London: Routledge.

[14] Lee, Debbie (2017). *Slavery in the Romantic Imagination*. Philadelphia: University of Pennsylvania Press, 6, 223.

[15] See introduction to this volume by Hologa and Lange, 10.

[16] Spark, Muriel (2013). *Mary Shelley: A Biography*. Manchester: Carcanet Press.

[17] Seymour, Miranda (2018). *Mary Shelley*. London: Simon & Schuster UK.

[18] Gordon, Charlotte (2016). *Romantic Outlaws: The Extraordinary Lives of Mary Wollstonecraft and Mary Shelley*. London: Windmill Books.

[19] Sampson, Fiona (2018). *In Search of Mary Shelley: The Girl Who Wrote Frankenstein*. London: Profile Books.

[20] Seymour (2018), 172.

[21] *Ibid.*, 137.

[22] Mellor, Anne K. (2012). *Mary Shelley: Her Life, Her Fiction, Her Monsters*. London: Routledge, 25.

[23] Feldman, Paula R. and Diana Scott-Kilvert (eds.) (1987). *The Journals of Mary Shelley, 1814-1844,* Vol. 1*: 1814-1822*. Oxford: Clarendon Press, 20.

[24] Bennett, Betty T. (1994). *Selected Letters of Mary Wollstonecraft Shelley*. Baltimore: The Johns Hopkins University Press, 41, 101.

[25] Gordon (2016), 139.

[26] *Ibid.*, 136.

[27] Canning, George (1824). "Amelioration of the Condition of the Slave Population in the West Indies." *Hansard Parliamentary Debates, 2nd Series*. 2018. Web. 08 May 2022. https://api.parliament.uk/historic-hansard.

[28] Seymour (2018), 335.

[29] Bennett (1994), 145.

[30] Lee (2017), 193.

[31] *Ibid.*, 363.

[32] Young (2008), 5.

[33] Mulvey-Roberts (2018), 75.

[34] Lee (2017), 184.

[35] Kitson, Peter (2008). *Romantic Literature, Race, and Colonial Encounter*. New York: Palgrave Macmillan, 86.

[36] Halberstam, Jack (1995). *Skin Shows: Gothic Horror and the Technology of Monsters*. Durham, NC: Duke University Press, 9.

[37] See Shelley (1996).

[38] Volney, Constantin-François (2010). *Volney's Ruins: Or, Meditations on the Revolutions of Empires*. Charleston, SC: Nabu Press.

[39] See introduction to this volume by Hologa and Lange, 9.

[40] Lorde, Audre (2018). *The Master's Tools Will Never Dismantle the Master's House*. New York: Penguin Books.

[41] Malchow (1996), 18.

[42] Mellor (2012), 88.

[43] Sterrenburg, Lee (1978). "*The Last Man:* Anatomy of Failed Revolutions." *Nineteenth-Century Fiction*, 33.3, 324-347.

[44] Seymour (2018), 137.

[45] Feldman et al. (1987), 476-477.

[46] Stoker, Bram (1996 [1897]). *Dracula*. Eds. Nina Auerbach and David J. Skal. New York: W.W. Norton.

[47] Arata, Stephen D. (1990). "The Occidental Tourist: *Dracula* and the Anxiety of Reverse Colonization." *Victorian Studies* 33.4, 621-645.

[48] Bewell, Alan (2003). *Romanticism and Colonial Disease*. Baltimore: The Johns Hopkins University Press, 303.

[49] Rousseau, Jean-Jacques (2009 [1755]). *Discourse on the Origin of Inequality*. Oxford: Oxford University Press.

[50] Bewell (2003), 306.

[51] Sterrenburg (1978), 328, 331, 323.

[52] Blanning, Tim (2011). *The Romantic Revolution*. London: W&N.

[53] Friedrich, Caspar David (1818). *Der Wanderer über dem Nebelmeer*. Hamburger Kunsthalle.

[54] Géricault, Jean-Louis A.T. (1818-19). *Le Radeau de la Méduse*. Louvre Museum.

[55] Bewell (2003), 313.

[56] Gibbon, Edward (2000). *The History of the Decline and Fall of the Roman Empire*. New York: Penguin Books, 297.

[57] Yeats, W.B. (2008). *W.B. Yeats: The Major Works Including Poems, Plays, and Critical Prose*. Oxford: Oxford University Press, 91.

[58] Kitson (2008), 2.

[59] Prince, Mary (2000 [1831]). *The History of Mary Prince: A West Indian Slave*. New York: Penguin Books.

[60] Lee (2017), 224.

[61] Malchow (1996), 39.

[62] Saafawi, Ahmed (2018). *Frankenstein in Baghdad: A Novel*. New York: Penguin Books, trans. Jonathan Wright.

Bibliography

Arata, Stephen D. (1990). "The Occidental Tourist: *Dracula* and the Anxiety of Reverse Colonization." *Victorian Studies* 33.4, 621-645.

Bennett, Betty T. (1994). *Selected Letters of Mary Wollstonecraft Shelley*. Baltimore: The Johns Hopkins University Press.

Bewell, Alan (2003). *Romanticism and Colonial Disease*. Baltimore: The Johns Hopkins University Press.

Blanning, Tim (2011). *The Romantic Revolution*. London: W&N.

Bohls, Elizabeth A. (1994). "Standards of Taste, Discourses of 'Race', and the Aesthetic Education of a Monster: Critique of Empire in *Frankenstein*." *Eighteenth-Century Life*, 18, 25-36.

Brantlinger, Patrick (2016). "Race and Frankenstein." *The Cambridge Companion to Frankenstein*. Ed. Andrew Smith. Cambridge: Cambridge University Press, 128-142.

Canning, George (1824). "Amelioration of the Condition of the Slave Population in the West Indies." *Hansard Parliamentary Debates, 2nd Series*. 2018. Web. 08 May 2022. https://api.parliament.uk/historic-hansard.

Feldman, Paula R. and Scott-Kilvert, Diana (eds.) (1987). *The Journals of Mary Shelley, 1814-1844,* Vol. 1: *1814-1822*. Oxford: Clarendon Press.

--- (1987). *The Journals of Mary Shelley, 1814-1844,* Vol. 2: *1822-1844*. Oxford: Clarendon Press.

Friedrich, Caspar David (1818). *Der Wanderer über dem Nebelmeer*. Hamburger Kunsthalle.

Géricault, Jean-Louis André Théodore (1818-1819). *Le Radeau de la Méduse*. Louvre Museum.

Gibbon, Edward (2000). *The History of the Decline and Fall of the Roman Empire*. New York: Penguin Books.

Gordon, Charlotte (2016). *Romantic Outlaws: The Extraordinary Lives of Mary Wollstonecraft and Mary Shelley*. London: Windmill Books.

Halberstam, Jack (1995). *Skin Shows: Gothic Horror and the Technology of Monsters*. Durham, NC: Duke University Press.

Kitson, Peter. *Romantic Literature, Race, and Colonial Encounter*. New York: Palgrave Macmillan.

Lee, Debbie (2017). *Slavery in the Romantic Imagination*. Philadelphia, PA: University of Pennsylvania Press.

Lorde, Audre (2018). *The Master's Tools Will Never Dismantle The Master's House*. New York: Penguin Books.

Malchow, H.R. (1996). *Gothic Images of Race in the Nineteenth Century*. Redwood City, CA: Stanford University Press.

Mellor, Anne K. (2012). *Mary Shelley: Her Life, Her Fiction, Her Monsters*. London: Routledge.

Mulvey-Roberts, Marie (2018). *Dangerous Bodies: Historicising the Gothic Corporeal*. Manchester: Manchester University Press.

Prince, Mary (2000 [1831]). *The History of Mary Prince: A West Indian Slave*. New York: Penguin Books.

Rousseau, Jean-Jacques (2009 [1755]). *Discourse on the Origin of Inequality*. Oxford: Oxford University Press.

Saafawi, Ahmed (2018). *Frankenstein in Baghdad: A Novel*. New York, NY: Penguin Books, trans.by Jonathan Wright.

Sampson, Fiona (2018). *In Search of Mary Shelley: The Girl Who Wrote Frankenstein*. London: Profile Books.

Seymour, Miranda (2018). *Mary Shelley*. London: Simon & Schuster UK.

Shelley, Mary (2003 [1831]). *Frankenstein, or The Modern Prometheus*. Ed. Maurice Hindle. New York: Penguin Books.

--- (2019 [1818]). *Frankenstein, or The Modern Prometheus*. Ed. Nick Groom. Oxford: Oxford University Press.

--- (1996). *The Novels and Selected Works of Mary Shelley*. Vol 5. Eds. Nora Crook, Pamela Clemit, Betty T Bennett. London: Routledge.

--- (2008 [1826]). *The Last Man*. Ed. Morton D. Paley. Oxford: Oxford University Press.

Smith, A.L. (2004). "'This Thing of Darkness': Racial Discourse in Mary Shelley's *Frankenstein*." *Gothic Studies* 6.2, 208-222.

Smith, Andrew (ed.) (2016). *The Cambridge Companion to Frankenstein*. Cambridge: Cambridge University Press.

Spark, Muriel (2013). *Mary Shelley: A Biography*. Manchester: Carcanet Press.

Sterrenburg, Lee (1978). "*The Last Man*: Anatomy of Failed Revolutions." *Nineteenth-Century Fiction* 33.3, 324-347.

Stoker, Bram (1996 [1897]). *Dracula*. Eds. Nina Auerbach, David J. Skal. New York: Norton.

Volney, Constantin-François (2010). *Volney's Ruins: Or, Meditations on the Revolutions of Empires*. Charleston, SC: Nabu Press.

Yeats, W.B. (2008). *W.B. Yeats: The Major Works including Poems, Plays, and Critical Prose*. Oxford: Oxford University Press.

Young, Elizabeth (2008). *Black Frankenstein: The Making of an American Metaphor*. New York: NYU Press.

Paul Almonte

"How Did Such an Age Come About?" The Anti-Woke Romanticism of Yukio Mishima

> Would he be able to die young – and if possible free from all pain? A graceful death – as a richly patterned kimono, thrown carelessly across a polished table, slides unobtrusively down into the darkness of the floor beneath. A death marked by elegance.[1]
>
> Yukio Mishima

> Drawing our brine cart along, how briefly we live in this sad world, how fleetingly![2]
>
> Yukio Mishima

1. Introduction: Romanticism Across Culture and Time

Insistent in its claim to echo "a certain 19th-century Romanticism" that "would never disappear",[3] Yukio Mishima's tetralogy, *Sea of Fertility* (1970), offers a compelling example of Romanticism's global impact on cultural thought – including nineteenth-century tensions between revolution and reaction repeated in our own age's conflicts between despotic rulers and populist uprisings throughout the world. Mishima's version of Romanticism sheds light on its abilities and failures to extend what he calls the "consolations of nature"[4] beyond the singular, privileged aesthete, and toward genuine community building. Like the British Romantics, Mishima intertwines personal, insular psychologies with attempts at social and political engagement among class and caste systems.

William Wordsworth serves as a particularly useful comparison. In *Tintern Abbey*, for example, he uses the recuperative powers of the abbey's "beauteous forms" to escape life's frustrations, angers, and despairs. "Thoughts of deep seclusion" transport Wordsworth from "hours of weariness" and the "heavy and weary weight / Of all this unintelligible world is lightened", turning him from "darkness" to a "life and hope for future years":

> These beauteous forms,
> Through a long absence, have not been to me
> As is a landscape to a blind man's eye:
> But oft, in lonely rooms, and 'mid the din
> Of towns and cities, I have owed to them,
> In hours of weariness, sensations sweet,
> Felt in the blood, and felt along the heart;
> And passing even into my purer mind
> With tranquil restoration: – feelings too
> Of unremembered pleasure: such, perhaps,
> As have no slight or trivial influence
> On that best portion of a good man's life,
> His little, nameless, unremembered, acts
> Of kindness and of love.[5]

Wordsworth's experience and memory of the French Revolution saw him torn between the excitement and value he felt toward the French Revolution and his more conservative belief in societal hierarchy. In his 2020 biography, *Radical Wordsworth*, Jonathan Bate defines the conflict thus: "[Wordsworth] was aware of the tricks of memory. His past has 'self-presence' [...] in his heart and yet there is such a gap – a ' vacancy' – between the lived experience [...] and the mind of the poet as he nears the age of thirty and begins to write down his memories that 'sometimes when I think of them I seem / Two consciousnesses – conscious of myself, / And of some other being.'"[6] Bate describes Wordsworth acknowledging the woke part of his desire for the French Revolution to have taken firmer root in creating a government of the people:

> The act of feeling [...] was the first step towards an acknowledgment of [...] human rights and thence to a revolution in the social relations that constrained both France and Britain. In mingling the language of democratic politics with that of strong feeling, Wordsworth was channelling the spirit of Jean-Jacques Rousseau via Michel Beaupuy, yoking the cult of sensibility embodied in *La nouvelle Héloïse* to the revolutionary clarion call of Rousseau's *Social Contract*, with its idea that government should be based not on the inherited authority of the few but on the 'general will' of the people.[7]

But, as Bate goes on to note, Wordsworth's revolutionary belief does not hold:

> He was beginning to question his own complicity with the revolution, to upbraid himself. His own loyalties were by now divided [...] He was, of course, writing [...] a decade after the event, circling back in retrospect. And he would revise his account on several occasions in later years, moderating the language of books nine and ten of *The Prelude* in order to distance himself more and more from his youthful self, as the politics of his middle age and later years revolved to conservatism [...] In the act of writing, it is his mature self in flight from the young idealist he once was.[8]

This is the debate – egalitarian principles and actions versus the preservation of the historical social and political order – which Mishima engages in, too. Seeking meaning and solace in a cultural grace he fears is dying, Shigekuni Honda, the tetralogy's central voice, confronts the corrupting pressures of twentieth-century Japanese society through his experience with a series of reincarnations of his beloved friend, Kiyoaki. A young man of the Japanese upper class, Kiyoaki dies bereft after a forced separation from his beloved, Satoko, who is betrothed to an imperial prince: "[T]he tie that bound him to Satoko had been cut by the shining blade of imperial sanction."[9]

Framed within this classic Romantic mortality/immortality trope, between a Keatsian "Cold Pastoral"[10] eternity and a lived history that will die, this article asks the following: Does Mishima's Romanticism stand at odds with history, where the past is just so many corroded "relics of grandeur"[11] and presumed eternally meaningful ideals simply false visions? If Mishima's narrator/poet/historian cannot put memory's fragments back together to resemble anything but "the sight of a moonbeam shining into a corner of a ruined palace",[12] what, then, if anything, is truly recovered, restored, or redeemed, and for whom? Will an 'anti-wokeness' reign through Honda's attempts to maintain the old class order or does the societal decay Mishima describes ironically suggest a positive message at the tetralogy's close: a new, woke order replacing the old?[13] Will there be a "life and hope for future years?"[14] In challenging his readers to answer these questions, Mishima casts the tension within a Romantic inwardness, a "war of emotion": "The kind of war no one can see, only feel [...] and just as in the old wars, there will be casualties [...;] it's the fate of our age".[15] Wordsworth and Keats are

Mishima's poetic foils as Honda, his "sylvan historian", narrates what Kelly calls the story of Japan's "national decline":

> Before quitting his opulent home that November day, Mishima sealed and posted to his publisher the manuscript of *The Sea of Fertility*, a tetralogy of novels over which he had laboured for five years. If he had meant the work to be his magnum opus, it was doomed to be occluded by his suicide. These four books – *Spring Snow*, *Runaway Horses*, *The Temple of Dawn* and *The Decay of the Angel* – are a saga of 20th-century Japan: a story of national decline that nonetheless proposes redemption through the endurance of a certain soul, forceful enough to be reborn ad infinitum.[16]

Each of three subsequent reincarnations – Isao, an idealistic soldier who participates in a violent coup to fight what he regards as the decadence and degradation of Japanese culture and government, Ying Chan, a beautiful young princess and, Toru, an equally beautiful young man whose passions run toward violence, not love – are first defined by a purity to which Honda is drawn. This purity, though, is shadowed by indications of mortality (understood as physical decay and questionable ethics or morality) as Honda searches for an integration of time and eternity akin to what Wordsworth finds in poems like "The Ruined Cottage"[17] and Keats describes in "Ode to a Nightingale" ("Thou wast not born for death immortal Bird! / No hungry generations tread thee down"[18]). In pursuing and chronicling these reincarnations, Honda seeks a connection of human and environment that reconciles Kiyoaki's mortal loss with his seemingly perfect love: "[L]ooked at from this vantage point, all the phenomena below and all the phenomena of the past seemed to lie before him on a single rain-soaked map".[19] "Surrounded by unbroken silence [...] was a world untouched by blemish of any kind [...] But could such a still and perfect world, which eschewed all intimacy, really bear any relation to the familiar world he knew?"[20]

Eliding for now the interpretive impact of Mishima's own dramatic suicide (he committed ritual *seppuku* as protest against what he viewed as Japan's decadence and moral decay), Kelly's suggestion of "redemption through the endurance of a certain soul"[21] is, perhaps, the central argument in the tetralogy with which one must come to terms. The idea of redemption foregrounds the late-Romantic/Modernist idiom in which Mishima worked and which is our interest here. Honda pursues these manifestations of his dead friend – culminating in a full-circle return to Kiyoaki's beloved, Satoko – to seek meaning, closure, a unification of all things: a Romantic integration of earth and eternity. In Honda's engagements with the various reincarnations, Mishima juxtaposes beautiful yet problematic memories (defining them as "relics of grandeur"[22]) with contemporary concerns (e.g. Japan's "national decline"[23]). The reincarnations lead, as Kelly notes, to the final encounter Honda has with Satoko, the original object of Kiyoaki's Romantic desire and Honda's half-century-long idealisation of her, who has spent the last sixty years shut away in a convent.

2. The Ethics of Narration

Mishima's poetic descriptions of life, love, and beauty throughout the tetralogy raise questions about the definition and redeeming value of "truth"[24] within Keats's famous odes – "Ode to a Nightingale" and "Ode on a Grecian Urn" – and their contrast between the spiritual power of an imagined eternity and a lived history that will die. Mishima locates Honda's narration in something akin to Keats's contrasts of hope and despair, visions or "waking" nightmares where "haply the Queen-Moon is on her throne", but for him, "there is no light":[25]

> The classically elegant garden is an incline. The gold dust of all-powerful beauty and pleasure drifts down. Absolute freedom soaring in emptiness is torn away like a rending of flesh. The shadows gather. The light dies. Soft power drips and drips from the beautiful fingers. The fire flickers in the depths of flesh, the spirit is departing. The brightly checkered floor of the pavilion, the vermillion balustrades, have faded not at all. Relics of grandeur, they will be there when the angels are gone.[26]

But do these poetic moments achieve truly instructive, impactful, and lasting effects? That is, are they woke? Do they move from acknowledgement of inequality to ethically acting on that awareness or is Mishima decrying Romanticism's failure by hiding the ugliness, the brutality, the corruption – the reality – of life in walled-off gardens, falsely painted pictures, or decayed and meaningless mausoleums of the mind? This is what is at stake in Honda's narration and his life. Does the claim that "they will be there when the angels are gone"[27] suggest an emptiness that makes a memory or hope akin to that expressed in "Grecian Urn" a false one? In *Spring Snow* (1990), for example, Mishima describes the difficulty of this move from the safety of solitary or solipsistic musing to living in – and impacting – the tumultuous social and political world around us. "In the midst of the turmoil of history", his narrator notes, "each one of us builds his own little shelter of self-awareness and we can never leave it".[28] These "little shelters," Mishima seems to suggest, are akin to the "emptiness" of Keats' "Cold Pastoral":[29]

> A pervasive aura of desolation carries the reader into the tetralogy's final instalment, *The Decay of the Angel*, a work of pitch-black pessimism that sees the Japan of 1970 nearly consumed by a rising tide of modern detritus. The septuagenarian Honda places his faith in one more seeming renewal of Kiyoaki – an arrogant, ingrate youth named Toru – but in the process he is harried and abused almost to death, so leaving him to wonder whether he ever read the augurs correctly or has been living an epic delusion all along.[30]

For Mishima, it seems, no idealism akin to Wordsworth's initial observation of the French Revolution's change to the social order informs his view of Japanese society. Mishima is not advocating an openness to society; the opposite rather: an anti-wokeness that wants caste systems preserved. Seemingly hinting at a critique of the imperial order, given that Satoko was betrothed to a prince, Koyiaki's love for her ironically may become a symbol of the desire to preserve it. As the tetralogy proceeds, Honda himself becomes a direct actor in Mishima's explorations of these Romantic ideals, human frailties, and mortality. Acknowledging his own base desires, Honda worries that there can be no Romantic integration (for him or anyone) of ideal love and physical passion: "[T]ime dripped away like blood. Old men dried up and died. In payment for having neglected to stop time at the glorious moment when the rich blood, unbeknownst to the owner himself, was bringing rich drunkenness".[31] A series of questions is raised about what Honda comes to understand about himself and the Romantic world he creates through the reincarnations: is the attempt at being a "sylvan historian"[32] within this – or any such – corrupted world a viable or honest artistic response to it? Is his storytelling deluded or wilfully exclusionary in terms of class? To illustrate these questions, we return to Wordsworth. A central premise of his Romantic project might be said to be the endurance of the privileged positions of his narrator, the Wanderer, and himself. In contrast to the extremely challenging life and death of the woman whose story is recounted in *The Ruined Cottage*, Wordsworth's emphasises humanity's "chearfuless" (*sic*) and the emotional survival of the two storytellers via their woke empathy at the end:

> 'Every smile',
> Said Margaret to me here beneath these trees,
> 'Made my heart bleed,' At this the old Man paus'd
> And looking up to those enormous elms
> He said, 'Tis now the hour of deepest noon,
> At this still season of repose and peace,
> This hour when all things which are not at rest
> Are chearful, while this multitude of flies
> Fills all the air with happy melody,
> Why should a tear be in an old man's eye?
> Why should we thus with an untoward mind
> And in the weakness of humanity
> From natural wisdom turn our hearts away,
> To natural comfort shut our eyes and ears,
> And feeding on disquiet thus disturb
> The calm of Nature with our restless thoughts?[33]

Reflecting on this story of the young woman's demise, the men assert their own emotional comfort. They applaud their empathy and thereby grant themselves peace, with the old man suggesting that any excessive grieving or care over the woman's experience is not warranted. Indeed, "wisdom" demands they give up their sorrow and be "chearful":

> I stood, and leaning o'er the garden-gate
> Reviewed that Woman's suff'rings, and it seemed
> To comfort me while with a brother's love
> I blessed her in the impotence of grief.
> At length upon the hut I fix'd my eyes
> Fondly, and traced with milder interest
> That secret spirit of humanity
> Which, 'mid the calm oblivious tendencies
> Of nature, 'mid her plants, her weeds, and flowers,
> And silent overgrowings, still survived.
> The old man, seeing this, resumed and said,
> "My Friend, enough to sorrow have you given,
> The purposes of wisdom ask no more;
> Be wise and chearful, and no longer read

The forms of things with an unworthy eye.
She sleeps in the calm earth, and peace is here".[34]

This is troubling. The letting go seems too easily achieved. A woke concern for the poor too easily presumed; the life "calmly" buried in the ground is too easily mourned as a means to their own psychological peace. The "comfort" the male narrators/listeners take in "reviewing that Woman's suff'rings" and claiming to "trace" humanity's "secret spirit" from it feels like a false empathy; such lip-service "blessing" of her pain empties Romanticism of its woke claim to care.

There is the problem, too, of Wordsworth's later and continual revision of his work, "in order to distance himself more and more from his youthful self", as Bate notes, as "the politics of [Wordsworth's] middle age and later years revolved to conservatism".[35] The encounters and memories of Margaret are read from an even further patronising remove as Wordsworth renounces his earlier wokeness: "Actions have consequences; once violence begins, a cycle of retribution will follow. Does that mean, Wordsworth wonders, that the pure ideals of liberty, equality and fraternity will never be realised throughout society and that the task of the writer may be to think about individual choice and liberty instead?"[36] This is the same position in which we see Honda. Juxtaposing "The Ruined Cottage" with Honda's encounters with Kiyoaki's reincarnations is fruitful as Mishima, too, has been searching for what is surviving or, more properly, what *should* survive in the "secret spirit of humanity."[37] The narrative position Wordsworth evinces at the end of "The Ruined Cottage" is one Honda has been struggling with throughout the tetralogy. His privileged position as a storyteller and member of the upper class seems to allow Honda a condescending absolution. But in his search to reconnect with the reincarnated versions of Kiyoaki, Honda's Romantic perspective, actions, and narrative authority are called into question. At stake is an ethics of narration.

Before Honda takes centre stage, Kiyoaki's thoughts and feelings of a world gone wrong predominate. "How," he asks, "did such an age come about, an age which had defiled everything that once was sacred?"[38] Mishima is beginning to explore here what we might call a sinister Romanticism – a more direct acknowledgement of darker societal behaviours that Romanticism's aesthetic constructions, like Keats' famous lines at the end of "Grecian Urn" – "Beauty is truth, truth beauty, – that is all / Ye know on earth, and all ye need to know"[39] – only elide. Here, the "sylvan historian" makes a more critical comparison between an ideal, bucolic past and a corrupted present. Kiyoaki's is no temporary "melancholy fit"[40] but a true death wish:

> He was oblivious of the outside world. The clear, calm mirror of his soul had now been shattered. There was a turmoil in his heart that churned with the force of a tropical storm. But what emotion now had him in its grip? It must be called delight. But it was a delight so irrational, so passionate, that it was almost unearthly [...] There was something sinister, ominously threatening about it. Long ago he had resolved to recognize his emotions as his only guiding truth and to live his life accordingly [...]. That principle had now brought him to his present sinister feeling of joy, which seemed to be the brink of a racing, plunging whirlpool. There seemed to be nothing left but to throw himself into it.[41]

The truth of beauty here is a suppressed, but growing darkness:

> This, he knew, was further proof of the hidden, savage essence of the elegance he had cultivated for so long. Surely the simplest solution was for them to die together, but he felt that something far more agonizing was called for.[42]

For Honda, heart and environment both were bereft. And, as much as he tries, no poetic "comfort of the warmer sun"[43] would be forthcoming:

> The elegance that had been so conscious a part of him had withered. His heart had become desolate. Nowhere in himself could he find the kind of graceful sorrow that inspires poems. He was empty now, his soul a desert swept by parching winds.[44]

The novel ends by posing a Keatsian question: can one create a beauty "untouched by blemish of any kind"[45] but also not devoid of the human element? As *Spring Snow* concludes, its language evokes a darkening, destructive melancholy (which in the next instalment, *Runaway Horses*, will be called "threatening sorrows"[46]): "Like unto a violent torrent [...] beings in existence thus are annihilated from moment to moment."[47] After the failure to see Satoko, Kiyoaki's condition deteriorates, and the last pages of the novel are his death knell and the passing of the narration to Honda. A crucial part of the conclusion is Honda romanticising (or memorialising) the beauty of Kiyoaki's death mask:

197

Despite the contortions, however, it was beautiful. Intense suffering had imbued it with an extraordinary character, carving lines into it that gave it the austere dignity of a bronze mask. The beautiful eyes were filled with tears.[48]

3. Acting in a World Gone Wrong

The ethical or woke question, as we might call it, then, is how to act in a corrupted world. Kiyoaki's love affair with Satoko might have represented an attempt to break the cultural stranglehold of royalty and caste. But Kiyoaki dies and Satoko is convent bound, where she will remain the rest of her days. The royal, reactionary authority holds. And so it is left to Honda and Kiyoaki's reincarnations to embody and engage the question of what Kiyoaki's gesture symbolises. Whereas Wordsworth's narrators comfortably proclaim the validity of their professed empathy for Margaret (via their woke care for the poorer classes), Honda acknowledges his corrupted self and conflicted narratorial position. He recognises that caste distinctions remain and should be upheld. While Kiyoaki gets his "elegant" – if not exactly "easeful" – death, his reincarnations do not. Honda's long life, tracing Mishima's critique of twentieth-century Japanese culture's move away from imperial respect and Samurai tenets, becomes one of physical and moral decay where no signs of woke virtue or Romantic idealism remain. Neither gracefulness nor grace endure; only, it seems, a poetic and ethical emptiness:

> [A]n intolerable idea had come to [Honda]. He found he could not help thinking that the crystal vessel of beauty and purity he sought had already fallen to the ground and lay in fragments, and that he was stubbornly refusing to acknowledge it.[49]

The question for the subsequent novels is whether Honda rescues or renews the idealisation emphasised in the first novel: the "truth" of suffering and the "contortions" of a mortal life have apparently made art of Kiyoaki's face, "carving" in it a romanticised meaning, the "austere dignity,"[50] that were Honda to be a "sylvan historian"[51] might reinforce the beauty and truth of the broader Japanese hierarchy of which Kiyoaki was a part. The following novels answer whether Mishima really believes in this idealisation, or this woke interpretation. In *Runaway Horses*, Mishima again muses on the ethical response of character, narrator, and writer to a world falling to the "weariness, the fever, and the fret",[52] if you

198

will. As in *Spring Snow*, a love story predominates between Isao, the young soldier who wants to restore the previous regime, and Makiko, his older lover. It is intertwined with Isao's capture and trial for his role in plotting to overthrow the current government. Seeing him as Kiyoaki's reincarnation, Honda serves as Isao's trial attorney. Early on, before he becomes aware of Isao's intentions, there are moments when Honda feels genuine poetic fusions of nature and humanity, art, and life, that seem to maintain psychic calm and reflect social peace. Describing a classic Romantic trope, he calls it the "consolation of nature:"

> He saw nothing but the lines of buildings, passive beneath the falling rain. In the pervading coolness, the consolation of nature, Honda began to reflect [...] Now as he looked from this vantage point, all the phenomena below and all the phenomena of the past seemed to lie before him on a single rain-soaked map.[53]

Mishima often offers such Wordsworthian recoveries, but the poetic memory represented through the instructive revisioning that Honda is undertaking in recounting these reincarnations of Kiyoaki does not reach the sublime: "Its eye upon the supreme moment. But the moment does not come. The anxiety resolves into a gentle poetic mood."[54] The "mood" is a fine one, but simply aesthetic, not a transcendent feeling that connects all: words like "worn," "ruined," "ravaged", and "fragmented" counter the hope that "elegance" becomes transcendence:

> But despite all this, the mood inspired as like the outpouring of a dark and ineffably elegant mist, like the sight of a moonbeam shining into a corner of a ruined palace to fall upon a mother-of-pearl furnishing. Because the light passed through a worn and ravaged bamboo blind, the elegance of the shattered fragments shone all the more.[55]

Honda hopes his narration can adequately capture the love he has witnessed in Kiyoaki and help maintain a societal whole through this story of pure love: "All incongruity was wiped away at that moment. I, whose eyes had witnessed so miraculous a transformation, could myself hardly remain unchanged".[56]Here, again, is an attempt to bring together, to fuse or integrate what Keats does not or cannot reconcile in "Grecian Urn". Kiyoaki's effacement left the mortal world unhappy but only fleetingly so. His supposedly "miraculous transformation" into Isao is reigniting human love[57] and signalling a societal restoration, a respect for culture and love for all people. Even Honda claims to change, his "callow faith"[58] giving way to admitting to the presence and value of love. But will this be a true woke recognition: an understanding of the worth and needs of others that activates a change in behaviour, that reconciles or heals anything human? Honda's telling of Isao's suffering again echoes Wordsworth's narrators in "The Ruined Cottage". But whereas Wordsworth ultimately describes an integrative empathy, Honda sees fracture. "'There's no doubt that he's heading straight for tragedy'", Honda says of Isao. "'It will be beautiful, of course, but should he throw his whole life away as a sacrificial offering to such a fleeting beauty.'"[59] This "fleeting beauty" is Romanticism as empty solace: "[A]n intolerable idea had come to him. [Honda] found he could not help thinking that the crystal vessel of beauty and purity he sought had already fallen to the ground and lay in fragments."[60] Such Romantic set-pieces abound, but do not redeem. The moment cannot be sustained; the integration of mortality and immortality fails:

> Isao shut his eyes and gave himself over greedily to the image of Makiko before him a moment ago. Her beautiful smiling face with its fair skin – he wanted to store this image in his heart just as it was, unflawed. But if he were too eager, it would shatter like a mirror that has slipped from one's grasp.[61]

Both the impossibility of his continuing connection with Makiko and the failure of the revolution lead Isao to the cleansing power of *seppuku*, ritual suicide: if society cannot be redeemed, its decadent course not changed, then a sacrifice must be made: For Isao, presaging Mishima's own suicide, words are idle, action is paramount:

> The sins I refer to have nothing to do with the law. And the greatest sin is that of a man who, finding himself in a world where the sacred light of His Majesty is obscured, nevertheless determines to go on living without doing anything about it. The only way to purge this grave sin is to make a fiery offering with one's own hands [...] and then to commit *seppuku* immediately. With death, all is purified.[62]

But will all truly become purified through his death? Has anything on earth, anything mortal, been changed for the better? The tetralogy's third novel, *The Temple of Dawn* (1990), plays a key role in answering these questions by defining the meaning and ethics of Mishima's increasingly anti-woke Romantic narration. In it, Honda's own human desire – carnal and base, as he admits – complicates his attempt to idealise the stories of

200

Kiyoaki's reincarnations. His desires and actions are now clearly implicated in these narratives. For example, a Lolita-like desire for Ying Chan has Honda voyeuristically invading her space, a behaviour he had humiliatingly, if not repentantly, been caught exhibiting publicly before: "from the moment he had peeped through the luminous hole in the back of the bookcase, she had become an inhabitant of a world created by his perception [...] contaminated by the moment he laid eyes on it".[63] Honda claims to want a pure nightingale. "[H]e wanted to see a soaring Ying Chan," but bound by what he recognises as his base actions and perceptions, "she did not soar".[64] The ugliness of his narration exposes him to himself. A Wordsworthian recovery would now be a mockery. "He was empty now, his soul a desert".[65] It now became clear that Honda's ultimate desire, what he really, really wanted to see could exist only in a world where he did not. In order to see what he truly wished to, he must die. [...] It would mean Honda's exit from a world contaminated by perception.[66]

At the end of this novel, like the first one, a beauty is stricken and dies. Ying's twin sister recounts to Honda Ying's death from a snake bite in her garden with a strange laughter heard by her lady-in-waiting before she came upon the prostrate woman: "According to [her], Ying Chan was alone in the garden [...] although there was no one else there, she was heard laughing. The lady-in-waiting thought it strange that she should be laughing all by herself".[67] Despite the beauty of that last sentence, no poetic sublime recovers the narrative. "The laughter ceased and almost at once turned into shrill screams. The lady-in-waiting rushed up to find Ying Chan on the ground, her thigh bitten by a cobra". All that is left is the "pretentious illusion" of Honda's "most ugly of dreams".

> Nothing was more unattractive than the fact that both the force moving one to the noblest or most just of deeds and that inspiring the most obscene pleasure and the most ugly of dreams should spring from the same source and be accompanied by the same warring palpitations [...] Perhaps the root of temptation lay not in carnal desire but in this pretentious illusion of silvery sublimity.[68]

Drawing direct attention to the Romantic movement – to that "certain nineteenth-century romanticism that would not disappear"[69] – Mishima begins the last novel, *The Decay of the Angel* (1990), with a description of idyllic hope and fusion which Honda had hoped to find through Kiyoaki's previous reincarnations. "Toru went to the east window and pulled back the glass to let in the beauty of the last moments before sunrise

[…] Toru could almost see dots of houses on the far slopes. Above them was a vision of a rose coming into bloom".[70] But the image offers only a fleeting connection: "[I]n the mists of early summer such an appearance was a gradual separation from the inchoate".[71] Again, a presumably eternal Edenic site and feeling is immediately undercut or juxtaposed with decay or ruin and, in an obvious Romantic trope, shrouded in a mist that obscures the vision. The historian, the poet, the memory can neither put the "shattered fragments of a poem that had once been alive inside [Kiyoaki]"[72] back together nor maintain beauty's reign. Echoing the contest between beauty and ugliness with which he concluded *The Temple of Dawn*, Mishima offers an extended description of a sea that is at once beautiful and ugly:

> Seeing went beyond being, to take wings like a bird. It transported Toru to a realm visible to no one. Even beauty there was a rotted, tattered skirt. That had to be a sea never defiled by being, a sea upon which ships never appeared. There had to be a realm where at the limit of all the layers of clarity it was definite that nothing at all made an appearance, a realm of solid, definite indigo […][73]

A central question of *The Decay of the Angel* is which parts of the mortal lives and consciousnesses of Toru (the fourth reincarnation) and Honda redeem anything of the ideal, the beautiful, the eternal, the spiritual. Toru announces a desire to commit evil against a pure, beautiful girl and does so. He then attacks Honda, who had adopted him. Toru's punishment is a failed suicide that leaves him blind and beholden to an ugly acolyte, Kinue. Mishima is here pushing his Romantic contrasts toward a sinister ugliness, toward these more "threatening sorrows".[74] The melancholic has become the sinful and, perhaps worse, the prosaic, the mundane. The supposed transcendent power of beauty originally symbolised in the feelings evoked by Kiyoaki's death mask is here mocked by Toru's reliance on the ugly Kinue. Unlike Kiyoaki, Toru neither finds a beautiful mortal love nor meaningful death. As Honda wryly notes: "[Y]ou have had no destiny. The beautiful death was not for you".[75]

We sense another despairing death coming. The hopeful Keatsian contrasts of "Grecian Urn" and "Nightingale" will not be integrated or resolved. Honda already sees the sinister, the decay and corruption in Toru's mind as it reminds him of his own "most obscene" pleasure.[76] These characters – from Toru to Isao from *Runaway Horses* – are merely sacrificial lambs, their stories not ones of fusion with a transcendent ideal

passed down from Kiyoaki, but of Romanticism's ruin in the midst of modern corruptions: "The old wars are finished, a new kind of war has just begun; this is the era for the war of emotion. The kind of war no one can see, only feel [...] and just as in the old wars, there will be casualties [...] it's the fate of our age – and you're one of our representatives".[77]
But does Honda achieve any sort of effective or positive position as a "sylvan historian"? Does he achieve a poetic awareness that truly understands or makes sense of what the various reincarnations mean? Will he rescue anything of Kiyoaki's love or the culture from which he came? In asking these questions, we must also remember Honda's own fallen status as a "disgraced voyeur". Again, unlike Wordsworth's narrators in "The Ruined Cottage", Honda is deeply implicated in this corrupted world. Starting with the third novel, Mishima has been very explicit in not allowing Honda a safe narratorial distance, or a too easily assumed idealist (woke) perspective. Honda recognizes that he no longer believes in the integrative hope (personal and collective) reflected in Kiyoaki and Satoko's love:

> [I]t weighed on him to think that he must visit Satoko as Kiyoaki's representative, bearing memories. Sixty years had gone by and the words were still in his ears [...] But the journey was too much for him. Old and ugly and stained with sin as he was, the complications seemed only to increase.[78]

Mishima describes Honda this way – fully, ashamedly human – to heighten the contrast with the isolated, convent-enshrined Satoko. The fallen Honda and the pure Satoko are juxtaposed in one last Edenic *tableaux* that becomes a contest for Kiyoaki's Romantic meaning. Will Honda, in his final thoughts on and feelings for Satoko, redeem the Romanticism that he had doubted, that he called "callow"[79] at key points during his life and pilgrimage? Will a "Grecian Urn"-like balance between mortal realities and eternal verities return and hold? Will this woke Romanticism purify and be purified by the convent garden environment?[80] Or, will the uglier, modernist recastings that foreground the sin and corruption of humanity win? Will the voice of the "sylvan historian" be refused in favour of "a self-awareness that knew nothing of love, that slaughtered without raising a hand, that relished death as it composed noble condolences, that invited the world to destruction while seeking the last possible moment for itself"?[81]

"For Honda it had been sixty years, for Satoko had it been the time it takes to cross a garden bridge from shadow into sunlight".[82] This sentence captures the essence of Mishima's questions regarding memory and the Romantic project, and the narrator, author, or poet's role in it: how to define and present time, the activities and experiences that make up a life and juxtapose them with hopes and claims about eternal veracities, beliefs and moments of universal emotional value. Mishima offers Romantic paradoxes ("soft though hard") in describing the aged Satoko, lines that seem to integrate a "beauty that cannot die" with a real life. As Honda first sees her, Satoko is poised between a beautiful sensuality ("the lips were still moist"[83]) and a transition to an eternal, artistic image:

> [A]ge had sped in the direction not of decay but of purification. The skin seemed to glow with a still light; the beauty of the eyes was clearer, shining through something like a patina. Age had crystallized into a perfect jewel. It was cold though diaphanous, roundly soft though hard, and the lips were still moist.[84]

But the encounter with Satoko does not go as Honda had hoped. Having allowed him the chance to recount the story of hers and Kiyoaki's shared passion and his romanticised death because of their separation, Satoko refuses the memory: "Calmly, without a touch of emotion, she said 'It has been a most interesting story, but, unfortunately I did not know Mr. Matsugae. I fear you have confused me with someone else'".[85] The sylvan history Honda wants will not be redeemed. Unlike the lover on Keats's famous urn, the memory of Kiyoaki and Satoko he wants to preserve will "fade".[86] It will not endure, let alone prevail: "Kiyoaki […] Who might he have been?"[87] The emotional connection is denied; no poetic fusion acknowledged. Satoko, the one person who could validate Honda's narrative and to whom his lifetime pilgrimage for Kiyoaki has been made, rejects it. However politely, she mocks the Romanticism of Honda's story: "The Abbess laughed and seemed to sway gently. 'Your interesting letter seemed almost too earnest'".[88]

So, the purification and melding of which Honda speaks – and for which Mishima had hoped – remains cold. Despite Edenic descriptions, the pastoral claim did not take root. Keatsian "silence and slow time" cannot patina over or suppress the mortal lives – love, corruption, decay – Mishima describes. Rejecting his Romantic reading of her life, Satoko refuses the mantle of "unravish'd bride of quietness" despite what Honda imagines being her dreams of "sixty years".[89] For Satoko, Honda's woke story does not sustain except as a false icon. She will not allow herself to be placed into a frieze akin to the image on Keats's urn and falsely used. In so refusing to acknowledge Kiyoaki and rejecting Honda's telling of the story, Satoko shakes Honda to his very core. His sense of self and his stories/memories of the various incarnations of Kiyoaki dissolve into doubt. "[W]ho knows," he wonders, "perhaps there had been no I".[90] Honda becomes the Keatsian voice at the end of "Nightingale": mortal and uncertain whether the "wings of poesy" have achieved anything permanent:

> Forlorn! the very word is like a bell
> To toll me back from thee to my sole self!
> Adieu! the fancy cannot cheat so well
> As she is fam'd to do, deceiving elf.
> Adieu! adieu! thy plaintive anthem fades
> Past the near meadows, over the still stream,
> Up the hill-side; and now 'tis buried deep
> In the next valley-glades:
> Was it a vision, or a waking dream?
> Fled is that music: – Do I wake or sleep?[91]

With his characters and central narrator trapped in the "midst of woe", Mishima's Romanticism fails as a "friend to man". Honda is "forlorn", "tolled back" to his base self. The hopeful idealism (or woke absolutes and purifications) is emptied here at the tetralogy's end: "If [Satoko] still carried with her all the hypocrisy of that other world, then there must be doubts about the validity of her conversion when she entered this one. The dreams of sixty years seemed betrayed in that instant".[92] No artistic or spiritual refuge survives. Honda's Romantic idealisations – his wokeness – are just relics of the corrupted, failed society, rather than its saving, or transcendent grace. "In flight from a host of threatening sorrows" and with Satoko ultimately an empty cipher, Honda finds not "consolation in nature",[93] but desolation. The garden remains, but to no purpose: "There was no other sound. The garden was empty. He had come, thought Honda, to a place that had no memories, nothing".[94]

Mishima's Romanticism is finally a dark and desolate one. The conclusion of *The Decay of the Angel* strips personal and poetic memory of any consolation, any solace. Honda's encounters with Kiyoaki's reincarnations do not cohere or redeem Honda's original belief that "perhaps Kiyoaki had seen something" all those decades ago, felt some "expression of intense joy, the kind to be found nowhere but at the extremity of human existence".[95] Left "in the midst of the turmoil of history"[96] while Satoko remains ensconced behind her self-imposed walls, Honda finds no reconciliation of art and life, no integration of loves, castes, or cultures. Ultimately, Mishima judges the Romantic melding of one's individual passions with the desire to do more than just acknowledge issues of injustice and rights within the "turmoil of history" as failed. With his politics exclusive rather than inclusive – "anti-woke" in its privileging of emperor and caste – Mishima leaves his characters only "little shelter[s] of self-awareness" where they can hide from the need to act. Through this dark interpretation of Romanticism's application to contemporary society (as that "self-awareness that knew nothing of love, that slaughtered without raising a hand"[97]), Mishima helps us understand Romanticism's continuing transnational trace and impact and how Romantic considerations of aesthetics and ethical action cross cultures and time.

Notes

[1] *Ibid.*, 198.

[2] Mishima, Yukio (1990). *Runaway Horses*, New York: Vintage Press, 210.

[3] Mishima, Yukio (1990). *The Decay of the Angel*, New York: Vintage Press, 11.

[4] *Ibid.*, 21.

[5] Wordsworth, William (1798). "Lines Composed a Few Miles above Tintern Abbey, on Revisiting the Banks of the Wye, During a Tour, July 13, 1798". *The Gutenberg Project*, lines 24-36. Web. 10 October 2020. https://www.gutenberg.org/files/12145/12145-h/12145-h.htm#section2

[6] Bate, Jonathan (2020). *Radical Wordsworth: The Poet Who Changed the World*. New Haven and London: Yale University Press, 70.

[7] *Ibid.*, 188.

[8] *Ibid.*, 190.

[9] Yukio Mishima (1990). *Spring Snow*, New York: Vintage Press, 177.

[10] John Keats (1820a). "Ode on a Grecian Urn." *The Poetry Foundation*, line 45. Web. 20 October 2020. https://www.poetryfoundation.org/poems/44477/ode-on-a-grecian-urn.

[11] Mishima. *Spring Snow*, 54.

[12] *Ibid.*

[13] "We should all by now have learned the hard lesson, that there are no 'elect'" Mishima notes in *Spring Snow*, 211.

[14] Bate (2020), 193.

[15] Mishima. *Spring Snow*, 198.

[16] Kelly, Richard T. (2011). "Rereading: *The Sea of Fertility* Tetralogy by Yukio Mishima." *The Guardian*. 3 July 2011. n.pag. Web. 10 October 2020. https://www.theguardian.com/books/2011/jun/03/rereading-yukio-mishima-sea-of-fertility-tetralogy.

[17] Book One of *The Excursion*, but also identified as "The Ruined Cottage", a title which better fits Mishima's language and themes.

[18] John Keats. (1819). "Ode to a Nightingale." *The Poetry Foundation*, lines 70-71. Web. 20 October 2020. https://www.poetryfoundation.org/poems/44479/ode-to-a-nightingale.

[19] Mishima. *Runaway Horses*, 21.

[20] *Ibid.*

[21] Kelly (2011), n.pag.

[22] Mishima. *Decay of the Angel*, 54.

[23] Kelly (2011), n.pag.

[24] That is, questioning what appears to be Keats' privileging of a purely aesthetic sense of meaning at the end of "Grecian Urn": "Beauty is truth, truth beauty, – that is all/ Ye know on earth, and all ye need to know." John Keats (1820), line 45.

[25] Keats (1819), lines 36, 38.

[26] Mishima. *Decay of the Angel*, 54.

[27] Mishima. *The Decay of the Angel*, 54.

[28] Mishima. *Spring Snow*, 230-231.

[29] Keats (1820a), line 45.

[30] Kelly (2011), n.pag.

[31] Mishima. *Decay of the Angel*, 105.

[32] Keats (1820a), line 3.

[33] Wordsworth, William (1814). *The Excursion, Book One* ("The Ruined Cottage"). *The Gutenberg Project*, lines 184-198. Web. 10 October 2020. https://www.gutenberg.org/files/56361/56361-h/56361-h.htm.

[34] *Ibid.*, lines 921-941.

[35] Bate (2011), 191.

[36] *Ibid.*, 192.

[37] Wordsworth (1814), line 932.

[38] Mishima. *Spring Snow*, 72.

[39] Keats (1820a), lines 49-50.

[40] Keats (1820b). "Ode on Melancholy." *The Poetry Foundation*, line 11. Web. 20 October 2020. https://www.poetryfoundation.org/poems/44478/ode-on-melancholy.

[41] Mishima. *Spring Snow*, 177.

[42] *Ibid.*, 257.

[43] Wordsworth (1814). line 621.

[44] Mishima. *Spring Snow*, 358.

[45] Mishima. *Runaway Horses*, 21.

[46] *Ibid.*, 320.

[47] Mishima. *Spring Snow*, 384.

[48] *Ibid.*, 388.

[49] *Ibid.*, 247-248.

[50] *Ibid.*, 388.

[51] Keats (1820a), line 3.

[52] Keats (1819), line 23.

[53] Mishima, *Runaway Horses*, 21.

[54] *Ibid.*, 144.

[55] *Ibid.*, 211.

[56] *Ibid.*, 112.

[57] That is, his and Makiko's connection.

[58] Mishima. *Runaway Horses*, 112.

[59] *Ibid.*, 251.

[60] *Ibid.*, 247-248.

[61] *Ibid.*, 298.

[62] *Ibid.*, 322.

[63] Mishima. *Temple of Dawn*, 278.

[64] *Ibid.*, 279.

[65] *Ibid.*

[66] *Ibid.*, 301.

[67] *Ibid.*, 304.

[68] *Ibid.*, 304-305.

[69] Mishima. *Decay of the Angel*, 11.

[70] *Ibid.*, 14.

[71] *Ibid.*, 11.

[72] Mishima. *Spring Snow*, 358.

[73] Mishima. *Decay of the Angel*, 14.

[74] Mishima. *Runaway Horses*, 320.

[75] Mishima. *Decay of the Angel*, 207.

[76] Mishima. *Temple of Dawn*, 278.

[77] Mishima. *Spring Snow*, 198.

[78] Mishima. *Decay of the Angel*, 47.

[79] Mishima. *Runaway Horses*, 112.

[80] Echoing Keats here: "Ah, happy, happy boughs! that cannot shed / Your leaves, nor ever bid the Spring adieu; / And, happy melodist, unwearied, / For ever piping songs for ever new." (1820a), lines 21-24.

[81] Mishima. *Decay of the Angel*, 68.

[82] *Ibid.*, 232.

[83] *Ibid.*

84 *Ibid.*

85 *Ibid.*, 234.

86 Keats (1820a), line 19: ("She cannot fade, though thou hast not thy bliss, / For ever wilt thou love, and she be fair!")

87 Mishima. *Decay of the Angel*, 233.

88 *Ibid.*, 234

89 *Ibid.*, 232.

90 *Ibid.*, 235.

91 Keats (1819), lines 81-90.

92 Mishima. *Decay of the Angel*, 235.

93 *Ibid.*, 21.

94 *Ibid.*, 236.

95 Mishima. *Spring Snow*, 389.

96 Mishima. *Decay of the Angel*, 230.

97 *Ibid.*, 68.

Bibliography

Bate, Jonathan (2020). *Radical Wordsworth: The Poet Who Changed the World*. New Haven and London: Yale University Press.

Keats, John (1819). "Ode to a Nightingale." *The Poetry Foundation*. Web. 20 October 2020. https://www.poetryfoundation.org/poems/44479/ode-to-a-nightingale.

--- (1820a). "Ode on a Grecian Urn." *The Poetry Foundation*. Web. 20 October 2020. https://www.poetryfoundation.org/poems/44477/ode-on-a-grecian-urn.

--- (1820b). "Ode on Melancholy." *The Poetry Foundation*. Web. 20 October 2020. https://www.poetryfoundation.org/poems/44478/ode-on-melancholy.

Kelly, Richard T. (2011). "Rereading: *The Sea of Fertility* Tetralogy by Yukio Mishima." *The Guardian*. 3 July 2011. n.pag. Web. 10 October 2020. https://www.theguardian.com/books/2011/jun/03/rereading-yukio-mishima-sea-of-fertility-tetralogy.

Mishima, Yukio (1990). *Spring Snow*. New York: Vintage Press.

--- (1990). *Runaway Horses*. New York: Vintage Press.

--- (1990). *The Temple of Dawn*. New York: Vintage Press.

--- (1990). *The Decay of the Angel*. New York: Vintage Press.

Wordsworth, William (1814). *The Excursion, Book One* ("The Ruined Cottage"). *The Gutenberg Project*. Web. 10 October 2020. https://www.gutenberg.org/files/56361/56361-h/56361-h.htm.

--- (1798). "Lines, Composed a Few Miles above Tintern Abbey, on Revisiting the Banks of the Wye, During a Tour, July 13, 1798". The *Gutenberg Project*. Web. 10 October 2020. https://www.gutenberg.org/files/12145/12145-h/12145-h.htm#section2.

List of Contributors

Paul Almonte, American University of Sharjah, English Department, Sharjah, United Arab Emirates and LCC International University, English Department, Klaipeda, Lithuania.

Sérgio Das Neves, School of Social Sciences and Humanities, Institute for Studies of Literature and Tradition, NOVA University Lisbon, Lisboa, Portugal.

Lorenz A. Hindrichsen, Copenhagen International School, English Department, Nordhavn, Denmark.

Marie Hologa, Faculty of Culture Studies, Institute for Language, Literature, and Culture, TU Dortmund University, Germany.

Theadora Jean, Department of English, Royal Holloway, University of London, UK.

Maria Juko, Independent Scholar, Hamburg, Germany.

Md. Monirul Islam, Department of English, Presidency University, Kolkata.

Sophia Lange, Faculty of Culture Studies, Institute for Language, Literature, and Culture, TU Dortmund University, Germany.

Monika Lee, School of Humanities, Brescia University College, London, Ontario, Canada.

Katie Smith, Independent Scholar, Lancashire, UK.